ORIENTATION MAP:
BOTSWANA IN SOUTHERN AFRICA

25°E

Luanda

ANGOLA

ZAMBIA

Lusaka

MALAWI

MOZAMBIQUE

Harare

NAMIBIA

ZIMBABWE

BOTSWANA

— 23½°S Windhoek

VENDA

Pretoria
Jhb

Maputo

23½°S —

BOPHUTHATSWANA

SOUTH AFRICA

Durban

Cape Town

25°E

ITE 19

ambezi

Mpandamatenga

NAL PARK

Nata

ROUTE 8 (1)

KUBU
ISLAND

Mosetse

Plumtree

ROUTE 8 (2)

ROUTE 8 (1)

Sowa Pan

Mosu

thakane ROUTE 8 (3)

Francistown

Tonata

Shashe

Mmashoro

Serule

Selebi-Phikwe

Pont Drift

Limpopo

Serowe

Paje

Baines Drift

Platjanbridge

Palapye

Zanzibar Saambou

Martins Drift

Mahalapye

Machaneng

Dinokwe

Parrs Halt

Buffels Drift

Limpopo

Mochudi

Sikwane
Derdepoort

Tlhokweng Gate

Ramotswa

ioneer Gate

Zeerust

labama

ikeng

50   100   150   200   250 km

LEGEND

——————	Major road
- - - - -	Road follows valley
⌇	Major river
•	Towns and villages
∗	Places of interest
▪▪▪▪▪▪▪▪▪	Game reserves and national parks

ROUTE no. ➤ Routes refer to the publication *Visitors' Guide to Botswana* by Mike Main, John & Sandra Fowkes, published by Southern Book Publishers, 1987 (not applicable to this publication)

N

NEWMAN'S

BIRDS
OF BOTSWANA

Kenneth Newman

in conjunction with the Botswana Bird Club

The authors wish to acknowledge the contribution of the Botswana Bird Club Atlas Project in providing distributional data and for sharing such data prior to Atlas publication.

SOUTHERN
BOOK PUBLISHERS

ISBN 1 86812 194 1

First edition, first impression 1989

Set in Universe 8 on 9 pt
by Unifoto (Pty) Ltd. Cape
Printed and bound by CTP Book Printers Cape

BD9753

FOREWORD

Traditionally Botswana's birds have always been referred to in books covering the entire region south of the Cunene/Caprivi/Zambezi borders. In this context much of the information relevant to Botswana has come from interpretation of data from neighbouring countries, except possibly in the case of the Okavango Delta. But, even for the Delta, data collected by visitors is no substitute for data generated on a more regular basis. It is from this latter approach that we will begin to get a better appreciation of the birds of Botswana.

I therefore very much welcome the publication of this fieldguide concentrating on Botswana. Whilst it is not intended to be the definitive statement on our birds, since there is still much work to be done, this book, by stimulating our ability to identify and recognise some 550 species, will greatly help towards encouraging the good quality data we need. The book represents a much improved picture of the status and occurrence of our birds compared to the regional publications.

Much of the credit for initiating the development of this local understanding belongs to the Botswana Bird Club and its members. Since the Bird Club is a branch of the Botswana Society, it gives me great pleasure, in my capacity as the Society's President, to acknowledge the Bird Club in this way.

Any fieldguide is particularly dependent on the quality of its illustrations. Kenneth Newman has an enviable and deserved reputation as a bird artist. He is also a keen ornithologist in his own right. Furthermore, by his many visits to Botswana, Mr Newman has demonstrated an appreciation of our birdlife. I should therefore like to express my sincere gratitude to Mr Newman for getting together with the Botswana Bird Club and for jointly producing this most welcome fieldguide to the birds of Botswana.

P. S. Mmusi

The Hon. P. Mmusi
VICE PRESIDENT
Botswana

CONTENTS

ACKNOWLEDGEMENTS

Species distribution maps are fundamental to the usefulness of any bird field-guide and are dependent on data made available by field ornithologists. For many years this has been a rather haphazard process entirely dependent on reports published in the literature of the various bird clubs and on birds collected by museums. The comparatively recent institution of bird atlasing, whereby data gathering has been placed on an organised basis throughout southern Africa, has made it possible to obtain a much clearer and more accurate overall picture of bird distributions. In this regard I am particularly appreciative of the generosity of Dr Hew Penry, organiser of the Botswana Bird Club Atlas Project, and the Botswana Bird Club committee, in agreeing to the use in this fieldguide of hitherto unpublished data.

The co-operation of members of the Botswana Bird Club is also greatly appreciated. In particular my sincere thanks are due to Nigel Hunter, Don Aldis, Michael Bird, Brian and Di Bushell, Wendy Borello and Janet Barnes, each of whom has either refereed my distribution maps, species accounts and early text drafts, or contributed in other ways.

From the start I freely plundered the many articles published in the pages of the *Babbler*, the magazine of the Botswana Bird Club, and I take this opportunity to acknowledge the contributions of the various authors whose work and diligence in the field helped me to form a much clearer picture of Botswana's avifauna.

A special thanks to 'The Deception Valley Team', ten bird-wise friends who accompanied me and lent their support on a central Kalahari birding expedition during a very hot February 1987, namely: Duncan Christie, Ian Davidson, Andy Egginton, Peter Ferrett, Rodney Forster, Russell Friedman, John Hosken, Peter Lawson and Bob and Rosalind Levitt. Their contributions, unflagging enthusiasm and companionship in scorching daily temperatures will long be remembered.

Finally I wish to acknowledge those friends who demonstrated their support for this book by so willingly parting with the data they had themselves collected in the course of various expeditions to Botswana's remoter regions. These are: Colin Bell, Chris Brown, Duncan Buchart, Richard Coombe, 'Buster' Culverwell, Ian Davidson, Donald and Anita Fabian, 'Map' Ives, Chris McIntyre, Mark and Delia Owens, Dallas Reed, Hennie Rawlinson, Keith Stannard and Peter Steyn.

KN

INTRODUCTION

The Republic of Botswana occupies a central position in the southern African subcontinent, though its northern tip touches the Zambezi River which is usually considered to be the boundary between central and southern Africa. Its southern border meets the northern Cape Province of The Republic of South Africa, the north-east is bounded by Zimbabwe, the south-east by the Transvaal Province, mainly along the Limpopo and Marico rivers, while to the west lies the vast and varied territory of Namibia.

Natural habitats

Much of Botswana lies on Kalahari sands, a feature that extends into neighbouring Namibia, Cape Province and Zimbabwe, but here the similarity ends. Botswana's Kalahari sands, allied to its own climatic patterns and geomorphological processes, have produced a landscape that is in the main rather different to its neighbours. Of course at the edges the vegetation is similar on both sides of the international boundaries. While Botswana could be described as a semi-arid puddle of sand in the centre of the southern African subcontinent, such a generalisation masks the great variety of natural habitats that occur within its four major ecosystems. These four ecosystems consist of the Okavango/Linyanti/Chobe system; the Makgadikgadi Pans system; the Eastern thornveld and the Kalahari system.

In the north-east of Botswana, and in striking contrast to much of the rest of the country, is the huge inland waterway commonly referred to as the Okavango swamp, but more accurately the Okavango Delta, a great green wetland paradise and one of the natural wonders of Africa. Here, still on Kalahari sand, the great Okavango River spills in from Angola and spreads out into a maze of channels and lagoons of sparkling clear water. Within the Delta's waterways are vast beds of reeds and papyrus and countless islands supporting massive trees. Slowly these waters seep in a south-easterly direction, and what has not already evaporated, finally loses itself in the Kalahari sands, but not before providing home and food to millions of water and water-associated birds. Dominant over all and spectacular by its presence is the majestic African Fish Eagle whose ringing call is as much part of the Delta as the fish it eats. Within these waterways and lily-covered lagoons are countless herons, ducks, ibis, storks, plovers, jacanas, cormorants, darters and many others, while the riverine woodland of the islands and main streams supports as colourful an array of birds as one could wish to find anywhere in Africa, from the huge Pel's Fishing Owl to the diminutive Brown Firefinch. The Okavango Delta is a bird paradise second to none.

Apart from the Okavango Delta, the Kwando, Linyanti and Chobe Rivers provide similar habitat albeit on a much smaller scale. The riverine forests of these waterways provide a belt of mature, broadleafed shade trees. This habitat in conjunction with the swampy areas produces a virtual replica of the avifauna of the Delta, though such 'specials' as Bradfield's Hornbill and Narina Trogon become a little easier to find. This scene continues along the Chobe River where huge breeding colonies of Carmine Bee-eaters may be seen in spring and where Longcrested Eagles and Western Banded Snake Eagles may be found. Still in the north and north-east, but away from the waterways, the relatively higher rainfall allows the broadleafed woodlands found in Zimbabwe and the Caprivi Strip to spill over into Botswana. Such woodland brings with it some of the 'Miombo' specials such as Greencapped Eremomela, Angola Rock Thrush and Stierling's Barred Warbler.

Away from the better drained soils and extending south-eastwards to the

3

MAJOR VEGETATION REGIONS IN BOTSWANA

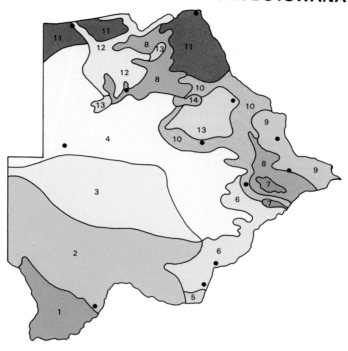

1. Arid scrub savanna

2. Southern Kalahari tree and bush savanna

3. Central Kalahari tree and bush savanna

4. Northern Kalahari tree and bush savanna

5. *Acacia eriobola* tree savanna

6. *Acacia* mixed woodland and *Combretum* bushveld on clay loam and sandy soils

7. Mixed *Mopane*/Croton/ *Combretum* close-tree savanna on rocky hills

8. *Mopane* tree and bush savanna

9. Mixed *Mopane*/*Arcacia*/broad-leafed woodland

10. Mixed *Mopane* tree and scrub savanna/*Acacia* mixed woodland along drainage lines

11. Mixed broadleafed woodland interspersed with grassland and *Mopane*

12. Aquatic grassland/riparian forest

13. Grass savanna

14. Palm savanna/Northern Kalahari tree and bush savanna

Francistown/Palapye region are large tracts of *Mopane* (*Colophospermum mopane*), a favourite place for locating Arnot's Chat. However, this habitat is interrupted by the Makgadikgadi Pans, another of Botswana's specials. When they hold water the pans boast huge numbers of flamingoes, pelicans, avocets and waders. Caspian Terns also appear and breed. The pans are surrounded by grasslands in which Pinkbilled Larks and Yellowthroated Sandgrouse are good finds, as well as coursers, plovers and other larks.

The eastern thornveld runs from the Francistown region all the way down to the Lobatse area covering the Botswana part of the Limpopo catchment. In the northern part *Mopane* is dominant but, south of the winter frost line, *Acacia* and *Combretum* woodland takes over. As well as *Mopane* a feature of the northern part is the regular occurrence of granite hills, many of which contain the localised and elusive Boulder Chat. The *Acacia/Combretum* woodland, like woodland anywhere, provides for a rich and varied birdlife: raptors, woodpeckers, hornbills, babblers, flycatchers, shrikes and waxbills. In addition there is the Limpopo riverine strip with its specials such as the Longtailed Glossy Starling and Pygmy Kingfisher.

In the extreme south-east, adjacent to the Mafekeng region, the woodland gives way to more open, grassy areas, the only region in Botswana where the Orangethroated Longclaw occurs. It is also excellent for larks, including the localised Shortclawed Lark. Lesser Kestrels favour the area in summer and Sociable Weavers make use of the scattered but dominant *Acacia eriobola*.

Much of the rest of the country falls within the Kalahari ecosystem. This landscape is by no means monotonous. The scenery is a shifting mosaic of low shrubs and bushes interspersed with patches of woodland. Even where the open areas are predominant, islands and belts of woodland occur. Within such woodland the birdlife can be very rewarding with almost every granivorous and insectivorous family represented. Waxbills, canaries, weavers, bee-eaters, cuckoos, sandgrouse, orioles, woodpeckers, shrikes and warblers can all be found. In the more open areas larks, Black Korhaans, Blackchested Prinias, Titbabblers, Black Crows and Greater Kestrels are frequent. This habitat is much more rewarding than a first impression often suggests.

In years of good rainfall the vegetation is supplemented by a plentiful growth of grass which triggers the arrival of seedeaters such as the Scalyfeathered Finch. Such nomadic breeders as the Monotonous Lark and Kurrichane Buttonquail can also become temporarily plentiful.

Contained in this ecosystem are three additional habitat features worthy of mention. Firstly, though the Kalahari is extremely sandy, the sand dunes are really only a predominant feature of the extreme south-west. Unlike the dunes of Namibia and the Cape Province these do not contain an endemic lark such as the Dune or Red Lark. Secondly, along the watershed between the Orange River and Limpopo system, i.e. from the Ghanzi/Namibia border (latitude 22° S) to the Lobatse region, there is a concentration of seasonal pans which, in wet years, can greatly increase the variety of birdlife. Thirdly, as the Limpopo enhances eastern Botswana, so do the Nosop (Nossob) and Molopo riverine habitats enhance the birdlife of the drier south and south-western regions.

Finally, in regard to habitat, the growth of towns such as Francistown, Gaborone and Lobatse has meant a growth in water and sewage impoundments. These man-made habitats have greatly added to the variety of birdlife in these otherwise relatively dry localities. See pp. 329-336 for typical habitat pictures.

Bird numbers

Some 550 bird species in total have been accepted for the Botswana national bird list. These are species known to live in the country at some time of the year, including the various rare vagrants which are from time to time recorded. In addition there is a 'shadow list' of birds known to occur close to Botswana's borders in neighbouring territories and which, although they have not yet been recorded in Botswana, can logically be expected to occur from time to time. All of these birds are illustrated and described in this fieldguide in the expectation that, once their rarity is appreciated, more will be learned of their localities and frequencies.

Total numbers of birds within the country fluctuate within a year and also from year to year. Annual fluctuations are brought about primarily by the arrival each spring of large numbers of birds from elsewhere in Africa (intra-Africa migrants) and from the northern hemisphere (Palaearctic migrants).

Whilst Botswana may not have the numbers of Palaearctic migrants in terms of species, it does appear that its habitats may be very significant for a large percentage of the world's population in regard to such species, for example, as the Redbacked and Lesser Grey Shrikes and Icterine Warbler. Even the relatively isolated islands of woodland within Kalahari scrub appear to attract the European Oriole, Cuckoo and others.

Of the intra-African migrants there are two categories. The first are those that regularly breed in Botswana but spend as much time *away* from their breeding grounds as in them. To this category belong such groups as kingfishers, cuckoos, rollers and the Wahlberg's Eagle. The second type refers to the winter visitors from further south, presumably escaping from the colder climate with its greatly reduced food supply. Such species include the Fairy Flycatcher and Fiscal Flycatcher.

On a more local scale, many bird species may undergo irregular movements within Botswana. Such movements may be triggered by rainfall, temperatures, food, breeding requirements or a combination of these and other factors not yet properly understood. Certainly rain and drought have a marked influence on birds. On the one hand we see extensive movements of waterbirds into the arid central and southern Kalahari following rare good rains in that region, on the other inhibited breeding during drought years by all but the hardiest of arid-land species.

Species status in Botswana

Users of this fieldguide may at first be surprised to see how many birds are listed as rare or are put into the category of 'Status not established.' These statements merely reflect the state of our present knowledge of many species. Now that such statements are in print, however, it is sincerely hoped that concerned readers will appreciate the urgent need for further information about our birds.

The true status of many bird species in Botswana is dogged by a paucity of reliable sight records. In a country so vast and so sparsely populated reliable observers are extremely few and are active mostly in the north, east and south-east of the country. Many regions where the rarer birds might be expected to occur, the borders with neighbouring territories and the central and south-central Kalahari for example, are seldom visited by people knowledgeable in bird identification, and so the presence or occasional occurrence of some species may go unrecorded. The growth of tourism in recent years has only partially remedied the situation since tourism also tends to centre on already well-trodden ground.

Most recent records of birds in Botswana, and some understanding of their distributions and frequencies, have been obtained by a comparatively small band of dedicated enthusiasts from the Botswana Bird Club (see Acknowledgements) who have travelled far and wide to little known regions in an effort to produce an accurate bird atlas for the country. Theirs is a continuing task but the results of the first ten years of atlasing is expected in about 1990. This fieldguide has benefitted from this fieldwork as any comparison with the status and distribution statements made in this and previous regional books will demonstrate. The information presented in this book therefore represents an up to date but still cautious picture. The publishing of the Botswana Atlas, further information collected during a wet spell in particular, and the regular input of data by field observers will provide the opportunity for improvements.

The Botswana Bird Club would be pleased to receive details of any interesting bird species recorded by either residents or visitors. If the bird does not appear to be in this fieldguide, if it is described as rare or if it is observed beyond the limits of the range shown, the facts of the observation should be reported in writing to the Club. In this regard, however, it must be stressed that all new bird records should be accompanied by a careful and accurate description of the species seen: why the observer is certain of the bird's specific identification as opposed to other, similar species, the date and location of the observation and, if possible, the names and addresses of others who may also have seen it. Only detailed reports of this nature can be considered for the national records. The address of the Botswana Bird Club is P.O.Box 71, Gaborone.

Looking at birds

Binoculars are an essential part of the birdwatcher's equipment; many of the smaller birds cannot be properly studied without them. Many good makes are available and 7 x 30, 8 x 35, or 10 x 40 are recommended; the first figure relates to magnification and the second to the diameter in millimetres of the front, or objective lens. Generally speaking the greater the diameter of the front lens in proportion to the rear, or eyepiece, the more light is gathered and transmitted thus creating a brighter image, and the wider the field of view. Today it is possible to obtain binoculars that are light and compact with a good magnification. Large, heavy binoculars are both tiring to carry and difficult to hold steady. Many people also use a telescope to study distant, difficult-to-identify species.

When looking at an unfamiliar bird it is a good plan to adopt a simple six-point system to help remember its salient features once it has flown or hopped out of sight: **1** Note its approximate size. This can be done by comparing it with a well-known species: thus is it larger or smaller than a sparrow, a pigeon or a guineafowl? and so on. **2** Note its general colour scheme, e.g. black upperparts, white underparts and a bold white bar on its wing. **3** What is its beak shape: short and conical like that of a sparrow, or longer and more finely proportioned, or is it long and curved; what colour is its beak? **4** What shape are its legs: are they long, short or normal, and what colour are they? **5** What habitat is the bird in: grassland, forest, bushveld, wetland or mountains? **6** What is the bird *doing*: is it walking, hopping, swimming, feeding amidst leaves, running up branches, etc.? These six simple checks should be memorised and will take the observer a long way towards establishing a bird's identity. A good plan is to use a notebook in which all the important features of a bird can be listed for future reference and diagnosis.

Species descriptions

In the descriptive text for each species, opposite the illustration of that species, the bird's most used vernacular name is given first in **bold** capital letters. In some cases a bird will have a second vernacular name which is also in wide use, and this appears in brackets after the first name. Immediately following the vernacular name is the scientific name of the bird, known throughout the world regardless of language. This appears in *italic* type and refers to the bird's genus and species in that order.

The use of scientific names calls for some explanation for the benefit of those unaccustomed to them. Birds, in common with all other forms of animal life, have all been placed in distinct groups for clarity of expression. It is all very well for the layman to refer to a 'Willie Wagtail' — his friends may well understand which bird he means, but in other countries, even in other parts of the same country, these popular names may in fact refer to totally different species. The Australian 'Willie Wagtail' is a very different bird to its African namesake. Even the accepted vernacular name sometimes varies from country to country. Thus, based on an international system of scientific nomenclature originated in the eighteenth century by the Swedish naturalist, Carl Linnaeus, all animals (and this includes birds) have been placed in clear groups or taxa, using names based on Latin or, in some cases, ancient Greek, which obviates any risk of confusion. No two birds can have the same scientific name. Firstly all animal life is placed in classes, and birds belong to the class Aves, mammals to the class Mammalia, insects to Insecta, and so on. These classes are then divided into major groups known as orders. The orders are subdivided into families, the families into genera (genus in the singular), and the genera into one or more species. A species can be further divided into races or subspecies.

When the above system of scientific nomenclature is applied to the common House Sparrow, its credentials look like this:

Class:	Aves
Order:	Passeriformes
Family:	Ploceidae
Genus:	*Passer*
Species:	*domesticus*

Thus, within the bird family PLOCEIDAE there is a genus known as *Passer*, and within that genus a specific bird known as *domesticus*. The name *Passer domesticus* can be regarded, in human terms, as surname and given name, although the sequence is reversed. The use of an animal's scientific name ensures that serious students throughout the world will at once know, without any possibility of confusion, to which species one is referring. Within the genus *Passer* there are several other species all closely related to *P. domesticus*: *P. diffusus*, the Greyheaded Sparrow, *P. motitensis*, the Great Sparrow and *P. melanurus*, the Cape Sparrow to name but a few. The present form of the local southern African House Sparrow is descended from a species introduced into Natal from India earlier this century. The Indian race differs in minor respects from the nominate European race and is given the subspecific name of *Passer domesticus indicus* or, again in human terms, a second given name. In fact the nominate race of the House Sparrow *Passer domesticus domesticus* (identical specific and subspecific names denote that the bird is of the nominate race), was also introduced from Europe to various places in the old Cape Colony and elsewhere at about the same time. It interbred with the Indian race and seems to have been subjugated, very little trace of its specific plumage pattern being now discernible in the southern African bird. The third or trinominal name is used in this fieldguide only in rare instances where it has been felt necessary to draw attention to the subspecific status of a bird.

When writing scientific names it is customary to write them in *italic* characters, to use an initial capital letter for the generic name and small or lower-case letters only for the specific and subspecific names.

8

Following the bird's names in the descriptive text is a brief statement of its known status. This is an attempt to give the reader an idea of the bird's relative abundance, whether it is rare, common, etc., and whether it is a seasonal visitor, a resident or a vagrant. These terms are set out and explained at the end of this chapter. It should be understood that the term 'common' for instance relates to the bird's frequency *within its preferred or normal habitat*, and not to the whole of Botswana. Following the foregoing information each species is briefly described. This is not a feather-by-feather description of its plumage (the illustrations make this unecessary) but an attempt to highlight specific characters that are diagnostic and distinguish it from other, similar species. In cases where a bird closely resembles another species attention is drawn to the fact, and the page reference of the similar species given for comparison.

It is inevitable when describing birds that certain names used for parts of its anatomy may be unfamiliar to the reader. Familiarity with the 'Topography of a Bird' drawing (below) is therefore recommended.

TOPOGRAPHY OF A BIRD

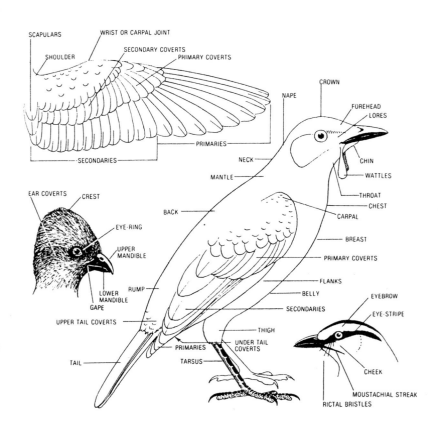

The bird's voice is then described as a further aid to establishing its identity. Most birds call or sing, and many do both. In fact the division between the more elaborate calls and the simpler songs is a fine one. Unfortunately any attempt at committing bird vocalisations to paper in the form of the written word is at best an approximation, influenced by the writer's ability to interpret them. Calls, consisting mostly of single-syllable notes, are the easiest to express in words, and may suggest a similar-sounding language phrase. Birds songs, on the other hand, especially the more complicated (frequently the most beautiful), are notoriously difficult to express clearly and are all too often impossible. In such cases an attempt has been made to give the more frequently uttered notes in the song or to describe it as 'melodious' and so on. At this point it is appropriate to draw the reader's attention to the set of bird song tapes by Len Gillard entitled 'SOUTHERN AFRICAN BIRD CALLS'. These tapes containing over 500 bird calls complement this fieldguide and are strongly recommended to those seriously interested in the birds of Botswana.

Finally, at the end of each descriptive text, the bird's measurements are given, followed by its reference number. It is not practicable to give a bird's measurements as it appears in the field since birds hold themselves in different ways at different times. A long-necked bird may hold its head and neck outstretched or tucked in; some birds have a hunched posture while others of similar size may habitually stand erect. The measurements supplied therefore represent those for a dead bird lying flat on a table, neither stretched nor compressed. Should the bird have long legs which stretch beyond its tail, these are included in the total measurement. In a few cases only, when a species has seasonally long tail-plumes, the measurements with and without the plumes are given.

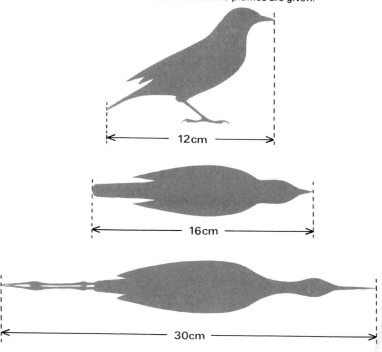

The bird's reference number is that used for it throughout southern Africa and serves as a cross-reference to other fieldguides for the region. This number is also shown on the distribution map for the species.

Distribution maps

Each species description is accompanied by a small distribution map showing the areas in Botswana in which it is likely to occur. Only very rare species do not have a map and, in these cases, the localities where they have been seen are given if known. These species ranges are rough guides only, based on present-day knowledge of the bird's occurrence. In time many will be modified as our knowledge is updated. Solid areas are the normal ranges, solid spots are known local ranges of isolated populations, and open circles indicate where a species has been recorded but is not regular. Because birds are highly mobile creatures they frequently appear in the most unlikely places, and one should be ever watchful for species occurring beyond the range shown on the maps. Comparison with the master map on the end pages of this fieldguide will provide an accurate key to the locations shown on the species distribution maps or in the text.

The colour plates

The birds depicted in this fieldguide have been drawn, so far as is possible, in such a way as to reveal their characteristic shapes, colours, markings and stance, or 'jizz' as it is known in ornithological parlance. Where several species on a plate closely resemble each other they are all drawn, at risk of monotony, in a similar stance to facilitate direct comparison. All the main figures on a plate are in approximate proportion to each other and, wherever possible, all birds in a family are drawn to the same proportions whether on the same plate or not. In a few cases it has been necessary to depict large birds to a smaller scale than others on the same plate, and in such cases they are clearly separated by a solid line. Secondary figures showing birds in flight, or in some cases showing immature plumages, are often drawn to a smaller scale than the main figures.

It is customary in bird books to present species in strict taxonomic order, that is to say in the order used by the national checklist. This usually means that one starts with the Ostrich and the grebes, continues with seabirds, herons, ducks, etc., and finishes with canaries and buntings. In this fieldguide this order of presentation has been applied with elasticity. Since its basic purpose is to help with bird identification, and in the knowledge that many users may be unfamiliar with the various bird families and their characteristics, some species that have a visual resemblance to birds of another family have been illustrated with those they most closely resemble.

Terms used to indicate bird status and abundance

Vagrant	a species not normally seen in southern Africa
Very rare	a species recorded once or twice in five years
Rare	a species recorded 10 times or less in a year in suitable habitat
Uncommon	a species recorded 30 or less times a month in suitable habitat
Fairly common	a species recorded 1-10 times a day in suitable habitat
Common	a species recorded 10-50 times a day in suitable habitat

11

Very common	a species recorded 50-100 times a day in suitable habitat
Abundant	a species recorded 100 or more times a day in suitable habitat
Seasonal	a species seen at certain times of the year only
Localised	a species seen only in restricted areas of suitable habitat
Resident	a species which breeds in southern Africa
Visitor	a non-breeding species (Palaearctic or intra-Africa migrant)
Summer	(In Botswana) mid-September to mid-March
Winter	(In Botswana) mid-March to mid-September
Passage migrant	a bird seen temporarily at a point that it passes through during migration; alternatively 'bird of passage'

Symbols used on the colour illustrations

♂ denotes MALE
♀ denotes FEMALE
J denotes an immature bird
Br denotes breeding plumage
N-Br denotes non-breeding plumage

WHERE TO WATCH BIRDS IN BOTSWANA

Most visitors to Botswana tend to migrate towards the Okavango Delta and Chobe National Park. This is not surprising but there are other areas that can be rewarding to the birder, and so some guidance to locating these is included here.

Before leaving the Okavango and Chobe, however, a few points may prove helpful. The Delta is a vast region and guidance about the birds you may wish to see is probably best obtained from the local tour operators. Most such operators have some knowledge about the birds, but there are a few who specialise in birdwatching tours and advertise this facility.

Chobe also has local tour operators of whom, again, some specialise in birdwatching. However, working the Kasane rapids can prove very rewarding: one of the few places to see the elusive Halfcollared Kingfisher. To get there turn off the main road by the large baobab tree at the end of the Kasane airstrip where a gravel road takes one a hundred or so metres towards the rapids, and from which point they can be heard about two hundred metres away. Also driving between Kasane and Ngoma via Serondella is usually very rewarding, as is a boat trip from Kasane upstream along the Chobe River.

For those wishing to work the Makgadikgadi Pans the easternmost pan, known as Sua Pan, is probably the better bet. Assuming one is driving from Francistown this pan is easily reached by turning left at the first baobab tree before the town of Nata. At this point a gate gives access and a sand road leads to the pan (four-wheel drive is recommended). Local advice can be obtained from the owner of the lodge just beyond Nata, which in itself is a good birding area.

Another good destination for birding is the Limpopo catchment known as the Tuli Block. Perhaps the best area is the private Mashatu Game Reserve at the northern end where, again, local agents are available for advice. There are other farms offering visitors accommodation and good birding, near Martins Drift for example.

Most people coming to Botswana pass through Francistown and Gaborone *en route* to some more exotic destination, but for those who like birding at any opportunity, a pause at these localities will prove worthwhile. Descriptions of these areas in some detail therefore follow.

In Francistown, as good a place as any, are the grounds and neighbouring riverine habitat of the motel situated some 5 km outside the town on the Tati River. Longtailed Shrikes, Tropical Boubou and, during the summer, the European Marsh Warbler can be expected among a considerable variety of species. Any granite hill in the surrounding region is worth exploring for the Boulder Chat.

However, the greatest birding attraction of the **Francistown** region must be the Shashe reservoir, Botswana's largest man-made lake. There are three good areas of interest to birders around the lake, and the map below indicates their positions.

AREA 1: This locality is the easiest to find and is consequently the most popular, especially at weekends.

Some 25 km south of Francistown and 2 km north of the Shashe River bridge, there is a turning marked with a signpost to Shashe Dam. A 3 km drive along a badly corrugated road leads to the Shashe Waterworks, where one is expected to sign in as a visitor. No charge is made nor prior permission needed to enter. Turn right after the gate and follow the signs to the camping and caravan site. Mudflats and *Mopane* woodland add diversity to this area and one has a good view across the expanse of water. In the shallower parts and perched on the dead trees one can expect the Darter, Grey and Goliath Heron, Openbilled Stork and Little Egret. Waders are attracted to the muddy shoreline while the Hottentot Teal, Knobbilled Duck and Whitefaced Duck have been recorded. Cattle may destroy some of the taller reedbeds but one may locate Moorhen, Common Waxbill and, with luck, Little Sparrowhawk.

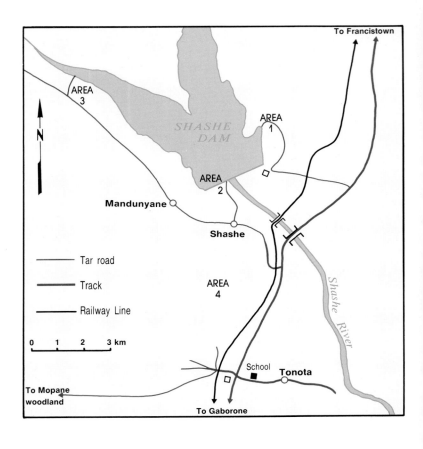

To Francistown

AREA
3

AREA
1

SHASHE
DAM

AREA
2

Mandunyane

Shashe

AREA
4

Shashe River

Tar road

Track

Railway Line

0   1   2   3 km

School   Tonota

To Mopane
woodland

To Gaborone

14

AREA 2: The spillway area, south of the dam wall, has some well-established reedbeds and permanent shallow pools. These are relatively uncommon habitats and may yield some interesting and unusual birds. To get there cross the railway line at the turning to Shashe village. Travel in a northerly direction through the village where there are a number of diverging tracks which, however, meet at the edge of the village where the soil is characteristically white. At 2,3 km from the railway crossing, take the sharp right-hand bend and travel through overgrazed lands and scrub *en route* to the spillway. There is a shallow but sandy stream bed to cross and, at the cattle grid, take a sharp left turn past the Mazeruru artisan's compound. Follow the track round to the right; it is sandy in places but negotiable by vehicles with good clearance. The dam wall will become apparent along this track which leads to its western end.

Among the reedbeds Water Dikkop, Greenbacked Heron, Red Bishop, European Sedge and African Marsh Warblers may be found. For those with patience Baillon's Crake may turn up, especially when the area becomes flooded during the summer rains.

AREA 3: Turn off the main road to Shashe village, cross the railway line and travel north-west through the villages of Shashe and Mandunyane. Passing through *Mopane* woodland and some 10 km from the railway crossing one finds a track leading off to the right. Passing through more *Mopane* and farmlands one sees a cattle grid beside a small water tower. The track, which is sandy in places, leads down to the water's edge and a small pump house situated at the end of a short spit.

At the end of the dry season some extensive mud flats are exposed, and these have produced a wide variety of waders and ducks. This area, being less accessible, is visited only by the occasional fisherman and is consequently less disturbed by tourists. A walk to the north follows a river channel where the *Acacia* woodland adjoins the water. This is a rich riverine habitat attracting a colourful variety of birds such as Gymnogene, Yellowbellied Bulbul, Tropical Boubou and Orangebreasted Bush Shrike.

AREA 4: An area worth visiting, if one has a little more time to spare, is the well-developed *Mopane* woodland some 30 km from the main road. To get there from Francistown, drive past Shashe village and turn right towards the petrol station which is opposite the road leading to Tonota village. Drive past the garage and over the railway crossing. Immediately after the railway take the furthest left fork where the road diverges into four separate tracks. For the first 10 km one travels through unspectacular lands and woodland. The vegetation becomes increasingly more interesting the further west one goes until more mature *Mopane* woodland is reached.

Arnot's Chat can be expected here together with Redbilled Helmetshrike.

Some 440 km south of Francistown lies **Gaborone** (pronounced Haboroni), the capital of Botswana. In 1988 the Botswana Bird Club produced, as a supplement to their magazine *Babbler*, 'The Birds of the Gaborone area'. This can be obtained through the Botswana Society office at the museum. Birding localities and directions for getting to them are given in two parts. Part A describes localities close to or in Gaborone itself, as follows:

A. MUSEUM: close by the Mall, at the opposite end from the National Assembly, on Independence Avenue opposite the Roman Catholic Cathedral.

A. NGOTWANE SEWAGE PONDS: follow the directions for the Ngotwane River but turn right opposite the filling station and garage. The sewage ponds and the outflow area can also be reached a short distance further on, immediately before the Ngotwane River bridge, through the Eucalyptus plantation on the right.

A. MARU-A-PULA SEWAGE PONDS: from the Francistown road take Nyerere Drive and go straight on at the first roundabout. The second turning on

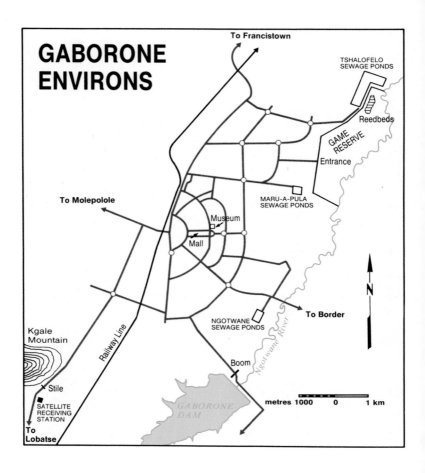

the right (before the Roads Training Centre) is a short gravel road leading directly to the sewage ponds. The outflow from the ponds, at the far end, passes into the game reserve. Permission to enter sewage pond property within the City can be obtained from the City Engineer's Department, but viewing from the perimeter fence is perfectly feasible at any of them.

A. GABORONE GAME RESERVE: from the Francistown road take Nyerere Drive and continue straight on at the first roundabout. The road soon bears sharply to the left and, before the bridge over the Segoditshane River, the access road to the Game Reserve will be seen on the right. An extensive view over the main reedbeds in the Game Reserve can also be obtained from the Tsholofelo Sewage Ponds.

A. TSHOLOFELO SEWAGE PONDS: follow directions for the Game Reserve but continue on over the Segoditshane River and turn right at the next roundabout. Continue on to the Botswana Power Corporation National Control Centre and Segoditshane Substation, on the right, then turn right immediately afterwards onto a gravel road. Continue straight on this road until a survey beacon is passed on the right. Bear left and the sewage ponds are reached shortly afterwards.

A. KGALE HILL: on the right of the Lobatse Road opposite the earth satellite station 5 km from Gaborone. There are stiles over the fence.

A. GABORONE DAM: take the Kaunda Road from Khama Crescent, turn right at the first roundabout, pass the Trade Fair Ground on the left and take the first gravel road thereafter (fairly rough). Bear left after 100 m. This leads to a boom at the foot of the dam wall. A permit, obtainable from the Water Utilities Corporation offices off the old Lobatse Road, is needed for access by vehicle. Beyond the boom follow the road along the base of the dam wall and through a gate to the dam itself. The road continues for some 17 km, leading to a private farm.

This section deals with localities a little further afield:

B. SIR SERETSE KHAMA INTERNATIONAL AIRPORT: take the Francistown Road out of Gaborone and turn left immediately after the rail crossing.

B. KOLOBENG RIVER: take the Molepolole Road to Mogoditshane, turn left to Gabane and, in Gabane, turn sharp right. After passing through Kumakwane the road crosses the Kolobeng River where there is a signpost to the remains of Livingstone's house. The section of the river to the left is the more interesting. This road can be quite sandy.

B. NGOTWANE DAM: access to the dam itself is no longer possible, except by private arrangement with the owners of smallholdings fronting onto the dam. The area around the dam wall and the intake to Gaborone Dam can be visited by taking the Lobatse Road for some 15 km, turning left onto the old Lobatse Road, crossing the bridge over the railway line and turning right onto a rough track immediately before the Metsemeswaane River (the bridge over the river has been removed).

B. MOSELESELE SAFARI PARK: along the Lobatse Road 17 km from Gaborone, the Park is signposted on the right-hand side.

B. MOGOBANE DAM: turn right off the road to Lobatse 40 km from Gaborone (15 km beyond the Ramotswa turning) onto a fair gravel road signposted to Ranaka/Mogobane. The dam is immediately before Mogobane village some 8 km from the Lobatse Road.

The Gaborone region, as defined by the 50 km x 50 km half degree square, boasts over 380 bird species, so there is plenty to find. Perhaps the more rewarding include Short-toed Rock Thrush, Crimson Boubou, Whitethroated Robin, Whitecrowned Shrike, Burntnecked Eremomela, Cutthroat Finch, Natal

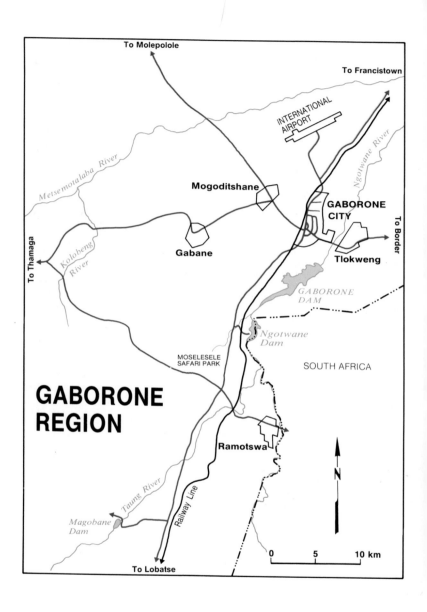

To Molepolole

To Francistown

INTERNATIONAL AIRPORT

Metsemotalaba River

Mogoditshane

Kolobeng River

Gabane

To Thamaga

Ngotwane River

GABORONE CITY

To Border

Tlokweng

GABORONE DAM

Ngotwane Dam

GABORONE REGION

MOSELESELE SAFARI PARK

SOUTH AFRICA

Ramotswa

Taung River

Railway Line

Magobane Dam

N

0   5   10 km

To Lobatse

Francolin and, during summer, migrants such as Icterine Warbler.

Anyone with more than a day or two in Gaborone should try to visit the south-east corner beyond Lobatse. Here the woodland gives way to more open grassland and a change of emphasis in the birdlife. Up to ten larks can be seen including the special Shortclawed Lark. Black Korhaans, Black Crows and Greater Kestrels become common. There are several good localities which are detailed as follows:

BAROLONG FARMS: The open grass savanna with scattered trees and numerous small pans in this upper part of the Molopo River catchment are unlike any other part of eastern Botswana. In contrast to the Kalahari there are extensive arable lands. General access is by the main road from Ramatlabama to Pitsane, and by the two secondary roads leading respectively northwest from Ramatlabama towards Mmathethe and west from Pisane, but there are also numerous rough tracks.

Two grassy pans just west of Ramatlabama village are typical of this area, and are easily accessible. Turn west onto a graded road just 0,9 km north of the border control post. This road passes through Ramatlabama village and, 5 km west of the main road, crosses the edge of one of the pans, with the other 0,5 km to the south-west. As in all pans bird variety and abundance vary greatly according to wetness, and indeed this is no small part of the ornithological interest in this area. At various times species such as African Snipe, Marsh Owl and Orangethroated Longclaw have been found here. The surrounding grasslands have resident Black Korhaan and both Greater and Rock Kestrels, while in summer Lesser Kestrel can be abundant with Eastern Redfooted Kestrel and other migrant raptors turning up.

The region is also good for larks, including the Shortclawed and other resident species, while the Pinkbilled and Melodious Lark are occasional visitors. There are also scattered Sociable Weaver colonies in the Barolong Farms, with a local concentration between 4 km and 6 km due north of Ramatlabama village. To reach these nests take an ungraded track north from near the eastern end of the village, about 1,5 km west of the main road. One can continue north through the network of tracks and rejoin the main road at Rakhuna.

KGORO PAN: this is the biggest and best of the muddy pans and also has extensive rock outcrops. Drive west from the crossroads at Pitsane on a good graded road. After 15,5 km, at a bend in the road just at the start of the village of Good Hope, turn north on an ungraded track. Head as if to pass just west of Kgoro Hill (the most prominent hill in view). After some 3 km the large depression of Kgoro (or Good Hope) Pan will become visible and there are then several minor tracks which lead towards it.

After rains a good selection of waders are found here, including rare visitors such as Turnstone and both species of flamingo, while most of the few occurrences of Blue Crane in Botswana have been recorded at this pan. Rufouseared Warbler occurs in the surrounding scrub.

PITSANE PAN: although this lies within a loose-knit village it can also be worth a visit, particularly after rains. To reach it turn east past the grain silos at Pitsane crossroads, and follow the road across the railway. Pitsane (or Mabete) Pan is then about 0,5 km to the northeast.

LOBATSE lies within a block of enclosed farmland within which access is relatively restricted. However, access on foot to the hills within the township boundary can be gained at several points, such as via the road that leads west past the High Court. The wooded hills and open arable landscape to the west of Lobatse can also prove very rewarding, as seen along the roads leading past Diabo Pan.

DIABO AREA: this refers to the open grassland and cultivated lands around Dipotsana and Pelotshetlha. Some 14 km after taking the Kanye road 5 km south of Lobatse, there is a gate and dirt road (usable by two-wheel drive vehicles).

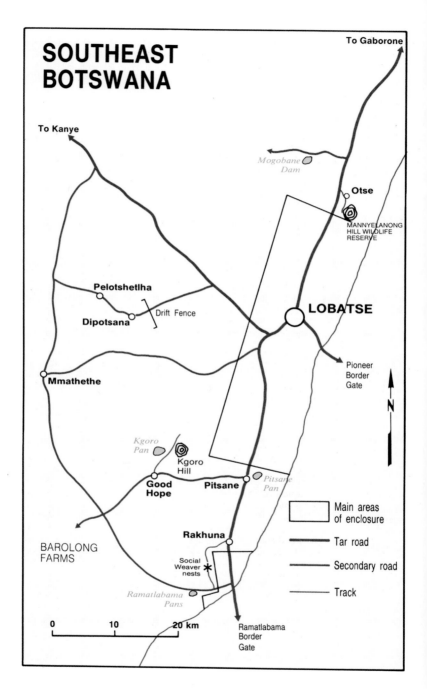

Follow this road passing through a drift fence after some 11 km. Another 3-4 km brings one to Dipotsana, which is a cluster of houses and a windmill in the middle of an open area.

This is another good locality for Shortclawed and Pinkbilled Larks, among others. Black Korhaan are plentiful and occasionally Whitebellied Korhaan can be found, as can Orange River Francolin, Namaqua Sandgrouse and the odd Secretarybird. Carry on to Pelotshetlha following the main track some 26 km from the turn-off. A further 8 km west brings one to the main Kanye/Mathete road. Look out for Chat Flycatcher along this stretch.

MANNYELALONG HILL WILDLIFE RESERVE: this reserve lies a short distance southeast of the village of Otse which is beside the main road north of Lobatse. The reserve was established in 1985 to help protect the one colony of Cape Vultures remaing in southern Botswana. The colony site, on the precipitous southern side of the hill, is clearly visible from the main road. To reach the base of the cliff take the turnoff at the northern end of the village, which is signposted to Otse and Moeding College. After 0,6 km cross the railway and then bear right on the graded gravel road. After a further 1 km turn right immediately below a small dam and cross a low concrete bridge. Just beyond the bridge turn left, following a dirt track around the contour east of the houses. Wildlife Department officials can be contacted at their house (about 0,8 km after the bridge) where a permit to visit the Reserve can be obtained for a small fee, but the Reserve has no formal opening hours. Continue on the same track to reach the colony.

Please note that the Cape Vultures are very susceptible to human disturbance, particularly during the breeding season (May to November). Excellent views can be obtained from outside the perimeter fence, especially as the morning air warms up and the vultures set out to forage, and in the late afternoon when they return.

In addition to the Cape Vultures, Black Eagle and Black Stork can often be seen from below the colony, as well as cliff-dwelling residents such as Rock Kestrel, Rock Pigeon and Mocking Chat. The Lanner Falcon is also resident in the general vicinity of Otse. The *Acacia* woodland around the base of Mannyelalong Hill is good for many of the more usual bird species of the area.

MOGOBANE DAM lies on the western side of Mogobane Village, north-west of Otse. To find the dam take the main road to about 5 km north of Otse and then drive west from the signposted turnoff. After another 5 km the road passes through a village; turn sharply left at a dairy farm then right to lead over a drift. The wooded valley below the dam can itself repay investigation, but to reach the open water continue west along the road for a further 1,5 km until the reservoir is seen. (This road continues on a picturesque route through the hills to Ranaka, then to Kanye or to Mosopa.)

Mogobane Dam is fairly shallow, and is best for water birds when the reservoir is about half full. Apart from a good range of waders in summer, 11 species of herons and 15 species of ducks and geese have been recorded at various times. The damp grass and reeds at either end of the reservoir and in the valley downstream are good for such species as Orangebreasted Waxbill, Fantailed Cisticola and a variety of widows and whydahs.

Further information can be found in articles by:

Wilson, J.R. (1984). 'The avifauna of the Lobatse area, south-east Botswana'. *Babbler 8*: 17-45.

Hunter, N.D. (1984). 'Preliminary notes on bird distribution and rarities in south-east Botswana.' *Babbler 7*: 14-22.

Gulls and terns. Family LARIDAE. Gulls are scavengers of coastal and inland waters. When feeding they pick their food, offal and other refuse, from land or from water, but do not plunge. Feeding flocks make loud screaming sounds. Terns differ from gulls in having more agile flight and more graceful proportions. Most have white underparts and grey upperparts with a black cap when breeding, this giving way to a white forehead when not breeding. The majority of terns, unlike gulls, plunge-dive to catch fish while others, especially those of inland waters, pluck insects and fish fry from the water's surface in hovering or dipping flight.

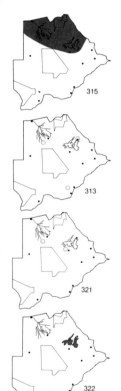

1 GREYHEADED GULL *Larus cirrocephalus.* Locally common resident. Adults have all-grey hood plus pale yellow eyes and bright red bills and legs as illustrated. The immature has a white head with dark smudges behind the eyes plus *ashy brown mottling on the upperparts and a black subterminal tail-bar.* Occurrence mainly centred on Chobe, Okavango Delta and Makgadikgadi Pans where, in favourable years, it is known to breed. Occurrence elsewhere occasional. 42 cm. **315**

2 LESSER BLACKBACKED GULL *Larus fuscus.* Rare summer vagrant. A large, distinctive white gull with black upperparts, yellow bill with a red spot near tip of lower mandible, pale straw coloured eyes with red eyerings and pale yellow legs. At rest the wings project well beyond the tail. Could occur singly at any large pan or dam but few records to date. 53-56 cm. **313**

3 GULLBILLED TERN *Gelochelidon nilotica.* Rare vagrant. A medium-sized tern with erect, gull-like posture. In breeding plumage has black cap, this reducing to a black mark behind the eye in non-breeding plumage. The *heavy, gull-like bill* is black, as are the longish legs. Feeds over water in dipping flight or by hawking insects at grass fires. When standing with other terns is noticeably taller. 38 cm. **321**

4 CASPIAN TERN *Hydroprogne caspia.* Rare to localised, seasonally common resident. Large size and massive red bill render this tern unmistakable. The immature has the upperparts mottled brownish. Usually singly or in small groups but large numbers when breeding. Flight leisurely, unlaboured. Hovers with bill directed downwards before plunge-diving, usually submerging completely, then takes off and swallows fish in flight. On Makgadikgadi Pans common when breeding after rains, otherwise occasional. 52 cm. **322**

5 BLACKHEADED GULL *Larus ridibundus.* Very rare vagrant; exact status not established. One record for Chobe region awaiting confirmation. Head may be blackish or speckled blackish on frontal half or white with black spot behind ear; see illustrations. Smaller than (1) with which it may mix. In flight shows more white on upper forewing. 35-38 cm. **319**

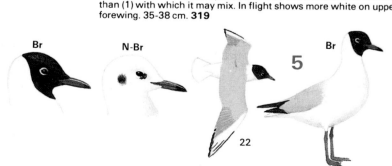

Br   N-Br   5   Br

22

1 WHISKERED TERN *Chlidonias hybridus.* Locally fairly common resident. Distinctive in breeding plumage, the sooty-grey body separated from the black cap by a white 'whisker' from bill to nape, bill and legs bright red. Non-breeding birds differ from the next species at this time mainly by presence of a *black streak extending from eye to nape, plus pale grey rump*; bill then black, legs dull red. Normally in small groups flying slowly back and forth over the water with slow, laboured wingbeats, the bill pointed downwards. Dips to the surface to seize food, occasionally shallow-plunging, or hawks insects in the air. Breeds in late summer at least in the Okavango Delta, nomadic and uncommon elsewhere. 23 cm. **338**

2 WHITEWINGED TERN (WHITEWINGED BLACK TERN) *Chlidonias leucopterus.* Common non-breeding summer visitor. Normally seen in non-breeding plumage when it differs from the previous species mainly in having a *black ear-patch* and spot before the eye plus a *white* rump and black legs. In breeding plumage, frequently seen in late summer, the entire body (except for white vent and tail) and underwing coverts are black, bill and legs dark red. Small groups or flocks occur over large waters, sewage ponds and occasionally pans. The flight is bouyant, erratic. Feeds by swooping for food on water, hawking it in the air or by hovering. Roosts in semi-submerged dead trees in water. 23 cm. **339**

Skimmers. Family RYNCHOPIDAE.

3 AFRICAN SKIMMER *Rynchops flavirostris.* Fairly common, localised resident. A brown and white tern-like bird with distinctive bill structure, this and the feeding action diagnostic. The immature has a streaky crown, upperparts with buff-edged feathers, the bill dark. Catches small fish by flying low over the water with the long lower mandible immersed in a skimming action. Flight elegant with powerful wing-beats. Small flocks occur on the Chobe and Okavango Rivers and the upper reaches of the Okavango Delta where they breed and rest on sandbanks. 38 cm. **343**

Cormorants. Family PHALACROCORACIDAE. Webb-footed, long-necked, hook-billed, fish- and frog-eating waterbirds which hunt their prey under water, then surface to swallow it. Swim with body partially submerged and habitually stand out of water with wings outspread to dry. Silent birds.

1 REED CORMORANT *Phalacrocorax africanus*. Fairly common resident. A small, long-tailed, crested cormorant, black to dark brown with paler, mottled underparts in the female. Immature lacks crest, has *entire underparts buffy-white*, never pure white; cf. next species. Singly or in small groups on most deep waters of northern, eastern and south-eastern Botswana. 60 cm. **58**

2 WHITEBREASTED CORMORANT *Phalacrocorax carbo*. Fairly common, localised resident. A large cormorant, adult all blackish except for pure white throat and breast, sometimes with a white thigh-patch. Immature with *pure white underparts*; cf. immature of previous species. Seen regularly on major dams, often resting in dead trees or on posts. 90 cm. **55**

Darters. Family ANHINGIDAE. Thin-necked, cormorant-like waterbirds with straight, unhooked bills. They catch fish under water by impaling them on their dagger-like bills, surfacing to swallow them. Swim with the body mostly submerged, only the long head and neck protruding above the surface, hence the popular name 'snake-bird'.

3 DARTER *Anhinga melanogaster*. Fairly common but localised resident. Distinguished from cormorants by long, thin neck with characteristic 'kink', and unhooked bill. Adult has lower neck rufous, upper neck dark brown with a white line extending backwards from the bill; upperparts with long, gold-buff plumes. The young bird, from nestling to immature, is buff coloured. Like cormorants the Darter perches with wings outspread to dry after fishing. Singly or in pairs on large waters and rivers, being most frequent in the Okavango Delta. 79 cm. **60**

Pelicans. Family PELECANIDAE. Huge, large-bodied waterbirds with short legs and webbed feet, long necks, long bills and a naked distensible pouch below the lower mandible. They catch fish by gathering in flocks and driving shoals into the shallows where they are scooped up in their bill-pouches. Walk awkwardly but soar effortlessly, sometimes to great heights.

4 WHITE PELICAN *Pelecanus onocrotalatus*. Fairly common localised resident. Adult told from the next species by larger size and all-white plumage (head and neck with a pale pink flush when breeding) except for a yellow breast-patch; the bill pink with blue-grey sides and yellow pouch. Immature as illustrated, darkest when youngest, becoming progressively paler with age. Occurs in flocks in the Okavango Delta and Makgadikgadi Pans, breeding in both localities; singly elsewhere. 180 cm. **49**

5 PINKBACKED PELICAN *Pelecanus rufescens*. Fairly common, localised resident. Adult distinguished from previous species by smaller size, pale grey-buff upperparts plus pale yellow bill and pouch; immature by rust-brown head, neck and upperparts. Usually in flocks on major waters, breeding in the Okavango Delta and Makgadikgadi Pans; single birds occur elsewhere. 135 cm. **50**

26

Herons. Family ARDEIDAE. Water-associated birds with moderately long bills, long necks and legs. Egrets are also a type of heron. When breeding many species have long, filamentous plumes on their backs or lower breast, or on both, while others have more or less permanent plumes on their napes. Again many species temporarily change the colours of their bills, facial skin and legs during the early part of their breeding cycle. Herons fly with their necks tucked into their shoulders, thus differing from storks, ibises and cranes. They seldom soar. Many herons are solitary in habit and secretive, others are gregarious and much in evidence. Most perch in trees and nest in reeds, trees or even on the ground. All have voices of a harsh, squawking nature heard usually when flushed. The four comparative silhouettes on the opposite page represent A: Dwarf Bittern (1); B: Squacco Heron (page 31); C: Little Egret (page 35); D: Grey Heron (page 37).

1 DWARF BITTERN *Ixobrychus sturmii.* Uncommon resident and summer visitor. Slate grey upperparts and heavily streaked underparts make adult appear all-dark at a distance but orange-yellow feet distinctive when flushed. Immature can be confused with that of (2) and (3) but *rufous underparts* and *rufous-tipped feathers* of upperparts, plus orange-yellow legs and feet diagnostic. The flight is direct and pigeon-like. Usually solitary (sometimes breeds in loose colonies) and largely crepuscular or nocturnal. Frequents pans, well-wooded rivers and bushes or thickets in floodwaters. When disturbed may adopt a 'sky-pointing' posture; see illustration. If flushed will perch in a tree. Occurrence often dependent on rainfall. 25 cm. **79**

2 LITTLE BITTERN *Ixobrychus minutus.* Uncommon resident and summer visitor. Bold marking of male unmistakable; female recognised by buffy neck and black cap. Immature differs from that of previous species in paler, less rufous underparts and olive (not orange-yellow) legs; from immature of the next species in tawny (not dark) folded wings. A diurnal species, solitary individuals usually well scattered in reeds and sedges where difficult to flush, 'sky-pointing' to avoid detection, although many birds can congregate at communal roosts in reedbeds at nightfall. Occurrence often dependent on rainfall. 26 cm. **78**

3 GREENBACKED HERON *Butorides striatus.* Locally common resident, commonest in the Delta. Upperparts appear grey-green, the feathers all clearly edged creamy, sides of neck and flanks grey, cap black; when flushed yellow feet prominent. Sexes alike. Immature identified by dark upperparts with *whitish spots on folded wings;* cf.immature of (1) and (2). Usually singly on wooded waters and papyrus beds, hunting by day from a dead tree in water or on shoreline. Will perch in a tree when flushed. 41 cm. **74**

4 RUFOUSBELLIED HERON *Butorides rufiventris.* Uncommon localised resident. All-dark heron with pale yellow facial skin and legs; rufous body and underwings distinctive in flight. Immature has buff-edged feathers to upperparts. Solitary and secretive on secluded, well vegetated backwaters. In the Okavango Delta breeds on islands of water figs *Ficus verruculosa* in association with other waterbirds, and is then conspicuous in the vicinity. 58 cm. **75**

1 SQUACCO HERON *Ardeola ralloides.* Locally common resident of northern waterways, uncommon summer visitor to the east. Distinctive in both breeding and non-breeding plumage; in flight resembles an egret but for buffy back. Occurs singly in secluded backwaters and flooded lands with emergent grasses, preferring to remain concealed in the vegetation. Most frequently seen in the Okavango Delta and Moremi Game Reserve where it breeds semi-colonially with other waterbirds on islands of water figs *Ficus verruculosa.* At nightfall large numbers congregate in regularly used reedbed roosts. 43 cm. **72**

2 BLACK EGRET *Egretta ardesiaca.* Uncommon to locally common resident; summer visitor only in the east. Entirely blue-black heron with black bill and legs and *yellow feet;* more robust, thicker-necked than the next species. Single birds or groups, sometimes large gatherings, at the fringes of flood pans, lagoons and dams, less often on rivers. When fishing habitually forms a canopy with its wings to exclude surface reflections. In the Okavango Delta breeds colonially with other herons and storks on islands of water figs *Ficus verruculosa.* 66 cm. **69**

3 SLATY EGRET *Egretta vinaceigula.* Uncommon, localised resident. More elegant, longer necked and more slate-grey than the previous species, with a rufous throat (most extensive in young birds) and *yellowish legs.* Occurs sparsely in the Chobe-Linyanti-Okavango region. Usually seen singly on quiet waters except at nightfall when numbers congregate to roost in favoured reedbeds. 60 cm. **70**

N-Br

1 WHITEBACKED NIGHT HERON *Gorsachius leuconotus*. Rare resident. Black hood, yellow facial markings and legs plus rufous plumage diagnostic; the white back-plumes present at all ages. When alarmed into flight makes a toad-like 'kraak'. Singly or in pairs sparsely distributed on quiet, well-wooded waters. In the Okavango Delta is found in secluded backwaters fringed by thickets, tall reeds or papyrus, elsewhere very rare but could be expected at well-wooded dams and rivers with permanent water. Entirely nocturnal in habits, roosting by day in a tree or reedbed. 53 cm. **77**

2 BLACKCROWNED NIGHT HERON *Nycticorax nycticorax*. Fairly common resident. Adult has characteristic black cap and black back contrasting with grey wings and white underparts; nape-plumes may be absent. Immature entirely different, resembling the next species but differing in smaller size, orange eyes, white spots to the tips of the feathers of the upperparts, and heavily streaked under-parts. Normally silent but emits a harsh 'quock' if flushed. Single birds or small groups frequent river backwaters, lagoons and dams at night, roosting by day in groups in trees or reedbeds. In the Okavango Delta can be seen at dusk flying in small flocks from roosts to favoured feeding grounds. 56 cm. **76**

3 BITTERN *Botaurus stellaris*. Rare, exact status not established. Occurrence poorly documented; may be resident in Okavango-Linyanti regions. Similar to the immature of the last species but much larger with a thickset appearance, more heavily streaked overall, with a black cap and yellow or red-brown eyes. In flight has a much greater wingspan than Blackcrowned Night Heron and the entire foot protrudes beyond the tail. Normal take-off call is 'squark', otherwise makes a far-carrying booming sound day or night during the summer when breeding. Solitary and highly secretive in seasonal and permanent marshes and backwaters in grassland. When alarmed adopts an upright 'sky-pointing' stance and is not easily flushed. 64 cm. **80**

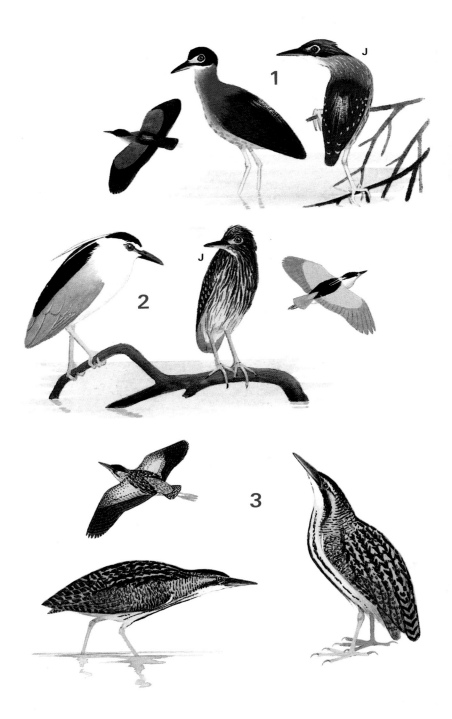

1 CATTLE EGRET *Bubulcus ibis.* Common resident and summer visitor. When breeding, October-March, adult has buff feathers on crown, back and breast, bill and legs coral to reddish, feet dusky. At other times adult entirely white, the bill yellow with black tip, legs dull yellow to dusky. Immature has black bill and legs, differing from next species in short bill, *black feet* and shorter, thicker neck. Does not feed at water but rests and roosts near water. Flocks attend cattle, to a lesser extent also wild ungulates, to glean insects disturbed by the grazing animals. Flocks often fly long distances daily between favoured roosts and feeding areas. Breeds colonially, usually in very large numbers, in trees or reeds over water. Widespread, most common in the east and north but vagrants may occur anywhere. 54 cm. **71**

2 LITTLE EGRET *Egretta garzetta.* Fairly common resident. More slenderly proportioned than the previous species with longer neck, long black bill and slender black legs with diagnostic *yellow feet.* Head plumes constant, breast and back plumes only when breeding. Gregarious at roosts and when breeding, otherwise mostly solitary. Occurs on still waters where it stands quietly in the shallows, or walks forward stealthily hunting. Most common on large, permanent waters but individuals wander widely. 64 cm. **67**

3 YELLOWBILLED EGRET *Egretta intermedia.* Locally common resident in the north, uncommon visitor elsewhere. Larger than previous two species, more heavily built, but smaller than the next. Plumes usually absent or reduced when not breeding, absent in immature. Bill normally yellow but orange with red base briefly when breeding; *upper legs yellow* but reddish briefly when breeding, lower legs and feet blackish-green. The neck has the characteristic 'kink' of the larger herons and, in profile, the long lower neck-feathers tend to stick out; cf. next species. Usually solitary but sometimes in loose groups, preferring to feed in the emergent grasses of floodplains and the well-vegetated fringes of pans. Roosts and breeds colonially with other herons. 68 cm. **68**

4 GREAT WHITE EGRET *Egretta alba.* Fairly common resident. Large, long-necked, long-legged egret with *normally orange-yellow bill*, thus frequently misidentified as the previous species but is much larger with *entirely black legs and feet.* The line of the gape extends back behind the eye; cf.(3). For a few weeks when breeding the bill is black, often with a yellow base, and filamentous plumes are present on the back. Single birds are usually seen standing motionless in shallows of large rivers, floodplains and dams. Gregarious when roosting and breeding. Most common in the northern regions but individuals are frequent in the south-east. 95 cm. **66**

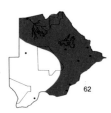

1 GREY HERON *Ardea cinerea.* Common resident. At rest differs from the Blackheaded Heron (4) mainly in having a white crown and heavy black eyebrow, *yellow bill*, absence of black on the hind neck plus pale yellow legs; in flight by *entirely grey underwings*. Immature is much paler than adult and immature of (4), also differing from that species by yellowish bill. Solitary in the shallows of quiet dams, rivers, lagoons and floodplains. Stands motionless for long periods when feeding, or stalks forward stealthily in a crouched attitude. Gregarious at roosts. Flight ponderous. 100 cm. **62**

2 PURPLE HERON *Ardea purpurea.* Locally common resident and uncommon visitor. Similar to the next species but much smaller, more slender, the neck thin and snake-like with a thin bill. Immature less brightly coloured about the neck, markings less clearly defined. Solitary and secretive, preferring the shelter of reeds and other emergent vegetation fringing lagoons and similar quiet waters. Most plentiful in the Okavango Delta where relatively large numbers congregate at nightfall to roost in favoured reedbeds. Breeds colonially with other herons, wandering widely at other times. 89 cm. **65**

3 GOLIATH HERON *Ardea goliath.* Uncommon localised resident. Larger than all other herons, more robustly proportioned, with slate-grey upperparts and rich rufous head, neck and underparts. Flies with ponderous wingbeats. Immature browner above, whitish streaked brown below. Singly or in pairs on large waters, feeding in deeper water than other herons where it stands motionless for long periods or stalks with slow strides. 140 cm. **64**

4 BLACKHEADED HERON *Ardea melanocephala.* Locally common resident in the east and south-east, uncommon in the north. Differs from the otherwise similar Grey Heron (1) by *entirely black* (or dark blue-grey) top to head and back of entire neck, plus slaty legs; in flight by *black and grey underwings*. Immature less black about head and neck, greyer than immature of (1), the foreneck with rufous markings. Normally feeds away from water, solitarily in grasslands, grassy road verges, agricultural lands, marshes and sewage ponds. Breeds in reeds or trees over water. Flight ponderous. 97 cm. **63**

Storks. Family CICONIIDAE. Large or very large, long-legged, long-necked birds with straight, stout bills. Fly with their necks out-stretched (with the exception of the Marabou Stork) and legs trailing well behind the tail. Leg colours often appear white as the result of soiling by defecation, a method of cooling down. They often rest with the lower part of their legs stretched forward on the ground (see illustration of immature Marabou Stork) and, on hot days, often soar to great heights. Bill-clapping is often used in greeting between pairs at the nest, but all species are otherwise silent.

1 SADDLEBILLED STORK *Ephippiorhynchus senegalensis.* Un-common resident. A large, strikingly coloured stork unlikely to be confused with any other; distinctive both at rest and in flight. Male has small, yellow pendant wattle at base of bill; female lacks this but has yellow eye-rings. Immature with grey instead of black markings, the white areas mottled with black, bill dull, blackish. Singly or in pairs in the shallows of large rivers, floodplains and marshes. Most frequent in the Chobe-Linyanti-Okavango region. 145 cm. **88**

2 MARABOU STORK *Leptoptilos crumeniferus.* Locally common resident, being most frequent in the northern regions, otherwise nomadic. Huge, bare-headed, bare-necked stork with a distensible fleshy pouch on the lower foreneck. Unlike other storks flies with the neck tucked in. Immature as illustrated, with woolly head fea-thers. Generally in flocks, large or small, frequently associating with vultures at animal carcasses and refuse dumps. Also gather at pools in rivers and floodlands to feed on trapped fish. Widespread and largely nomadic when not breeding, soaring to great heights and travelling long distances in search of food. Sometimes gather at rivers to bathe and rest, often spending days resting at one place. Large, regularly used breeding colonies exist in the Okavango Delta. 152 cm. **89**

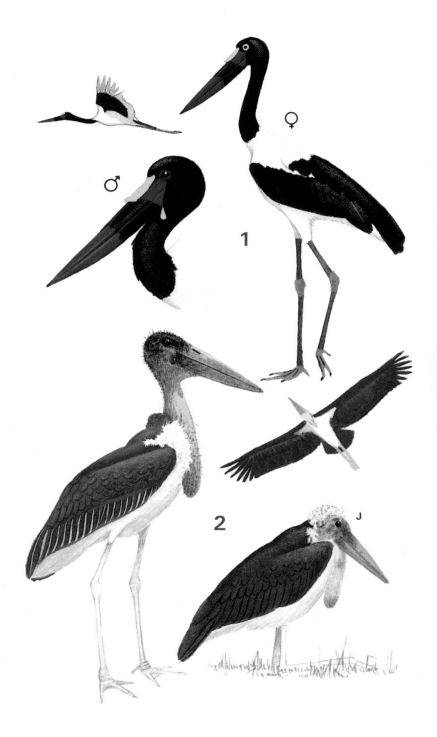

1 WHITE STORK *Ciconia ciconia.* Fairly common summer visitor. Unmistakable, large black and white stork with red bill and legs. Occurs in small, loose groups or large flocks feeding in grasslands, fallow farmlands and savanna, often in association with Abdim's Stork (3). Widespread and nomadic in summer. Flocks often soar and travel at great heights on hot days. May suddenly appear in a district and remain a few days to feed, then depart, this behaviour linked to infestations of agricultural pests. Numbers vary year to year. 117 cm. **83**

2 BLACK STORK *Ciconia nigra.* Uncommon resident. Similar to the next species but differing from it in larger sizer, red bill and longer, red legs. The immature has bill and legs yellowish-green, plumage duller. Occurs singly or in pairs but groups may gather to roost at night. Feeds at rivers and dams, breeds on cliffs, its distribution therefore linked to the hills of the south-east, east and north-west. 122 cm. **84**

3 ABDIM'S STORK *Ciconia abdimii.* Common summer visitor. Smaller, shorter-legged than previous species, the bill tawny, face blue, legs pink with red joints and feet. In flight this and the previous species difficult to distinguish one from the other unless seen at close range, but this species usually flocks, sometimes in hundreds. Feeds in grasslands, agricultural lands and savanna, often mixing with the White Stork (1). Like that species flocks soar to great heights and move about in response to insect infestations. 76 cm. **85**

1

2

3

1 YELLOWBILLED STORK *Mycteria ibis*. Fairly common localised resident and uncommon visitor. Distinguished by yellow, slightly down-curved bill, red face and forehead and pink legs; colours most intense when breeding, white plumage then with a distinct pink flush. Immature has head, neck and wing coverts pale brownish. Usually seen in small groups, occasionally larger flocks. Frequents floodpans, rivers and dams, favouring a woodland habitat. Feeds by wading and probing actively beneath the water, often with head submerged, while constantly moving. At times spreads one wing while feeding to diminish surface reflections. Groups rest at the waterside, often with other large waterbirds. Most common in the north. 97 cm. **90**

2 WOOLLYNECKED STORK *Ciconia episcopus*. Uncommon resident; sparsely distributed throughout the northern region, rarely in the southern half of Botswana. Identified by woolly white head and neck with black face plus white belly and undertail coverts, the *undertail coverts projecting beyond the black tail*. Immature lacks white patch at base of bill, generally duller. Usually singly in inundated grasslands in well-wooded areas; occasionally on dams and pans. 86 cm. **86**

3 OPENBILLED STORK *Anastomus lamelligerus*. Fairly common, localised resident. A small stork, appearing all-black with a tawny bill; at close range the open gap between the mandibles can be seen, but this is lacking in the young. Old birds have long, golden-brown lanceolate plumes on their backs and breasts. Usually in flocks in the wetlands of the northern regions, large flocks occurring in the Okavango Delta. Nomadic when not breeding, flying at great heights and for long distances between feeding grounds, thus producing occasional records elsewhere. Feeds on fresh water snails and mussels. Breeds colonially in trees standing in water, often in mixed colonies. 94 cm. **87**

Hamerkop. Family SCOPIDAE.

4 HAMERKOP *Scopus umbretta*. Fairly common resident. May occur anywhere beyond its normal range on occasion. Small, dull brown waterbird with a large, backward-projecting crest and heavy, conical black bill; immature similar. In flight makes a strange nasal 'wek...wek...wek...wek...'; at rest may make the same sound or a wavering, high-pitched 'wek-wek-warrrrrk' repeatedly. Singly, sometimes in groups when feeding, at almost any water point. Feeds in the shallows, stalking and shuffling its feet to disturb frogs and other aquatic creatures. On large waters may fly over the water and swoop down for food after hovering briefly. Builds huge, domed nest in waterside tree (see illustration) or on large rock. 56 cm. **81**

Flamingoes. Family PHOENICOPTERIDAE. Flamingoes usually occur in large flocks, sometimes many thousands together. Single birds and small groups are less usual. They prefer shallow saline waters and, unless breeding, are nomadic, remaining in one place only so long as conditions are suitable. Both species can occur in large numbers at Makgadikgadi Pans and Lake Ngami, where breeding is known; elsewhere they occur as erratic visitors. Individuals in a flock make a honking sound which, collectively, results in a continuous babbling. Immatures are grey-brown with a bill pattern similar to adults. Flamingoes fly with both neck and legs outstretched.

1 LESSER FLAMINGO *Phoenicopterus minor.* Common resident and uncommon visitor; see under family description. Distinguished by evenly coloured *dark maroon bill* which appears black at a distance; smaller and *pinker* overall than the next species. In flight the wing coverts are mottled with dark red. 102 cm. **97**

2 GREATER FLAMINGO *Phoenicopterus ruber.* Common resident and uncommon visitor; see under family description. Distinguished by *pink bill with black tip*; in company with the previous species is taller, whiter. In flight the wing coverts are an even scarlet. 140 cm. **96**

Ibises and spoonbills. Family PLATALEIDAE. Large waterbirds with longish legs, ibises with decurved bills, spoonbills with spatulate bills. Ibises feed by probing the ground with their bills, spoonbills feed in water. All but the Hadeda Ibis are normally silent.

3 AFRICAN SPOONBILL *Platalea alba.* Fairly common resident. Distinguished from other white waterbirds by pink legs and pink, spoon-shaped bill. Immature has wings and head streaked brown. Occurs singly or in small flocks on both regular waters and seasonal flood pans. Feeds with the bill submersed and partially open while being moved side-to-side as illustrated. Breeds colonially, often with other waterbirds, in reeds and trees in water, especially in the Okavango Delta. Nomadic when not breeding. 91 cm. **95**

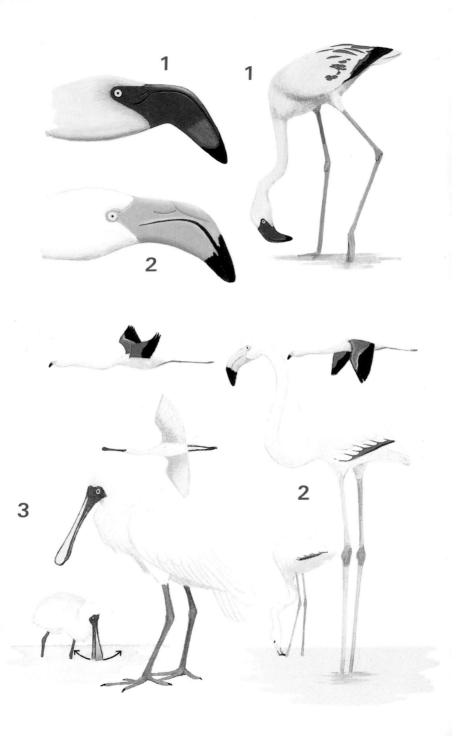

1 SACRED IBIS *Threskiornis aethiopicus.* Fairly common resident. Has curved black bill, black head, neck, legs and back plumes contrasting with otherwise white plumage. Immature has front of neck white, rest speckled, back plumes absent. Single birds or flocks frequent marshy ground adjoining dams, sewage ponds and floodplains in addition to moist agricultural lands. Breeds colonially in reedbeds or bushes with other waterbirds. Nomadic. 89 cm. **91**

2 HADEDA IBIS *Bostrychia hagedash.* Locally common resident. Identified by heavy body with fairly short legs, decurved bill and iridescent pink shoulder plus white cheek-stripes; in flight shows broad wings. Immature duller, fluffy-headed. Very noisy; when perched or in flight makes a raucous 'HA! ha-a-a...ha-ha-a-a...', often several calling in unison, mostly early morning and evening. Usually in small groups in marshes, agricultural lands, dams, sewage ponds and riverine woodland. Roosts in tall trees and flies to and from feeding grounds early and late in the day. 76 cm. **94**

3 GLOSSY IBIS *Plegadis falcinellus.* Locally fairly common resident, otherwise uncommon visitor. Slender, lighter-bodied than other ibises, bronze-brown in breeding plumage with iridescent green wings; at other times the head and neck flecked white; see illustrations. Immature has pink patches on bill and neck as illustrated. Flocks sometimes fly in large, V-shaped skeins, the birds identified by their slender appearance and protruding legs; cf. (2). Frequent permanent waters in the north, breeding in mixed waterbird colonies in the Okavango Delta. Occurs as visiting nomad in the east and south-east, sometimes in large numbers during seasons of good rains, when they feed at dams and sewage ponds. 71 cm. **93**

Finfoots. Family HELIORNITHIDAE.

4 AFRICAN FINFOOT *Podica senegalensis.* Rare; exact status uncertain. Very few records to date with no confirmed sightings for northern waters. Differs from any duck or cormorant in bright vermillion bill and legs; female with white throat. Normally silent but a clucking is sometimes heard when a bird is flushed. Solitary or in pairs on secluded, tree-lined waters where it swims unobtrusively beneath the overhanging branches. Swims with much of the body submerged, head and neck stretched forward with each foot-stroke; dives well. Shy and retiring. If disturbed patters vigorously across the water, feet making a distinct splashing sound. Sometimes leaves the water to rest on a rock or semi-submerged branch. Roosts at night on a low, overhanging branch. 63 cm. **229**

Geese and ducks. Family ANATIDAE. Members of this family in southern Africa are subject to considerable movements, both short and long range. These movements are not migrations since they form no regular pattern, but are dictated by rainfall patterns and breeding requirements. Thus duck numbers fluctuate markedly. Many species have bright, often metallic wing specula in both sexes. Some ducks have marked sexual plumage differences (sexual dimorphism) and all undergo an annual flightless period when they moult their wing feathers entirely. At these times they retire to the safety of large waters.

1 WHITEFACED DUCK *Dendrocygna viduata.* Common resident. Distinguished from female South African Shelduck (pp. 50-51) by black head and neck, banded flanks and erect posture. Immature with white face smudged brown. The call is a loud, shrill whistling 'swee-swee-sweeoo', often by many birds in a flying flock. Has long legs and an erect stance and swims with the body high in the water. In flight feet protrude beyond tail. Flocks, often hundreds, on large waters, especially those with surface and emergent vegetation, feeding mostly post-dawn and pre-dusk, loafing on shorelines and sandbanks by day. Numbers subject to much fluctuation. 48 cm. **99**

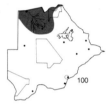

2 FULVOUS DUCK *Dendrocygna bicolor.* Uncommon to locally common resident; rare in the south-east. Fulvous colouring and cream-coloured flank feathers diagnostic; immature similar, duller. An erect-standing duck with long legs; in flight feet protrude beyond tail. Less vocal than the previous species, two resonant notes repeated 'tsoo-ee'. Gregarious and nomadic when not breeding, flocking sometimes in great numbers at Lake Ngami. Prefers quiet waters with surface and emergent vegetation, feeding post-dawn and pre-dusk, loafing and preening most of the day. 46 cm. **100**

3 WHITEBACKED DUCK *Thalassornis leuconotus.* Fairly common, localised resident; most common in the north, uncommon in the east and south-east. White back visible only in flight or when preening. Best identified by pale spot at base of bill, sharply tapering bill with deep base, and a humped back sloping down to submerged tail when swimming. Immature resembles adult. Makes a soft whistle 'cur-wee'. In pairs or small groups on lagoons and pans, especially temporary flood pans with ample surface and emergent vegetation. Moves to more permanent waters in times of drought. Feeds mostly on water-lilies and their seeds, obtained by diving. Quiet, unobtrusive, difficult to see among surface vegetation, remaining motionless when danger threatens; may dive. Seldom flies by day. 43 cm. **101**

1 PYGMY GOOSE *Nettapus auritus.* Locally common resident. Identified by small size, dark green upperparts and short, deep-based yellow bill; in flight by distinctive white upperwing-patches. Immature resembles female. Mostly silent but males make a soft twittering whistle 'choo-choo' or 'pee-wee' and a repeated, subdued 'tsu-tswi...tsu-tswi...'; females a weak quack and a twittering whistle. Pairs or groups on quiet northern waters: sheltered pans, lagoons and river pools with clear water and waterlilies. When alert remains motionless among the surface vegetation and is difficult to detect. Dives readily and perches in trees. 33 cm. **114**

2 SOUTH AFRICAN SHELDUCK *Tadorna cana.* Uncommon, localised resident and winter visitor. A long-bodied duck with horizontal stance. Female differs from Whitefaced Duck (pp.48-49) in grey (not black) head and neck; in flight both sexes differ from the next species in richer rufous body colouring and grey heads plus white face in female. Immature duller than adult; young female initially with white circles around the eyes, these extending over the face with maturity. Male utters a deep 'hoogh', 'how' or 'honk', female alternating with a harsher 'hark'; female hisses while accompanying young. Courting pairs are noisy and aggressive. Unless in moult pairs frequent shallow brackish pans and dams, mainly in the southeast. 64 cm. **103**

3 EGYPTIAN GOOSE *Alopochen aegyptiacus.* Common, widespread resident. Larger, longer-necked than previous species; long pink legs, pink bill and rufous eye-patches diagnostic. Immature similar, duller. Very noisy in social interactions, males making a husky wheezing sound, females a harsh, nasal, high-pitched 'hur-hur-hur-hur'. Both sexes extend their heads and necks while calling. Pairs or groups occupy small waters or sections of rivers, but large numbers gather on deep waters when in moult. Feeds mainly at night, flying at sunset to communal grazing grounds. Subject to local movement when not breeding and extending into more arid regions in response to rains. 71 cm. **102**

4 SPURWINGED GOOSE *Plectropterus gambensis.* Common resident. Very large size and glossy-black plumage unmistakable; male with a fleshy caruncle on the forehead. Female and immature browner with little or no white on underparts. Male may make a soft high-pitched bubbling 'cherwit' in flight, either sex a four-syllable 'chi-chi-chi-chi'. Unless breeding occurs in flocks on floodplains, swamps and dams. Feeds mostly early morning, evening or night. Subject to marked seasonal, long distance movements. Fly in staggered lines or V-formations. Regularly perches on dead trees. 102 cm. **116**

1 HOTTENTOT TEAL *Anas hottentota*. Uncommon resident. Distinguished by very small size; from the next species by grey-blue (not red) bill and buff colouring of underparts. When swimming the flank feathers usually overlap the wing to form a zig-zag dividing line. Normally silent. Pairs and flocks favour shallow reed-fringed pans, lakes, marsh pools and dams. Most active early morning and evening, much of the day spent resting on shoreline. Nomadic. 35 cm. **107**

2 REDBILLED TEAL *Anas erythrorhyncha*. Common resident. Larger than the previous species, differing in red bill and whitish, heavily speckled body. In flight shows a *cream-coloured* speculum. The few sounds made by this species are soft, audible only at close range. Frequently in large flocks (500 000 seen on Lake Ngami) on lakes, marsh pools, flood plains and dams, preferring open waters with ample submerged and peripheral vegetation. Swims and feeds actively by day during dry season; feeds by night and loafs by day during rains. Nomadic. 48 cm. **108**

3 SOUTHERN POCHARD *Netta erythropthalma*. Fairly common resident. Male dark bronze-brown with tawny flanks, red eyes and slate-grey bill; female duller, distinguished from female of next species by *white crescentic mark on sides of head* plus white throat and bill-base. In flight white specula extend full span of wings. No distinctive calls. Pairs or flocks frequent clear, deep permanent or temporary waters, feeding mostly mornings and evenings, otherwise resting. Nomadic. 51 cm. **113**

4 MACCOA DUCK *Oxyura maccoa*. Uncommon resident and visitor; most frequent in the south-east where known to breed. A small, squat, stiff-tailed duck with short, thick-based bill. Chestnut plumage, black head and bright blue bill of male unmistakable. Female and non-breeding male dull, speckled grey-brown pepper and salt pattern with dark brown back and cap, plus a *white stripe below eye*, and whitish upper neck and throat, bill dull grey. Generally silent. Small numbers occur on shallow, nutrient-rich dams and lakes with extensive fringing reedbeds. Seldom leaves water. Swims with body low, tail trailing, the tip submerged, or with tail stiffly erect. Dives frequently. Male often swims with head and neck stretched forward, tail erect, neck inflated while making bubbles in the water with the bill. 46 cm.**117**

1 CAPE SHOVELLER *Anas smithii.* Fairly common resident. Dull, brownish duck identified by large, black, spatulate bill and yellow-orange legs, yellow eyes in male, brown in female; cf. next species. In flight shows pale blue upperwings. Immature duller. Normally silent but male sometimes utters an explosive 'rrar' or a series of quiet, hoarse 'cawick' sounds with rising inflection, sometimes interspersed with a rapid, rattling 'rarararara'. Female may give a series of notes with downward inflection, a rippling chatter 'chacha-chachacha' or a persistent quacking. Pairs or small groups favour open, shallow saline pans, dams and temporary pools in marshes and rivers after flooding, also sewage ponds where water fertility is high. Nomadic and restless. 53 cm. **112**

2 EUROPEAN SHOVELLER *Anas clypeata.* Not yet recorded in Botswana but known elsewhere in southern Africa as a very rare, non-breeding vagrant. Non-breeding plumage of male differs from that of (1) in rufous flanks and whitish rear end to body plus greyer head, neck and upperparts; bill larger, paler, in both sexes. In flight probably inseparable from Cape Shoveller. Could occur anywhere. 51 cm. **111**

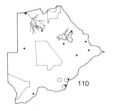

3 GARGANEY *Anas querquedula.* Rare summer vagrant; the three known records refer to the south-east but this species may occasionally occur in other areas. Male most likely to occur in non-breeding plumage, resembling female. A small, brownish duck with distinct streaks *above and below* the eyes; differs from female Maccoa Duck (pp. 52-53) in this, smaller size and smaller bill. Sits low in the water when swimming. Single birds may occur during summer on dams and pans. 38 cm. **110**

4 CAPE TEAL *Anas capensis.* Fairly common resident in the southeast, much less common in the north. A small, pale coloured duck with a pink, upturned bill; looks almost white in good light. In flight shows a predominantly white speculum with a dark green central patch. Immature resembles adult. Usually silent. In pairs or flocks on shallow pans, dams and lakes preferring brack waters, soda lakes. Feeds actively by day. Occurrences often sporadic according to rains, especially in the more arid regions. 46 cm. **106**

1

♂ ♀ ♂

♀ ♂

♂

♀ ♂

♀

N-Br ♂

3

♀

♀ ♂

♀

4

1 PINTAIL *Anas acuta.* Very rare summer vagrant; has been recorded on Lake Ngami but could occasionally occur on any water during summer. Male most likely to occur in non-breeding plumage, resembling female. Told by slender proportions, dull grey bill and brown, speckled plumage; long tail *may not be present.* In flight appears pointed-winged, underbody, underwing coverts and trailing edge of secondaries white, upperwings with bronze-green specula. Feeds by night, wary and inconspicuous by day. 51-66 cm. **109**

2 AFRICAN BLACK DUCK *Anas sparsa.* Uncommon, localised resident. Characterised by dark brown plumage with bold white spotting on wings and back; speculum green with white border. Immature browner, spots buffy, belly barred white. On water appears short-necked, long-bodied. Vociferous when flying, female making persistent loud quacking, male an almost imperceptible 'weep... weep...weep...'. During the day sedentary, territorial pairs frequent well-wooded streams and rivers where secretive and alert; at sunset move to larger, open waters, often many pairs together. Unpaired birds more restless, often occurring on dams by day. 51-54 cm. **105**

3 YELLOWBILLED DUCK *Anas undulata.* Common resident. Bright yellow bill with black central 'saddle' diagnostic; plumage brown, all feathers edged white, broadly on flanks and underparts, imparting an ashy appearance, head and neck dusky. In flight shows bright green specula. Immature has feathers edged buffy, underparts more heavily spotted. No distinctive calls but on taking off female makes loud, evenly spaced quacks. Pairs and flocks occur on a wide range of open waters, feeding mainly early morning and late afternoon; may graze in inundated grassland all day. Nomadic. 53-58 cm. **104**

4 KNOBBILLED DUCK *Sarkidiornis melanotos.* Fairly common resident. Male (much larger than female) distinguished by glossy dark blue upperparts, white underparts, the head and neck well speckled black (washed yellow when breeding) and a large fleshy caruncle on upper mandible. Female duller, lacking caruncle. First-year young (a) quite different from adult, having dark brown upperparts and pale buff underparts with distinct eye-stripe; sub-adult (b) like dull version of female, but underparts orange-buff. Mostly silent. Flocks, in which females usually outnumber males, frequent marshes, floodplains and temporary pans in woodland, less often dams, sewage ponds and rivers. Habitually perches in dead trees. Seasonal movements considerable. Flocks fly in V-formation or staggered line. 64-79 cm. **115**

Grebes. Family PODICIPEDIDAE. Small to fairly large, almost tailless waterbirds. Feed beneath the surface by diving, remaining submerged 20-50 seconds. Seldom seen on land but fly long distances to new waters at night. Breeding and non-breeding plumages differ. Small chicks are striped on the upperparts, the head stripes remaining until nearly fully grown. Ride on parents' backs when small.

1 DABCHICK (LITTLE GREBE) *Tachybaptus ruficollis.* Fairly common resident. Smaller than any duck. Rufous neck and creamy spot at base of bill diagnostic in breeding season; at other times differs from the next species in non-breeding plumage in duller (not white) underparts and dark (not red) eyes. The call is a shrill, descending trill. Single birds or loose groups occur on dams, pans and small rivers, seldom large rivers. Dives frequently and skitters across the water when chasing rivals. Nomadic. 20 cm. **8**

2 BLACKNECKED GREBE *Podiceps nigricollis.* Uncommon localised resident and visitor. Larger than the previous species, the dark upperparts contrasting with the silvery-white underparts, the eyes *red* at all times; in breeding plumage with black head but golden ear coverts not always present. Makes a quiet 'poo-eep' or a rapid chattering. Small groups occur on saline pans and sewage ponds. When preening habitually exposes underparts by rolling to one side on the water. Sparsely distributed and highly nomadic. 28 cm. **7**

3 GREAT CRESTED GREBE *Podiceps cristatus.* Rare, localised resident and visitor to the south-east. In non-breeding plumage differs from the previous species in white head with cap only black, darker ruby-red eyes, larger bill and larger overall size. Normally silent. Usually in pairs or groups of pairs on reed-fringed dams. On water, when preening, habitually exposes its white underparts by rolling as previous species. 50 cm. **6**

Coots, gallinules, moorhens, crakes and rails. Family RALLIDAE. Fairly large to very small, long-legged, large-footed mainly water-associated birds. Many have white undertail coverts and reveal them by habitually flicking the tail upwards. Coots and moorhens blackish with brightly coloured beaks and forehead shields; gallinules with green-blue plumage; crakes and rails with mostly cryptic colouring; the minute flufftails or pygmy crakes with marked sexual plumage differences. Crakes and rails mostly secretive.

4 REDKNOBBED COOT *Fulica cristata.* Locally common resident. The only all-black waterbird with white frontal shield and beak; legs and lobed feet grey. Immature ashy-brown, lacking the white shield. Normal call 'clukuk' or 'crornk'. Singly or many on permanent open waters with fringing vegetation. Swims, occasionally dives, or walks on shoreline, sometimes further afield in marshlands. Habitually stands on floating nests or pursues other coots and other species in noisy overwater chases. Absent from the drier regions but nomadic during rains. 43 cm. **228**

1 PURPLE GALLINULE. *Porphyrio porphyrio.* Locally fairly common resident; most frequent in the Okavango Delta. Large, striking, purple and green waterbird with red bill and frontal shield and pink legs. Immature duller, brownish with red-brown legs. Has a deep, explosive bubbling call plus various shrieks and groans. Singly or in pairs in marshes, vegetation fringing still waters and reedbeds associated with sewage ponds. Walks about on mud-flats and in reedbeds or wades in shallows. Is not secretive. 46 cm. **223**

2 LESSER GALLINULE *Porphyrula alleni.* Rare; status not yet established. Most records are from the north with one or two from the east and south-east. Small, dark blue and green, large-footed waterbird. Appears blackish at a distance. In breeding plumage bill and legs red, frontal shield blue in male, apple-green in female. In non-breeding plumage both sexes duller, bill, legs and frontal shield blackish-red. Immature brownish with green wash on wings and rump, underparts pale grey-buff, white on foreneck, breast and belly, frontal shield rufous-horn to dark green-blue, bill and legs blackish-red. Usual call six to eight rapid 'dug-dug-dug...' notes. Usually singly at pans, lagoons and marsh ponds where it climbs about in tangled reeds and other waterside vegetation feeding on the flowers and seeds. Shy, most active early morning. 25 cm. **224**

3 LESSER MOORHEN *Gallinula chloropus.* Rare summer resident. Small waterbird of blackish appearance. Much smaller than the next species, back and wings green-brown, head, neck and underparts blue-slate with white vent; bill yellow, culmen and frontal shield red, legs orange-pink, brownish or greenish. Immature has underparts more dove-grey becoming white ventrally, bill horn-coloured, yellow-ochre at base (lower mandible may have a blackish base), culmen blackish to red, frontal shield absent, legs grey-green to dull pink. The call is three to five rapid hoots 'tu-tu-tu-tu'. Sparsely recorded in reedbeds, flooded grasslands, swamps and marsh pools. Swims more than previous species but shy and secretive. 23 cm. **227**

4 MOORHEN *Gallinula chloropus.* Fairly common resident. Larger than the previous species, with *bright red bill* and frontal shield, tip of bill, and legs, yellow, flank feathers white. *Immature brown, bill yellow-green, no frontal shield;* cf. (3). The call is a high-pitched, descending 'kr-rrrrk'. Frequents dams, lakes and quiet rivers with ample fringing vegetation; usually in pairs. Swims more on open water than (3) but also feeds out of water on muddy shorelines and in marshlands. 30-36 cm. **226**

5 BLACK CRAKE *Amaurornis flavirostris.* Fairly common, localised resident. Small black waterbird with yellow bill and red legs; immature duller as illustrated. The call, often in duet, is an explosive, growling 'rr-rr-rr-rrrung' repeated two or three times, also various clucking notes. Single birds and scattered individuals are usually seen walking on surface vegetation or in rank shoreline vegetation of pans, dams and marsh pools; frequent in the channels of the Okavango Delta. Not secretive. 20-23 cm. **213**

J

1

♂Br

2

3

4

5

1 REDCHESTED FLUFFTAIL *Sarothrura rufa.* Rare, localised resident apparently confined to the Okavango Delta. Normal call a much repeated, ventriloquial 'ooo-ooo-ooo-ooo-dueh-dueh-dueh...' but also makes a quail-like 'ick-kick-kick-kick...' and a loud, rapid, squeaking 'dui-dui-dui...' up to 40 or more times, fading off at the end. Calls mainly at night and on dull days, usually the only clue to the species' presence. Extremely small size and highly secretive behaviour make this species extremely difficult to observe. Reluctant to flush but once airborne flies a short distance with legs dangling before plunging back into cover; seldom flushes a second time. 15-17 cm. **217**

2 SPOTTED CRAKE *Porzana porzana.* Very rare summer visitor. Told from other similar crakes by spotted neck and underparts and yellow bill with red base and black tip. The call, seldom heard in Africa, is a series of whip-like notes 'hwitt-hwitt-hwitt'. Recorded very occasionally from widely separated localities. Highly secretive and mainly crepuscular in marshes, floodlands and dense vegetation fringing permanent pans. Walks in a crouched attitude and is difficult to flush. 24 cm. **214**

3 BAILLON'S CRAKE *Porzana pusilla.* Rare, status not established; few records to date. Male illustrated; female has white throat and central breast. Makes a low, piping 'quick-quick'. Highly secretive in marshes, lush waterside herbage and flooded grasslands, diving into cover at the least disturbance. 18 cm. **215**

4 CORNCRAKE *Crex crex.* Rare summer visitor; recorded very occasionally from widely separated localities. A short-billed, tawny crake with blackish upperparts, chestnut wing coverts and barred flanks. Silent in southern Africa. Occurs during summer in rank grass, sedges on dry ground, fallow fields and airfields, sometimes near water. When flushed flies off with dangling legs, the chestnut wings conspicuous. 37 cm. **211**

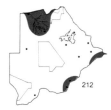

5 AFRICAN CRAKE *Crex egregia.* Rare summer resident. Heavily mottled upperparts and boldly barred underparts distinctive. Has a high-pitched chittering trill of eight or nine notes. Found in grassland, marshes, pans, rank vegetation and thickets, frequently away from water. Secretive but will visit rain puddles on quiet roads. 20-23 cm. **212**

6 STRIPED CRAKE *Aenigmatolimnas marginalis.* Status not established. An intra-Africa migrant, its occurrence in Botswana unconfirmed. Sexes differ as illustrated, the male more rufous. The call (heard at night) is a constant ticking like a wristwatch 'tak-tak-tak-tak...'. Behaviour much the same as the previous species. Should be watched for in the marshes and floodlands of the Linyanti-Okavango-Chobe region. 24 cm. **216**

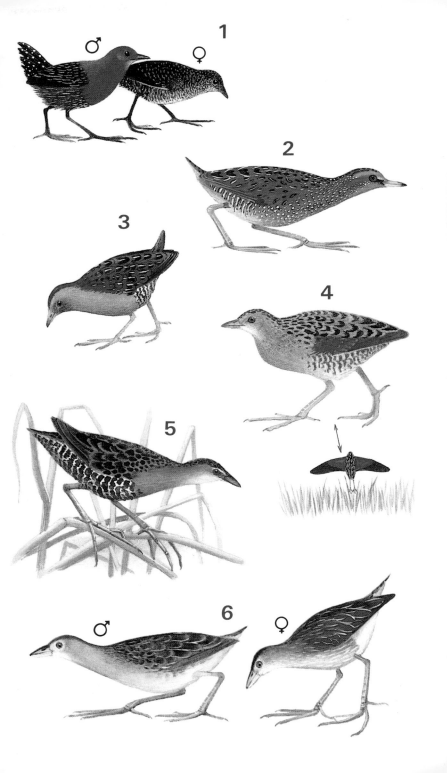

1 AFRICAN RAIL *Rallus caerulescens*. Rare to uncommon resident; most frequent in the north, very local elsewhere. Identified by long red bill and legs, brown upperparts and banded underparts. Immature sooty brown, white of throat extending to central breast, flanks barred rufous. The call is a trilling rattle 'creeea-crak-crak-crak...'. A shy, skulking bird of reedbeds and dense swamp vegetation, occasionally emerging at pool fringes. Moves with stealth and speed, flicking its tail continuously. 36 cm. **210**

2 PAINTED SNIPE (Family ROSTRATULIDAE) *Rostratula benghalensis*. Uncommon resident; probably sedentary in the north, more occasional in the east and south-east. Immature resembles male. Calls mainly at night, a long 'whooook' sound repeated. Pairs occur on muddy shorelines of pans, marsh pools and dams, usually close to waterside vegetation. Secretive by day but becoming active at dusk, walking with bobbing hind quarters. Unrelated to true snipes. 28-32 cm. **242**

Families CHARADRIIDAE **(plovers)** and SCOLOPACIDAE **(sandpipers, snipes and allies)**. Long- to fairly long-legged terrestrial and waterside birds, large plovers erect-standing, small plovers with horizontal, hunched posture. Sandpipers, generally called waders, are plover-like non-breeding Palaearctic migrants, most numerous in summer. On arrival in Botswana (September), or just prior to their departure (March), may show partial or even full breeding plumage. Waders shown in non-breeding plumage unless otherwise indicated.

3 GREAT SNIPE *Gallinago media*. Very rare summer visitor. Differs from the next species in larger size and bulky-bodied appearance, bold white markings on upperparts and more heavily banded underparts; bill less long than in (4). In flight upperwings more rufous than in (4), new plumage showing bold white markings *but in moulting birds* (*most common in southern Africa*) *this feature less apparent*; white outer tail feathers plus white tips to all but the central tail feathers visible at close range and when bird is settling. When flushed calls 'etch-etch' and flies straight with erratic side to side tilting action on *lazy wing-beats* before resettling. Very occasional in the Linyanti-Okavango region, favouring short grass around alkaline pans and drier ground than (4). 35 cm. **285**

4 AFRICAN SNIPE (ETHIOPIAN SNIPE) *Gallinago nigripennis*. Resident; fairly common in the north, localised elsewhere. Differs from (3) in whiter underparts (barring on flanks only), white or barred outer tail feathers *without white tips*, and longer bill. When flushed calls 'scaap' and *zig-zags at low level with fluttering wing-beats* before resettling. In breeding display flies high then zooms down steeply with fanned tail-feathers vibrating to produce a soft 'drumming' sound. Singly or in pairs in marshes and temporary floodlands, preferring wetter conditions than (3). 32 cm. **286**

5 CASPIAN PLOVER *Charadrius asiaticus*. Uncommon Palaearctic migrant. The male illustrated is in breeding plumage, quite often seen during late summer. Female may have rufous breast-band incomplete, dark lower edge always absent. The call, seldom heard in Africa, is a shrill 'ku-wit', loudest at night. Distribution fairly widespread but flocks prefer the drier edges of the Delta region, the more arid, short-grassed plains of Makgadikgadi Pans Game Reserve and the Deception Valley, not necessarily near water. Reluctant to take wing; most active at night. 21-23 cm. **252**

1 WHITEFRONTED PLOVER *Charadrius marginatus.* Rare resident and visitor; most frequent in the north, more occasional in the east and south-east. Differs from other small plovers in whitish underparts lacking any breast-bands; ochre wash on breast very pale. Immature resembles female. Makes a soft 'wit' or 'twirit' in flight. Singly or in small groups on sandy rivers, lakes and pans and in the Okavango system. Feeds at the water's edge in crouched attitude, frequently running rapidly short distances. Nowhere plentiful. 18 cm. **246**

2 CHESTNUTBANDED PLOVER *Charadrius pallidus.* Seasonally fairly common on Makgadikgadi Pans, rare visitor elsewhere. Female lacks black forecrown and lores. Makes a soft 'chuck' call on take-off. Singly or in loose flocks on saline pans and sandflats, less often on riverbanks. Feeds in shallows or on shoreline. 15 cm. **247**

3 RINGED PLOVER *Charadrius hiaticula.* Uncommon summer visitor. Single bold black band encircling breast and neck diagnostic; cf. Threebanded Plover (4). In flight differs from (4) in distinct white wing-bar; see illustration. The call is 'coo-eep' or 'too-li'. Singly or in small parties, often mixing with (4), on shorelines of pans, lakes, sewage ponds and dams. 18 cm. **245**

4 THREEBANDED PLOVER *Charadrius tricollaris.* Common resident. Identified by double black breast-bands separated by white band encircling neck; cf. Ringed Plover (3). Immature with the upper band brown, incomplete, the lower band flecked white, head uniformly brown. The call is 'wick-wick' or 'tiuu-it, tiuu-it'. Singly, in pairs or small parties on shores of almost any waters. Fairly widespread but nomadic to some extent. 18 cm. **249**

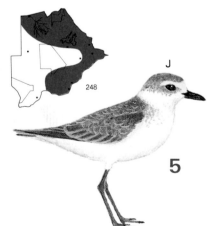

5 KITTLITZ'S PLOVER *Charadrius pecuarius.* Fairly common resident. Adult distinguished from other small plovers by buff breast extending back to legs. Immature lacks buff colouring and black head markings; see illustration. In flight calls 'tip-peep'; also has a trilling call 'trit-tritritritrit'. Small parties occur on the dry shorelines of pans, mudflats adjacent to lakes and dams, and on airfields. Nomadic when not breeding. 16 cm. **248**

66

1 LONGTOED PLOVER *Vanellus crassirostris.* Fairly common, localised resident. Distinguished by white frontal half of head, neck and upper breast contrasting with black nape, rear neck and breastband. The call is 'wheet' and, in flight, a clicking 'kick-k-k-kick-k-k-k'. Pairs or groups occur on quiet backwaters of the Chobe River and marsh pools and floodplains in the Linyanti-Okavango systems, their long toes adapted for walking on floating vegetation. 30 cm. **261**

2 BLACKSMITH PLOVER *Vanellus armatus.* Common resident. A pied plover with *grey wings and mantle*; cf. previous species. Immature as illustrated. The call is a metallic 'klink, klink, klink...' repeated loudly and continuously when disturbed. Pairs and small, scattered flocks frequent the shores of most still waters of any size, also marshes and floodplains. Will move into more arid regions beyond its normal range when water is present. 30 cm. **258**

3 CROWNED PLOVER *Vanellus coronatus.* Common resident. Distinguished by white circle surrounding black cap, plus mainly red bill and red legs; eyes usually pale yellow, sometimes dark brown. Immature similar, duller. At times very noisy, calling 'kie-weeet' on the ground or a repeated, shrill 'kree-kree-kreeip-kreeip...' in flight, day or night. Pairs and groups occur on dry, open ground, areas of short or burnt grass, on airfields and road verges. Often fly about in groups at some height calling repeatedly. 30 cm. **255**

4 WATTLED PLOVER *Vanellus senegallus.* Uncommon resident. Bright yellow bill, wattles and legs distinguish this plover from all but the next species, from which it differs in shorter wattles, white *only on forecrown*, a streaked neck, lack of white bar on folded wing and *brown breast extending to legs*. The call is a shrill 'kwep kwep kwep kwep kwe kwe kwekwe kwekwekwekwekwek' becoming faster with increased agitation. Pairs and small groups frequent grassy waterside localities: riverbanks, dam walls, lake shores and marshes, mostly in the north and east. 35 cm. **260**

5 WHITECROWNED PLOVER *Vanellus albiceps.* Rare, localised resident. Distinguished from the previous species by longer wattles (longer than the bill), a broad white band (dark edged in males) extending from bill to nape, *entirely white underparts* and a black wing bordered above by white; in flight wings appear mainly white; cf. (1). A noisy species, the call a sharp 'peep, peep-peep, peep...' uttered rapidly when flushed. Pairs and groups frequent sandbanks in rivers. 30 cm. **259**

1 GREY PLOVER *Pluvialis squatarola.* Rare summer visitor. Overall greyish appearance of non-breeding plumage (a) resembles a large, plump wader with stout black bill and black legs; in flight shows *black 'armpits'.* Both partial breeding plumage (b) and full breeding plumage possible September and April. Has a far-carrying whistle 'tlui-tlui' or 'pee-u-wee'. A coastal species, occurring in Botswana as a passage migrant. Singly or in small groups sporadically on pans, shallow dams, sewage ponds and lake shores. 28-30 cm. **254**

2 WHIMBREL *Numenius phaeopus.* Rare summer visitor; so far recorded only in the Gaborone region. A large wader with long downcurved bill; differs from the next species in *smaller size, shorter bill* and dark cap with pale central line. In flight shows similar white back to (3) but upperwings darker. Calls 'foo-eeee' or, in flight, a rippling 'peep-eep-eep-eep-ee'. A coastal species occurring as a rare and temporary vagrant in Botswana. 43 cm. **290**

3 CURLEW *Numenius arquata.* Rare summer visitor. A very large wader with *enormously long, downcurved bill.* In flight shows large white area on back and rump; cf. previous species. Calls include 'cur-lew', or 'corwe-corwe' or 'quee-quee-quee'. A coastal species occurring as a rare passage migrant to shallow waters in Botswana. 59 cm. **289**

1 MARSH SANDPIPER *Tringa stagnatalis.* Fairly common summer visitor. Clear white underparts like the next species but smaller, with *straight, slender bill* and yellowish legs. In flight shows white back and rump as (2) but upperwings show less contrast and feet protrude more. When put to flight calls 'tchick' *frequently.* Sparsely but widely distributed, singly or in small groups on shallow waters, including temporary floodlands, October-March. 23 cm. **269**

2 GREENSHANK *Tringa nebularia.* Fairly common summer visitor, a few all year. Has clear white underparts as previous species but is larger, with more robust, *slightly upturned bill* and green-grey legs. In flight from above shows extensive white back, rump and upper tail plus dark outer wings and less dark inner wings; feet protrude only slightly. On take-off calls 'tew-tew-tew'. Usually singly on shallow, nutrient-rich waters including rivers. Shy and difficult to approach. When flushed towers up and makes its triple call before flying off some distance. Fairly widespread, extending into the more arid regions if water is present October-March. 32 cm. **270**

3 RUFF *Philomachus pugnax.* Fairly common to locally common summer visitor. Male larger than female (called Reeve). Told by short, straight bill with slightly bulbous tip, featureless face, *boldly scaled upperparts*; legs orange in adult, grey-green in immature. In flight shows *white oval patches on sides of dark tail*. On arrival in Botswana (September), or prior to departure (March) males may show traces of breeding plumage; see small illustrations. Silent, but birds in a flying flock may call 'chit' in a twittering chorus. Singly, in groups or large flocks in shallows of dams, sewage ponds, pans, rivers and in marshes. 24-30 cm. **284**

1 PECTORAL SANDPIPER *Calidris melanotos*. Very rare summer vagrant; three confirmed records for Botswana. Differs from Ruff (pages 72-73) in smaller size, shorter yellow legs and well-streaked breast terminating in a sharp line and contrasting with white underparts; full breeding plumage more rufous. In flight no clear wing-bars but streaked back appears snipe-like. Usual call 'kreek' or 'prritt' one or more times. Takes off with erratic snipe-like action, then flies straight. Singly or with other waders on sewage ponds, dams, pans or moist grasslands. 20-23 cm. **279**

2 SANDERLING *Calidris alba*. Rare summer visitor. A small wader of very white appearance with dark shoulder-patch and short, thick bill; larger and paler than any stints (pages 78-79). Flight low, direct, white wing-bars conspicuous. When flushed calls a liquid 'blt-blt'. Sporadic on open shores of lakes, dams and pans feeding in a hunched, head-down posture and probing hurriedly. 19 cm. **281**

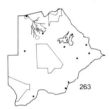

3 TEREK SANDPIPER *Xenus cinereus*. Rare summer visitor; few positive records. Distinguished by long *upcurved bill*, short, orange-yellow legs and pale grey-brown upperparts with a dark shoulder. In flight white secondaries and grey rump diagnostic. Calls 'tur-lip' or 'turr-loo-tew'. *Bobs its rear end up and down* and moves about rapidly while feeding, sometimes running at speed between bouts of deep probing with its bill. 23-25 cm. **263**

4 KNOT *Calidris canutus*. Very rare summer visitor; two confirmed records only for Botswana. Differs from other short-billed waders in plump-bodied appearance; frequently assumes semi-breeding plumage before departure in March. In flight wings appear long, pointed, white wing-bars conspicuous. Calls 'knut', sometimes in a series. A coastal species that feeds with slow forward movement while probing several times between steps. Single birds may occur occasionally on any waters. 25 cm. **271**

5 TURNSTONE *Arenaria interpres*. Rare summer visitor. Characterised by long-shaped body, hunched, head-in-shoulders appearance and horizontal stance plus striking plumage pattern. Flight or contact call 'kuiti-kuiti-kuiti' or, in mild alarm, 'tuck-a-tuck' given about five times then tailing off to 'ti-tititi'. Occurs as occasional passage migrant in the Delta or on dams and pans with stony or muddy shorelines, feeding by turning over small stones, caked mud and debris. If flushed flies off low, revealing extensive white back and wing-bars. 22 cm. **262**

1 GREEN SANDPIPER *Tringa ochropus*. Rare summer visitor; scattered records exist for the north, east and south-east. Differs from Wood Sandpiper (4) in having darker, less obviously spotted upperparts and longer bill; in flight larger white rump, barred tail and *dark underwing coverts*. When flushed towers up uttering a loud, shrill 'weet-a-weet', then makes off with erratic, snipe-like flight. Solitary on a variety of waters. 23 cm. **265**

2 COMMON SANDPIPER *Tringa hypoleucos*. Fairly common summer visitor; a few all year. Identified by white pectoral region showing above folded wing, medium-short, robust bill and *habit of frequently bobbing its hind quarters*. In flight shows no white rump but faint white wing-bar and outer tail feathers. When flushed flies off low with stiff wings bowed downwards below the horizontal and sporadic wing-flicking while uttering a shrill 'twee-wee-wee'. Singly on shores of rivers, dams and lakes August-April. 20 cm. **264**

3 CURLEW SANDPIPER *Calidris ferruginea*. Fairly common summer visitor. Small wader with *downward-curved bill*; in flight shows broad white rump. Calls 'tchirrrr', small groups becoming very vocal when chasing each other; in flight calls 'chiet-chiet'. Occurs usually in small flocks (occasionally large flocks) on dams and pans. Feeds in shallows, characteristically walking forward with head down while probing rapidly with its bill. 19 cm. **272**

4 WOOD SANDPIPER *Tringa glareola*. Common summer visitor; a few all year. Told by well-spotted upperparts, broad, distinct eyebrow, short, straight bill and fairly long legs. In flight shows *white underwing coverts*, differing mainly in this and bill length from Green Sandpiper (1); feet protrude beyond tail in flight. When flushed towers up and calls a flat, triple 'chiff-if-if'. Also has a high-pitched alarm call 'tch-tch-tch-tch-tch'. Solitary or in small groups on most shallow waters and flooded grasslands. 20 cm. **266**

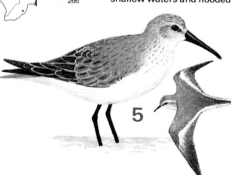

5 DUNLIN *Calidris alpina*. Very rare summer vagrant; one record only. May be confused with (3) but bill stouter, less decurved, upperparts darker and rump dark (not white). When feeding has a typical hunched, neckless appearance. Could occur on shoreline of any still waters. 14-15 cm. **812**

76

1 LITTLE STINT *Calidris minuta*. Fairly common to locally common summer visitor. Differs from next species in having black legs, thicker bill and paler upperparts. Early arrivals (September) sometimes show traces of breeding plumage. Utters a sharp 'chit' or rapid 'chitchitchit...'. Smallest of the regular summer-visiting waders, often seen in large numbers. Fairly widespread on pans, lakes and dams feeding at the waterline in hunched, head-down posture. Extends into more arid regions when water present. 14-15 cm. **274**

2 LONGTOED STINT *Calidris subminuta*. Very rare summer vagrant; one record to date. Fractionally smaller than the previous species, distinguished from it by having *longer*, greenish-yellow (not black) legs and richer, darker brown upperparts streaked with pale buff. Characteristically stretches its neck and stands very erect. Has a loud, trilling call 'chrree-chrree'. Feeds on shorelines of dams and pans, mixing with other waders, especially (1). 14 cm. **275**

3 TEMMINCK'S STINT *Calidris temminckii*. Very rare summer vagrant; one record to date. Very similar to previous species but has *yellow* legs and feet and fairly uniform, *unmarked* grey upperparts. In flight the outer tail feathers show white. 14-15 cm. **274**

Phalaropes. Very rare oceanic vagrants to inland waters. Swim buoyantly; feed from the water's surface with a pirouetting action.

4 REDNECKED PHALAROPE *Phalaropus lobatus*. Status not established; confirmed records for Botswana lacking. Occurrence possible on any still waters. Identified by thin bill (about same length as head) and *dark grey upperparts*; may have dark cap. 17 cm. **292**

5 GREY PHALAROPE *Phalaropus fulicarius*. Very rare summer vagrant. Recognised by short, fairly robust bill with (usually) yellow base and *uniform* pale grey upperparts. Recorded once in the southeast. May occur on any still waters. 20 cm. **291**

1 REDSHANK *Tringa totanus.* Rare summer visitor. Told by long red or orange legs and *moderately long, straight bill* with reddish base; from orange-legged Ruff (pp. 72-73) in plain upperparts and bill length. In flight the only wader with white triangular patches on the wings plus white back, rump and tail, the tail faintly barred. Calls 'teu-he-he' on take-off. Flight erratic with jerky, deliberate wing-beats, feet slightly protruding beyond tail. Individuals occasionally September-March. 25 cm. **268**

2 SPOTTED REDSHANK *Tringa erythropus.* Status not established; one record only provisionally accepted for Savuti. Lankier, more gracefully proportioned than the previous species, bill and legs longer, of overall greyish appearance with usually some spotting on the upperparts; whitish underparts. Posture fairly erect. In flight shows white only as oval patch on back; feet protrude more than in (1). The call is a deep 'cheewit'. Possible on any still, shallow waters. 30 cm. **267**

3 BLACKTAILED GODWIT *Limosa limosa.* Rare summer visitor; few records. Despite *straight bill and longer legs* is not easily told from the next species when at rest, but head, neck and breast are of uniform tone, *not* streaked. In flight broad, black tail-band and prominent white upper wing-bars diagnostic. May call a loud 'wicka wicka wicka'. 40-50 cm. **287**

4 BARTAILED GODWIT *Limosa lapponica.* Rare summer visitor. Stockier, shorter-legged than the previous species, bill long (longest in female) and gently *upcurved* not straight; head, neck and breast streaked. In flight tail shows numerous light bars, wings unbarred. The call is a deep 'god-whit'. Likely to occur occasionally on shallow dams, pans and marsh pools. 36-39 cm. **288**

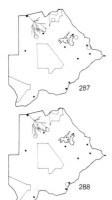

5 AFRICAN JACANA *Actophilornis atricanus.* Common to locally very common resident. Adult unmistakable with chestnut body, white head and neck with black crown, nape and mantle, blue frontal shield and long legs with enormously long toes. Immature (frequently mistaken for next species) has *black* stripe through eye and *black* crown; cf. next species which is much smaller. The call, while standing or flying, is 'kyowrrr'. Individuals walk on waterlily leaves and other surface vegetation of pans, lagoons, dams and river backwaters. Often chase one another in brief, low flight while calling loudly and stand with wings raised after settling. Very common in the northern wetlands, but occurs elsewhere in suitable habitat. 40 cm. **240**

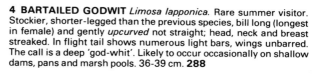

6 LESSER JACANA *Microparra capensis.* Uncommon to locally common resident. Very much smaller than the previous species (sparrow size minus feet). Differs from the young of (5) in pale feather-edges to brown upperparts giving 'scaled' effect; central mantle and back deep bronze-brown, *crown and eye-stripe chestnut*, underparts white. Immature has dark crown, the nape golden-chestnut. Silent except for an occasional 'kruk'. Occurs in similar habitat to (5) but shy and easily overlooked. 20 cm. **241**

Avocet and stilts. Family RECURVIROSTRIDAE. Elegant, long-legged, long-billed black and white wading birds, avocets with up-turned bills, stilts with straight bills.

1 AVOCET *Recurvirostra avosetta.* Uncommon to locally common resident and visitor; large flocks can occur in the Makgadikgadi Pans but irregular and few in number elsewhere. Thin, upturned bill and pied plumage diagnostic at all times. Immature dark brown where adult is black. The call is a liquid 'kluut', several birds sometimes calling together. Flocks, varying from a few individuals to many thousands, occur in shallow waters of salt pans, lakes and dams. Feeds by wading, sometimes swimming, moving foreward slowly, the immersed bill being swept side to side. 43 cm. **294**

2 BLACKWINGED STILT *Himantopus himantopus.* Common to very common resident and visitor. Long, slender bill and very long red legs diagnostic; long trailing legs also conspicuous in flight. Immature duller, as illustrated. The call is a loud 'kik-kik-kik-kik' or 'kyik'. Individuals, pairs or flocks at shallow pans, dams and lake shores. Wades with legs well immersed while feeding, the bill sweeping the surface. Widespread and highly nomadic when not breeding. 38 cm. **295**

Dikkops. Family BURHINIDAE. Also known as 'Thick-knees'. Plover-like birds with large heads and eyes, long legs, feet without a hind claw and tawny colouring. Normally walk with short, mincing steps. Nocturnal and crepuscular, spending the daytime resting in some concealed position. Sexes alike; young resemble adults.

1 SPOTTED DIKKOP *Burhinus capensis.* Fairly common resident. Distinguished from the next species by heavily spotted upperparts, no wing-bar and by habitat preference. Most vocal on moonlit nights, flying about restlessly and calling a shrill, eerie 'chwee-chwee, chwee-chwee, chwee, chwee, tiu-tiu-tiu...' tailing off at the end. Pairs frequent dry rocky ground with short grass, open fields and clearings within woodland. Rests by day under a bush or among rocks, running off in crouched posture if disturbed. Widespread. 44 cm. **297**

2 WATER DIKKOP *Burhinus vermiculatus.* Locally fairly common resident. Distinguished from previous species by distinct *grey wing-bar,* edged black, plus habitat. Starts calling at dusk, a piping, melancholy 'whee-wheeoo-wheeoo' and continues throughout moonlit nights. Single birds and small groups on well-vegetated banks of permanent rivers plus lakes, pans and marsh pools with fringing vegetation. Lies up during the day in reeds or beneath overhanging bushes. 40 cm. **298**

Pratincoles and coursers. Family GLAREOLIDAE. Pratincoles are gregarious, migratory and nomadic birds with very short legs in relation to body-length. At rest or in their elegant, often erratic, flight resemble large swallows. Feed mostly in the air in flocks. Their calls are of a 'kip-kip-kip...' nature. The related, terrestrial-feeding coursers are more plover-like with erect stance, but unlike plovers lack a hind toe. Sexes alike in both groups.

3 REDWINGED PRATINCOLE *Glareola pratincola.* Fairly common, localised resident and visitor. Told from the next species only with difficulty unless flying; has *rufous* underwings (not black) and white trailing edges to the inner-wings (secondaries). Occurs in flocks, sometimes large, on marshlands, burnt grasslands and pan-fringes in the north; rarely further south. Flocks may rise in great, wheeling columns and perform remarkable aerial manoeuvres. When settling stands briefly with wings raised. 25 cm. **304**

4 BLACKWINGED PRATINCOLE *Glareola nordmanni.* Fairly common, localised summer visitor. Differs from previous species in less red on gape, more extensive yellow-buff colouring on lower breast; in flight by entirely blackish underwings. Flocks, frequently hundreds, occur in short, open grassland including well-grazed cattle areas. Favours drier regions than (3), is thus commoner further south, otherwise behaviour same as (3). 25 cm. **305**

5 ROCK PRATINCOLE (WHITECOLLARED PRATINCOLE) *Glareola nuchalis.* Rare; status not established. Recorded once on Chobe River near Kasane. Smaller than (3) and (4), lacks a throat-patch, outer tail feathers only slightly elongated; narrow white collar and *red legs* diagnostic. Frequents boulder-strewn rapids, perching on rocks in the water and feeding over water. 18 cm. **306**

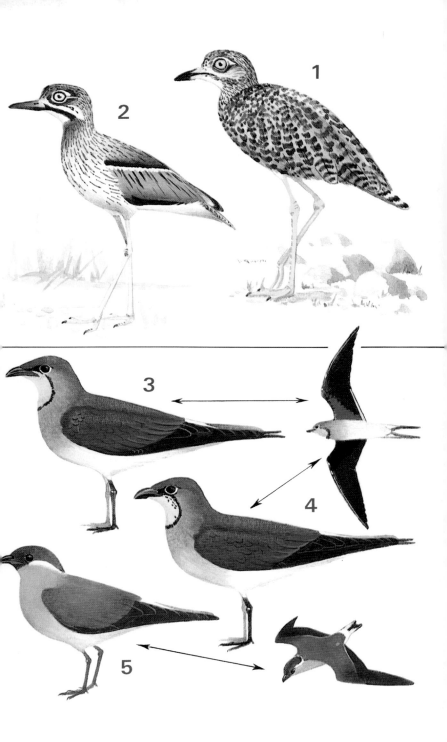

1 BRONZEWINGED COURSER *Rhinoptilus chalcopterus.* Uncommon resident. A large courser with *red legs* and distinctive head markings, these less clearly defined in immature. At night calls a shrill 'ji-ku-it' or a plaintive 'groraag'. A nocturnal species of well-wooded regions, roosting by day beneath a bush and feeding at night in open areas and on roads. Widely distributed, except in the south-west. 25 cm. **303**

2 TEMMINCK'S COURSER *Cursorius temminckii.* Fairly common resident. Small, white-legged *rufous-capped* courser; cf. next species. Immature speckled buff on crown and upperparts. May call a sharp 'err-err-err' in flight. Small groups are found in short-grass plains around pans, on ploughed lands and airfields. Stands erect then runs rapidly forward before stooping briefly to feed; occasionally bobs its head and tail. Nomadic. 20 cm. **300**

3 BURCHELL'S COURSER *Cursorius rufus.* Rare. Exact status not established. Differs from the previous species in having a grey back to the crown and showing a *white trailing edge patch to the inner wings* in flight. Immature has mottled upperparts. A quiet species, may call 'kok-kok-kwich'. Also bobs its head and hind quarters and jerks its body backwards and forewards or sideways. Habits and habitat very similar to (2) but much more sparsely distributed at widely separated localities. 23 cm. **299**

4 DOUBLEBANDED COURSER *Rhinoptilus africanus.* Fairly common resident. A distinctive, pale-coloured courser with two black bands encircling the lower neck and breast; immature very similar. Normally silent but may call 'pee-wee' if put to flight; also calls 'chik-kee, chik-kee, chick-kee-kee-kee-kee' while flying at night. Pairs and scattered groups inhabit grasslands and plains, fringes of pans and barren, calcrete flats. Active day and night and seemingly indifferent to hot conditions. Runs rather than flies. 22 cm. **301**

5 THREEBANDED COURSER *Rhinoptilus cinctus.* Rare, status not established; few records only for north and north-east. Darker than the previous species, with bold head markings and bands encircling the spotted upper breast (not encircling the neck); immature with lower band poorly defined. Largely nocturnal and crepuscular, resting in shade by day. The call 'chick-a-chuck-a-chuck-a-chuck'. Singly or in groups frequenting well-grassed woodland. Freezes when approached, usually with its back to the observer. 28 cm. **302**

Bustards and korhaans. Family OTIDIDAE. Large, long-legged, long-necked terrestrial birds, cryptically coloured, tails short, feet with three forward-facing toes. Most have elaborate displays involving plumage transformations, flight or unusual calls.

237

1 REDCRESTED KORHAAN *Eupodotis ruficrista*. Fairly common to common resident. Told from other small korhaans by creamy-white V-marks on the upperparts; shorter legged and shorter necked than Blackbellied Korhaan (4). Female has a broad white band across lower breast, reduced in male to small pectoral patches. Red crest of male seldom seen and is *not* a field feature. Territorial call of male starts with a series of clicks, increasing in speed and changing to a series of shrill, piercing whistles 'phee-phee-phee-phee...' repeated 5-10 or more times. Pairs call in duet, a rapid 'wuka-wuka-wuka...' before the male switches to the whistling call. In summer male flies steeply upwards to about 30 m and then tumbles as though shot. Widespread, frequenting less open regions than (3). 53 cm. **237**

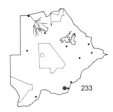

233

2 WHITEBELLIED KORHAAN *Eupodotis caerulescens*. Rare resident, mostly confined to grasslands of the extreme south-east. A small, distinctive korhaan, male with dark cap and throat plus blue-grey neck-front. The call, heard morning and evening, is 'takwarat' repeated several times in decreasing volume; this is sometimes preceded by several 'throat-clearing' sounds thus: 'aaa-aaa-aaa-takwarat-takwarat-takwarat...'. If flushed calls 'kuk-pa-wow' as it flies off. Occurs very sparsely in pairs and small parties. 53 cm. **233**

239

3 BLACK KORHAAN *Eupodotis afra*. Common to locally very common resident. Male distinctive, but female easily confused with other korhaans; note *back* of neck is black, bill pink with whitish tip, upperparts pale fawn with dark barring. Male calls a raucous, far-carrying 'krra-a-a-ak-wet-de-wet-de-wet-de-wet...' day or night; in flight calls 'kraak-araak-araak-araak-araak...'. Widespread though largely absent from the north and east. Territorial males highly conspicuous and noisy during hovering display flights. Females mostly inconspicuous. 53 cm. **239**

238

4 BLACKBELLIED KORHAAN (LONGLEGGED KORHAAN) *Eupodotis melanogaster*. Rare resident. Characterised by long legs (proportionately longer than any other korhaan), flying male by *white upperwings*. Male has *black* underparts extending in a line up the front of the neck to the chin; female has *white* underparts. Male calls while posturing as illustrated. Starting with (1), the neck is then stretched fully as in (2) and a dull 'waak' is uttered; next the neck is partially withdrawn and a throaty grunt is emitted followed by a short pause, then a sharp whip-like sound 'ooor-whip' is made before the head is again withdrawn. Singly or in pairs in open woodland and grassland. Male performs a courtship flight, descending with wings held aloft in a V-shape, head and neck arched back and black breast puffed out like a balloon. 58-65 cm. **238**

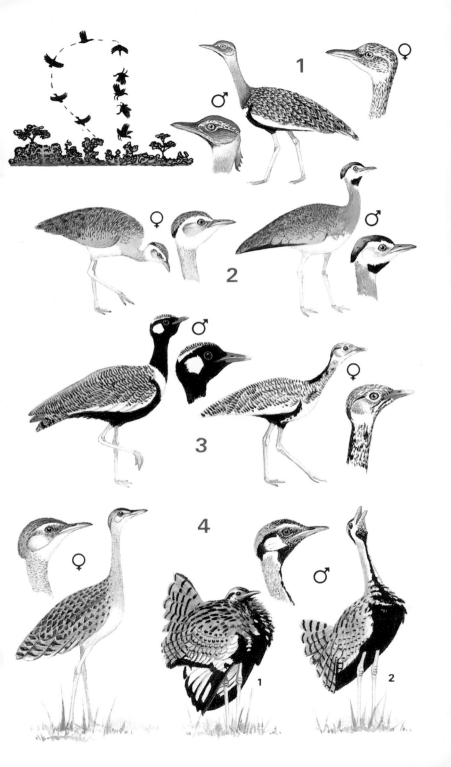

1 STANLEY'S BUSTARD (DENHAM'S BUSTARD) *Neotis denhami.* Rare visitor; few confirmed records. A large bustard, larger than the next species and differing in having a black cap with white central parting plus a *large black and white patch on the folded wing.* Non-breeding male with grey front to neck, breeding male with white neck. Smaller female with front of neck finely barred brown. Normally silent. In courtship male inflates its neck like a large, white balloon and erects its fanned tail to display the white undertail coverts; then visible at long distance. Favours grasslands and savanna. Very sparse in the north-east. 86-110 cm. **231**

2 LUDWIG'S BUSTARD *Neotis ludwigii.* Status not established; probably a rare visitor to the extreme south-west. No confirmed sightings in Botswana but has been seen just across the international boundary in the Kalahari Gemsbok National Park. Smaller than and similar to the previous species but *lacking any black on the head or folded wings;* cf. (1). The call, heard during courtship, is a deep-voiced 'klop...klop...klop'. At this time (October-November) male fluffs out its plumage and inflates its neck, revealing white underfeathers while calling at about ten-second intervals. A bird of desert and semi-desert. 86-110 ccm. **232**

3 KORI BUSTARD *Ardeotis kori.* Fairly common resident. Identified by huge size and crested head. Sexes alike but male about 20 per cent larger than female. In courtship male calls a deep 'wum, wum, wum, wum, wummmmm'. Singly, in pairs or groups in woodland, grassy plains and Kalahari scrub. Walks slowly with measured strides and flies reluctantly. In courtship male inflates its throat to spread outwards the white frontal neck feathers, the head with raised crest is drawn back, the wings are drooped and the tail deflected upwards and forwards to the neck, the white undertail coverts being splayed outwards conspicuously; see small illustration. 105-150 cm. **230**

Cranes. Family GRUIDAE. Large, long-legged, long-necked terrestrial birds, differing from storks in having short bills and being quite vocal. Like storks, they fly with their necks outstretched. Cranes indulge in elaborate dancing displays with spread wings when courting, this sometimes involving more than two birds. The three crane species occurring in southern Africa have become endangered or threatened in recent years as a result of persecution and harassment by man. In croplands they are often shot or poisoned by farmers while in their natural habitats they are frequently captured for zoos.

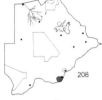

1 BLUE CRANE *Anthropoides paradisea.* Rare, status not established; very sparsely recorded from the south-east and Makgadikgadi Pans area. Distinctive blue-grey crane with bulbous head and long wing-plumes which appear as a trailing tail. Immature lacks these plumes. The call is a loud, rattling, nasal 'krra-a-a-a-r-r-r-k'. Nomadic. 105 cm. **208**

2 CROWNED CRANE *Balearica regulorum.* Rare resident and visitor; sparsely recorded from the Okavango and Makgadikgadi regions. Unmistakable; immature with crest and wattles less developed, of browner appearance. The call is a two-syllabled trumpeting sounding like 'ma-hem'. Frequents grasslands and marshes, though roosting in reedbeds or trees. 105 cm. **209**

3 WATTLED CRANE *Grus carunculata.* Locally fairly common resident. A very large crane with white head and neck and distinctive wattles at either side of the chin, these being absent in the immature. Seldom calls but can make a loud, drawn-out, bell-like 'horuk'. Pairs and small groups, sometimes flocks of 50 or more, on grasslands fringing lakes and lagoons, marshlands and large rivers. Most frequent in the Linyanti-Okavango region and at Magadikgadi Pans, often feeding in shallow water. Wary and difficult to approach. 120 cm. **207**

3

Buttonquails. Family TURNICIDAE. Very small terrestrial birds, superficially similar to true quails (see (3) and (4) below) but smaller and lacking a hind toe. Plumage similar in both sexes but females the more richly coloured. Immatures like males but with spotted breasts. They flush reluctantly, usually at one's feet, then fly low for a short distance before resettling.

1 KURRICHANE BUTTONQUAIL *Turnix sylvatica.* Fairly common to common resident. Told from the next species by whitish sides to the head, *pale yellow eyes* and heart-shaped spots on the sides of neck and breast. Female has a deep hooting call 'hooo...hooo...', repeated slowly. Pairs occur in well-developed grassland, savanna with good grass cover and fallow croplands. 14-15 cm. **205**

2 BLACKRUMPED BUTTONQUAIL (HOTTENTOT BUTTONQUAIL) *Turnix hottentotta.* Rare; status not established. Recorded once near Gweta. May prove more widespread, especially in the north-east. Told from the previous species by chestnut sides to head, brown eyes; in flight by dark rump. The call is similar to that of (1) but of even lower pitch. Habitat similar to (1) but sparse and irregular throughout its range. 14-15 cm. **206**

Quails and francolins. Family PHASIANIDAE. Terrestrial birds of mostly gregarious habits (quails excepted). Male francolins have legspurs (lacking in females) and crowing, ringing or cackling call-notes which are useful aids to identification. Immatures resemble adults but are duller. Quails are highly nomadic and irruptive, whereas francolins are more sedentary.

3 COMMON QUAIL *Coturnix coturnix.* Rare, status not established. One confirmed record for the south-west, all other sight-records lack confirmation. Told by pale underparts in both sexes; cf. next species. In flight difficult to tell from (4). The call is a penetrating 'whit-*whit*it, whit-*whit*it...' uttered day or night when breeding; if flushed calls 'pree-pree-pree'. Normally frequents well-grassed regions and cultivated lands. Namibian and South African records suggest this species may winter in the east, south and west of Botswana. 18 cm. **200**

4 HARLEQUIN QUAIL *Coturnix delegorguei.* Uncommon summer resident and winter visitor. Male told by bold black markings on white throat plus chestnut underparts. Female from female of previous species by dark 'necklace' across throat to ear-coverts. The call is a loud 'wit, wit-wit, wit, wit-wit-it', similar to the call of (3) but more metallic. Pairs occur in moist grasslands and in woodland with well-developed grass cover. Flushes reluctantly. Most common and widespread September-May but irruptive, numbers fluctuating year to year. 18 cm. **201**

1 COQUI FRANCOLIN *Francolinus coqui.* Uncommon resident. A small francolin with marked sexual differences as illustrated. The call is a piping 'be-quick...be-quick...' repeated six to eight times; territorial males also make a loud, high-pitched crowing 'kek, KEKekekekekekekekekekekek', second note loudest and all others diminishing in volume. Pairs and small coveys frequent well-grassed woodland and savanna. Habitually walks in a slow, stooped manner as the female illustrated, especially when crossing open spaces, and crouches motionless when alarmed. 28 cm. **188**

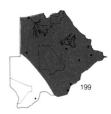

2 SWAINSON'S FRANCOLIN *Francolinus swainsonii.* Common resident. *The only red-necked francolin with black bill and legs;* basic plumage colour dark brown. Makes a harsh crowing call while perched on a branch, fallen log or termite mound 'krrraaak krrraaak krrraaak' fading at the end. Single birds and small coveys are found in thornveld, savanna and fallow agricultural lands, *running* away when disturbed, flying only if pressed. 34-39 cm. **199**

3 CRESTED FRANCOLIN *Francolinus sephaena.* Common resident. Identified by dark cap (the feathers of which are raised in alarm) and prominent white eyebrows, plus red legs and the habit of holding the *tail raised like a Bantam chicken*; in flight black tail conspicuous. The call is a shrill 'kwerri-kwetchi, kwerri-kwetchi', resembling the words 'beer and cognac, beer and cognac', and is heard mostly at dawn and dusk. Pairs and small coveys in woodland, savanna, wooded hills and riverine thickets, mostly keeping within cover. 32 cm. **189**

4 REDBILLED FRANCOLIN *Francolinus adspersus.* Common resident. Identified by red bill and legs, yellow skin surrounding eyes and *finely barred underparts*; cf. (5). Has a loud, harsh crowing call which increases to a frenzied cackling 'chak, chak, chak, CHAK, chakitty, chakitty, chakittychak, chakittychak'. Occurs in pairs and small coveys in Kalahari thornveld, low scrub and thickets, especially along rivers, but feeds on open ground. 30-38 cm. **194**

5 NATAL FRANCOLIN *Francolinus natalensis.* Common resident. Identified by entirely *black and white barred underparts*, bolder, more contrasty barring than in (3), plus red legs and red bill with a yellow base. Very noisy, the call a strident, cackling 'kek, kek-kek, kek, kek-kek, kek-kek-kek-kek, kwa-kekekek, kwa-kekekek, kwa-kekekek...' slowly fading at the end; when flushed flies off with much raucous cackling. Small coveys favour rocky, bush-covered hillsides, riverine woodland, wooded valleys and thornveld, usually in rocky situations and seldom far from water. 30-38 cm. **196**

1 ORANGE RIVER FRANCOLIN *Francolinus lavaillantoides*. Fairly common resident. The palest forms (a) occur in central and northern Botswana; elsewhere is more rufous about the head and underparts, more liberally spotted deep red as (b) and (c). The call, heard mostly mornings and evenings, is 'pirrie-perrie, pirrie-perrie, pirri-perrie...'. Occurs in small coveys in open grassland, Kalahari woodland with a sparse understorey, and around pans. Common in the south-eastern grasslands. Flushes with reluctance. 33-35 cm. **193**

Guineafowls. Family NUMIDIDAE. Differ from the related francolins in having bare heads surmounted by casques or plumes, unfeathered necks in adults, predominantly grey plumages and lack of leg-spurs. Highly gregarious unless breeding.

2 HELMETED GUINEAFOWL *Numidia meleagris*. Fairly common to common resident. Identified by blue neck, red helmet and horny casque on crown. Chick (a) is buffy-brown, striped darker; juvenile (b) predominantly brown, darker on upperparts, head-stripes remaining until casque has started growing; immature (c) resembles adult but has feathered neck, dark brown helmet and rudimentary casque. Normal adult call is a much-repeated 'ker-bek-ker-bek-ker-bek, krrrrrr...'; female also makes a continual piping 't-phueet-t-phueet-t-phueet...'. Flocks, sometimes very large, in grassland, thornveld and farmlands, going to water regularly in the evenings. 53-58 cm. **203**

1 OSTRICH (Family STRUTHIONIDAE) *Struthio camelus.* Common resident. Well-known, enormous, flightless bird. Immature like small, scruffy female; usually accompanied by adults. Male makes a lion-like roar at night. Usually in pairs or groups, sometimes with large creches of young birds. Occurs widely throughout Botswana (less frequently in areas of human settlement) and is found in all habitats except wetlands, being most common in the more arid zones. About 2 m. **1**

2 SECRETARYBIRD (Family SAGITTARIIDAE) *Sagittarius serpentarius.* Fairly common resident. Large, long-legged grey and black bird with long, loose black feathers projecting behind the head; adult with orange face, immature with yellow face. Normally silent, but sometimes makes a frog-like croak. Usually in pairs walking with measured strides in grassland, savanna or Kalahari scrub. Sometimes runs a short distance with spread wings and may also soar to a great height. Roosts on the top of thorn trees. Widely but sparsely distributed throughout the country. 125-150 cm. **118**

Vultures, kites, eagles, buzzards, hawks, harriers and Gymnogene. Family ACCIPITRIDAE. Diurnal birds of prey (raptors) characterised by hooked beaks suited to a mainly carnivorous diet. Each group hereafter described separately.

Vultures are typified by large size, heavy, hooked beaks, necks wholly or partially devoid of feathers (in many) and, for a bird of prey, relatively weak feet not suited to grasping prey. Vultures feed on carrion, soar with ease during much of the day, and bathe in ponds and rivers. Normally silent birds, but hiss and squeal when squabbling over food.

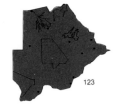

1 WHITEBACKED VULTURE *Gyps africanus*. Common resident. Adult difficult to distinguish from the next species (though smaller) unless the white back is seen, but at close range the eye is dark (not honey-coloured as (2)); plumage becomes pale with age. See underwing detail for in-flight comparison with next species. Immature darker than adult, lacks white rump, underparts with pale streaks, collar-feathers brown (not white), bare skin greenish, blackish on face. Widespread but with a preference for plains and wooded savanna and normally outnumbers all other vulture species in these habitats. Roosts and nests in large trees; cf. next species. 90-98 cm. **123**

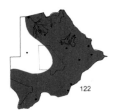

2 CAPE VULTURE *Gyps coprotheres*. Resident; uncommon generally to fairly common in east and south-east. Similar to the previous species but larger. Mature adult very pale (may have *almost white back*), bare skin blackish-blue, eyes honey-coloured; for in-flight comparison with previous species see underwing detail. Immature more rufous, warmer brown than immature of (1), streaking of underparts more cinnamon-buff, bare skin magenta-pink including bare patches at base of neck, these surrounded by white feathers. Breeds colonially on high cliffs (May-October), colonies then comprise many dozen pairs, otherwise singly or in groups anywhere. Ranges widely when not breeding. 105-115 cm. **122**

1 HOODED VULTURE *Necrosyrtes moñachus*. Fairly common resident of the northern region. A small, *thin-billed* vulture, adult with white downy feathers on a reddish face and neck plus white ruff and white 'pants' and legs. In flight appears square-winged and very dark; cf. flight pattern of (3). Immature all-brown including down on head and neck, face only pink; cf.immature of rare Egyptian Vulture (overleaf) which has a fully *feathered* head. Distribution mostly sparse but occasionally occurs beyond its normal northern range. 65-75 cm. **121**

2 WHITEHEADED VULTURE *Trigonoceps occipitalis*. Uncommon resident. Distinguished by large size, adult with white head, neck, underparts (female with white secondary feathers) plus heavy red and blue bill, pink face and legs. Flight pattern distinctive, female only showing white secondaries; see illustrations. Immature much browner on underparts, top of head brownish. Usually in pairs, generally outnumbered by other vultures at carrion but widespread in all habitat types. 78-82 cm. **125**

3 LAPPETFACED VULTURE *Torgos tracheliotus*. Fairly common resident. A huge, massive-billed vulture with crimson head and neck, streaked underparts and white 'pants', these contrasting with dark body and underwings in flight. Immature has dark 'pants' and varying amounts of white mottling in the plumage, sometimes with almost completely white back. Singly, pairs or small groups throughout. A powerfully built vulture which dominates all others at food sources. 98 cm. **124**

1 EGYPTIAN VULTURE *Neophron percnopterus*. Very rare vagrant; seen once in recent years (1976) on Boteti River. A small but distinctive whitish vulture with long, shaggy, buff head and neck feathers, and yellow face with slender bill. Pied flight pattern and diamond-shaped tail distinctive. Immature has dark brown plumage; cf. immature Hooded Vulture (previous page). Once common and widespread but now believed to be extinct throughout most of southern Africa. Further sightings should be reported, *with supporting evidence,* to the Botswana Bird Club. 64-71 cm. **120**

2 PALMNUT VULTURE *Gypohierax angolensis*. Very rare vagrant; old records exist for the north only. Adult white with black flight feathers and bare pink face; in flight told by distinctive pied pattern and *square black tail*; cf. previous species. Immature brown like immature of (1) but lacks loose head feathers; in flight shows square tail. Feeds on dead aquatic life ı ı shorelines of lakes and rivers; also on fruits of Raffia palms. Sper Js much of the day perched. New sightings should be reported, *with supporting evidence,* to the Botswana Bird Club. 60 cm. **147**

1

J

2

J

Milvus kites. Large, long-winged migrant raptors with V-shaped tails. Spend much of the day flying in leisurely fashion at low height while scanning the ground, their tails constantly twisting as they manoeuvre. Feed by scavenging and also catch various small animals. The Yellowbilled Kite is regarded by some authorities as a race of the Black Kite. However, since the former breeds in southern Africa while the latter is a non-breeding visitor, and since also the two birds have significant plumage and behavioural differences, the two are regarded as distinct species for purposes of this fieldguide.

1 YELLOWBILLED KITE *Milvus migrans parasitus.* Common to very common summer resident. Distinguished from the next species by *yellow bill*, brown head and more deeply forked tail. The immature has a black bill (only the cere is yellow), but is distinguished from all ages of the next species by more rufous underparts. In flight the adult sometimes calls 'kleeeuw', ending with a trill. Widespread late August - late March in all habitats; especially frequent along major roads. Nests in large trees, frequently near water. Usually singly or in loose groups but large numbers may gather at a food source, often mixing with the next species. Nomadic if not breeding. 55 cm. **126**

2 BLACK KITE *Milvus migrans migrans.* Uncommon summer visitor. Distinguished from the previous species by grey head, mantle and upper breast at all ages plus *black bill* (only the cere is yellow) and less deeply forked tail which appears square-cut when fanned. Immature greyish below with brown blotches. Call identical to (1). Nomadic; more often seen in flocks than (1), especially when flying termites are emerging, behaviour otherwise the same. 55 cm. **126**

Snake eagles, unlike true eagles, have *unfeathered legs*, heads with loose feathers giving a round-headed appearance, plus large yellow eyes. They either still-hunt by watching the ground from a perch or hunt while flying.

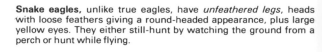

3 WESTERN BANDED SNAKE EAGLE *Circaetus cinerascens.* Rare localised resident. A small, robust, ash-brown eagle with a broad, dark terminal bar on the tail (a second bar is mostly obscured by the under tail coverts) and fine barring on the belly. In flight appears white with distinct underwing barring, *both tail-bars then visible*. Immature much paler, almost white about the head when very young but darkening with age, underparts whitish with ash-brown blotching; dark tail-bar present. Occurs in riverine forests and on wooded islands in the Chobe-Linyanti-Okavango regions where it still-hunts from a leafless branch in a tall tree. 55 cm. **145**

1 BATELEUR *Terathopius ecaudatus.* Common resident. A distinctive, bulky-looking black eagle with tawny wing coverts (more extensive in females) and scarlet face and legs; normally with chestnut back (a), less often with creamy-white back (b). In flight appears almost tailless, long wings gracefully tapered, male with widest black trailing edge. Immature progresses from uniform dull brown with slaty face and legs (c) to dark and light brown mottling with purple face and legs (d). In flight may call a loud, harsh 'schaaaaaaaw' in display or while attempting to pirate food; while perched may call a soft 'kau-kau-kau-ko-aaagh'. Flies with little wing-flapping, long, prolonged glides with a sideways rocking action as though balancing; sometimes makes wing-claps in flight. Usually singly at low altitude over a variety of habitats. Widespread. 55-70 cm. **146**

2 BLACKBREASTED SNAKE EAGLE *Circaetus gallicus.* Fairly common resident. Adult differs from the larger Martial Eagle (pp.118-119) in having *bare legs*, unspotted underparts and, in flight, predominantly white (not dark) underwings. Immature starts as (a) then progresses to stage (b), the head gradually darkening, underparts becoming clearer. Usually seen singly flying over open or lightly wooded regions. Flies high and often hovers motionless. Snakes when caught are taken into the air, killed and eaten in flight. 63-68 cm. **143**

3 BROWN SNAKE EAGLE *Circaetus cinereus.* Fairly common resident. Large brown eagle identified by whitish, unfeathered legs, large yellow eyes and erect stance when perched. In flight dark body and underwing coverts contrast with silvery-white flight feathers, the tail with four clear, dark bands. Immature starts with similar plumage to adult, less dark (a), then progresses to mottled stage (b). At all ages has downy white under-feathers, therefore even adult appears speckled when moulting. Singly in any woodland. Still-hunts from a bare branch, taking large snakes and killing them and eating them on the ground or in a tree. Occasionally hovers. Nomadic when not breeding. 71-76 cm. **142**

True eagles have fully feathered legs, this distinguishing them from snake eagles (previous page) and all other raptors. They also possess strong, large-clawed and often long-toed feet for grasping live prey, which is killed by crushing, and well-hooked bills. Most eagles hunt while flying, wheeling effortlessly in thermals (rising columns of warm air) and are therefore seldom seen perched during the warm hours of the day unless feeding.

1 BOOTED EAGLE *Hieraaetus pennatus*. Rare visitor; breeds in Namibia and Cape Province, when not breeding (November-August) ranges widely, may occur anywhere in Botswana. Occurs in two colour morphs, dark brown (a) and white or buffy (b), the latter most common. At rest differs from Wahlberg's Eagle (3) in more rounded head, pale buffy upperwing coverts showing as a broad bar on the folded wing and diagnostic white shoulder-patches. In flight tail square-ended when closed, slightly rounded when spread; wings held slightly forward while soaring, flight feathers black with pale 'wedges' at base of inner primaries and white shoulder-patches visible on dark plumaged birds. Upperwing pattern like *Milvus* kite (pp. 108-109) but tail not forked. In flapping flight makes four or five fast flaps followed by a glide. Immature similar to adult. 48-52 cm. **136**

2 LESSER SPOTTED EAGLE *Aquila pomarina*. In general a rare summer visitor, but sometimes temporarily common locally. A small brown eagle identified at rest by narrowly feathered 'stovepipe' legs; immature with white spots on folded wings. In flight from below appears broad-winged, the head protruding little, tail rounded. From above immature shows white patches at base of primaries, narrow white edges to upperwing coverts and a white crescent shape at base of tail (vestigial in adult); cf. larger Steppe Eagle (pp.114-115). Usually singly and sparsely distributed; occasionally large numbers may gather to feed at quelea breeding colonies (flock of about 300 observed in Tuli Block). Nomadic. 65 cm. **134**

3 WAHLBERG'S EAGLE *Aquila wahlbergi*. Fairly common summer resident. A small eagle with several colour morphs illustrated as (a), (b) and (c) with (a) probably most common. Other colour combinations also occur, e.g. dark head and white or pale brown body and *vice versa*. At rest the folded wing is more uniformly coloured than in (1), the legs less slender than in previous species. In flight shows fairly narrow, parallel wings and longish, *square tail held mostly closed*. Sometimes makes a whistling 'peeeeoo' in flight. Singly or in pairs in woodland and wooded savanna. Widespread but less frequent in arid regions. 55-60 cm. **135**

1 LONGCRESTED EAGLE *Lophaetus occipitalis.* Uncommon localised resident. A small eagle. At rest long, upstanding crest unmistakable; leg feathers may be white or black and white. Flight pattern also distinctive; see illustrations. Sometimes calls in flight, a shrill 'weee-er' or 'peerr-wee' repeated. Usually seen singly in woodland or riverine forests in the Chobe and Okavango regions. May perch prominently on an exposed branch. 53-58 cm. **139**

2 STEPPE EAGLE *Aquila nipalensis.* Uncommon summer visitor. Adult is a large, dark brown eagle with heavily feathered legs and, sometimes, a pale patch on the nape of the head. The gape is a prominent orange-yellow which extends back to a point *level with the back of the eyes.* Darker and plainer than the darkest Tawny Eagle (next species) to which it is closely related. Immature very like the next species but usually paler and shows much white in wings when flying including white trailing edge to wings and tail; cf.next species and Lesser Spotted Eagle (pp. 112-113). Nomadic. Occurs singly or in flocks in woodland, mostly in the eastern regions. May gather in large numbers at a termite emergence and at breeding colonies of queleas on which they feed, sometimes in company with the Lesser Spotted Eagle. 75 cm. **133**

3 TAWNY EAGLE *Aquila rapax.* Fairly common to common resident. Adult either tawny with or without dark brown mottling on wings (a and b), or chocolate brown with darker mottling (c); eyes pale brown. Immature may resemble adult or be very pale (d), then very similar to immature of previous species; eye dark brown. At all ages differs from previous species in yellow (not orange-yellow) cere and gape, the gape not extending backwards beyond the *centre of the eyes.* In flight adult shows little white in wings, none on upper tail coverts. Immature in flight similar to immature of (2) but white areas smaller, white trailing edge of wings less clear; indistinguishable at a distance. Widespread, normally singly or in pairs in well-wooded regions. 65-72 cm. **132**

114

1 AYRES' EAGLE *Hieraaetus ayresii*. Rare visitor; positively recorded only in the north and south-east. Superficially resembles the next species, but much smaller and usually darker. Some individuals (males?) only lightly spotted on white underparts (a) but majority heavily blotched as (b). Forehead may be white or dark; if dark gives appearance of cap extending below eyes as (b). Leading edge of wing frequently unmarked, then shows as a white shoulder-patch on folded wing. In flight underwings heavily barred appearing all-dark, tail with one broad, dark terminal band plus three narrow bands; cf. next species. Immature much paler, as illustrated. An agile, rapacious little eagle. Normally occurs very sparsely in well-developed, broadleafed woodland and heavily wooded hillsides. 46-55 cm. **138**

2 AFRICAN HAWK EAGLE *Hieraaetus fasciatus*. Fairly common resident. Much larger than the previous species, male usually less spotted on underparts than female. In flight shows characteristic white wing-patches, dark line on trailing edge of wing and broad terminal tail-band. Immature rufous on head and underparts as illustrated, later becomes white on central belly and breast, and more heavily spotted; cf. immature Black Sparrowhawk (p.131) which has *bare legs*. The call is a flute-like 'klu-klu-klukluee'. Usually in pairs in broadleafed and mixed open woodland, wooded hillsides or riverine forests. Perches, well concealed, in leafy canopy of tree, but pairs usually soar together, frequently in mornings. 60-65 cm. **137**

3 CROWNED EAGLE *Stephanoaetus coronatus*. Unrecorded in Botswana but may occasionally occur along the eastern border. Its presence in adjoining Zimbabwe is well known. Large, powerful eagle. Adult dark with crested head, heavily barred or blotched underparts; in flight heavily barred underwings and tail with rufous underwing coverts diagnostic. Young birds initially white on head and underparts (a), becoming progressively spotted and blotched with maturity (b). Very vocal within its territory, calling loudly during a daily undulating display flight 'kewee-kewee-kewee...' repeated as the bird rises and falls. Pairs frequent mature riverine forests with large trees, well-wooded hillsides and valleys, usually near water. 80-90 cm. **141**

1 AFRICAN FISH EAGLE *Haliaeetus vocifer.* Common resident. Well known, adult distinctive. Very young, free-flying birds (a) are easily mistaken for other brown eagles, but pale demarcation line of emergent white upper breast is usually detectable beneath the heavy brown markings. At one year plumage pattern begins to resemble that of adult though heavy brown streaks still remain on white breast and mantle (b). The ringing, far-carrying call is 'weee-ah, hyo-hyo' or 'heee-ah, heeah-heeah', the male's voice more shrill than that of female; calls while perched or in flight. Usually in pairs at large rivers, lakes, dams and pans. Common and conspicuous throughout the Chobe-Linyanti-Okavango region, regular at most permanent large waters elsewhere. 63-73 cm. **148**

2 MARTIAL EAGLE *Polemaetus bellicosus.* Fairly common resident. Distinctive, large, long-legged eagle, most similar to Black-breasted Snake Eagle (pp.110-111) but differing in spotted underparts and fully-feathered legs; in flight by dark (not whitish) underwings. Immature lacks dark head and breast, underparts white, unspotted as illustrated; cf. immature Crowned Eagle (p.117) which has entirely white head. Calls a loud, ringing 'kloo-ee, kloo-ee...'. Widespread in various wooded habitats. Hunts while flying or while perched in a leafy tree. 78-83 cm. **140**

3 BLACK EAGLE (VERREAUX'S EAGLE) *Aquila verreauxii.* Fairly common, localised resident. Large black eagle with white 'V' mark on its back. In flight has characteristic narrow-based wings with white 'flashes' at the base of the primaries. Immature mottled brown as illustrated, differing from Tawny Eagle (p.115) in rufous crown and nape plus pale legs heavily marked with dark brown. Pairs are resident in the eastern and south-eastern hill regions, preferring sheer rock cliffs on which they nest and roost, but immature birds frequently wander away from hills. 84 cm. **131**

Buzzards are medium-sized soaring raptors about the size of a small eagle, of robust build, bills aquiline but small, ceres large, eyes dark brown (honey-coloured in immatures), wings moderately long and well rounded, tails rounded when spread. During the day either perch in some conspicuous position or soar for long periods.

1 STEPPE BUZZARD *Buteo buteo vulpinus*. Common summer visitor. Adult variable, most commonly as (a) but dark form (b) and russet form (c) are frequently seen while other variations also occur. Diagnostic feature common to all except the very dark form is a distinct *pale zone across the breast*, which divides the streaked or smudged upper breast from the banded underparts. In flight wing pattern standard, with tonal variations only, the spread tail pale cinnamon with an indistinct, dusky terminal band. Immature has the entire underparts streaked or blotched as illustrated. This buzzard is much smaller than the Brown Snake Eagle (p.111) and lacks the large yellow eyes of that species. In flight sometimes calls 'kreeeeee', especially when two or more are flying together. Widespread September-March, commonly seen perched on roadside telegraph poles or circling overhead. Singly or in small, loose groups in grassland, scrub or agricultural lands, less often in well-wooded regions. 45-50 cm. **149**

2 LONGLEGGED BUZZARD *Buteo rufinus*. Status in Botswana not established; substantiated records lacking. Larger than the previous species, pale-headed with longer legs, wing coverts more rufous; a rare all-dark morph occurs (b). In flight normal morph shows pale head and upper breast, dark carpal patches, white patches at base of primaries, *dark vent* and unmarked tail. Perches much of day in similar manner to previous species. In flight hovers frequently. This species is rare anywhere in southern Africa. 51-66 cm. **151**

1 HONEY BUZZARD *Pernis apivorus*. Status in Botswana not established; no confirmed records but known to occur sparsely in adjacent territories. Slightly larger than a Steppe Buzzard (pp.120-121) but easily mistaken for it. Several colour morphs occur, (a) probably most common while a dark form (b) and one with entirely white underparts are known. Appears smaller-headed, longer-tailed than Steppe Buzzard and with *yellow* (not brown) eyes. In flight the small head protrudes well forward of the long wings, underwings heavily barred and with conspicuous *dark carpal patches*, tail with two dark central bands and one terminal band; cf. Steppe Buzzard. Immature as illustrated. Singly in well-wooded country. Perches well within the cover of trees or walks about the ground searching for wasps' and bees' nests, feeding on the grubs. 54-60 cm. **130**

2 JACKAL BUZZARD *Buteo rufofuscus*. Rare vagrant; sparsely recorded in the south-east. Chestnut breast and tail of adult distinctive. Flight pattern also distinctive with rounded wings and short, rounded, chestnut tail. Much paler immature (sometimes paler than illustrated) could be mistaken for larger, immature African Hawk Eagle (p.117) but has bare legs and, in flight, more rounded wings and tail. The call is a jackal-like, high-pitched 'kweh' or a mewing 'kip-kweeeu, kweeeu, kweeeeu' while flying. A bird of hilly regions and adjacent grasslands. 44-53 cm. **154**

3 AUGUR BUZZARD *Buteo augur*. Status not established; could occur as a casual vagrant from southern Zimbabwe where it is fairly common. Adult distinctive with almost entirely white underparts and chestnut tail; size and proportions same as previous species. Immature inseparable from immature of (2). Call same as (2). Prefers wooded hills with granite outcrops. 44-53 cm. **153**

1 LIZARD BUZZARD *Kaupifalco monogrammicus*. Uncommon, exact status not established; sparsely distributed with a few recorded sightings in the north and north-east. A small grey hawk resembling an Accipiter (pp. 126-131) but distinguished by diagnostic, vertical black streak on throat and two bold, white tail-bands (occasionally only one). Immature more buffy, throat-streak less clear. The call is a whistling 'pheeeoo, wot-wot-wot-wot-wot-wot' uttered frequently while perched or soaring. Singly in broadleafed woodland. Rests concealed in a tree canopy or on an exposed perch. Nomadic. 35-37 cm. **154**

2 BLACKSHOULDERED KITE *Elanus caeruleus*. Fairly common resident. Distinctive small raptor with pure white underparts, grey upperparts and black shoulder-patches; eyes ruby-red. In flight appears pure white with black wing-tips; cf. much larger Pallid Harrier (p.133). Immature more buffy on head, upperparts and breast, as illustrated. Usually silent, sometimes makes a weak 'weeet-weeet-weeet' when agitated. Singly or in pairs in grassland, Kalahari scrub, savanna and suburbia. Perches conspicuously on bare branches, roadside telephone poles and wires, often raising and lowering its tail repeatedly while watching the ground below. Graceful in flight, *often hovering* for periods of five to twenty seconds, and frequently hunts at dusk. 30 cm. **127**

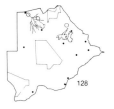

3 CUCKOO HAWK *Aviceda cuculoides*. Rare, exact status not established; possible resident. Adult distinguished by crested head and white underparts with bold rufous bands. In flight shows long wings and tail, both well banded as illustrated. Flight action buoyant and leisurely, wing-beats slow with spells of gliding. Immature with crested head and wing pattern similar to adult but underparts with bold, heart-shaped spots. Calls 'ticki-to-you' repeated slowly. Spends much time perched but also makes occasional, high soaring flights. Can be expected occasionally on the fringes of woodland and riverine forests in the north-east and Okavango Delta. 40 cm. **128**

Goshawks and sparrowhawks. True hawks (known collectively as Accipiters) characterised by short, rounded wings, fairly long tails and long bare, usually slender, legs and toes. Secretive, catching their prey (usually small birds) in a low, rapid aerial pursuit from the cover of a leafy tree, and frequently hunting at dusk.

1 LITTLE SPARROWHAWK *Accipiter minullus.* Uncommon resident. Adult recognised by very small size, yellow eyes, yellow legs and, in flight, by two conspicuous white spots on the upper tail. Immature by small size and heavy spotting of underparts. Call a single-syllabled 'ki' repeated rapidly. Occurs sparsely in well-wooded situations, riverine forests and wooded valleys. 23-25 cm. **157**

2 LITTLE BANDED GOSHAWK (SHIKRA) *Accipiter badius.* Fairly common resident. Adult identified by banded underparts *extending to the throat* (which has a dark central streak), deep red eyes and, in flight, by *lack of any white on rump or upper tail*; may sometimes show some white spots on the mantle. Immature by dark colouring of upperparts forming a *hood over the head*, dark central streak on throat, upper breast *streaked* brown, lower breast and belly *banded* brown, eyes and legs orange-yellow; cf. immature of next species. Call a metallic, two-syllabled 'kli-vit' repeated, also a plaintive 'tee-uuu'. Singly or in pairs in a wide range of wooded habitats; widely distributed. 30-34 cm. **159**

3 GABAR GOSHAWK *Micronisus gabar.* Fairly common to common resident. Normal adult (a) identified by grey throat and breast plus deep red eyes, red cere and legs and, in flight, by *broad white rump-patch.* Fairly common melanistic form (b) has same colours of soft parts but lacks white rump. Immature boldly streaked and blotched rufous all over head, neck and breast, banded rufous on rest of underparts, eyes yellow, cere and legs coral; cf.immature of previous species. Call a high-pitched, rapid piping 'pi-pi-pi-pi-pi...'. Frequents any woodland, often hunting in low flight over open country, otherwise from a perch within cover. 30-34 cm. **161**

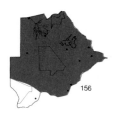

4 OVAMBO SPARROWHAWK *Accipiter ovampensis.* Uncommon resident. Adults identified by grey barring of underparts extending to the throat, cere and legs usually orange-yellow, occasionally red. In flight shows pale central tail feather-shafts on upper tail, small white rump-patch variable, often absent. Immature either pale (a) or rufous (b), lightly marked on underparts, cere and legs dull orange-yellow. A rare melanistic form occurs. Call a slow, repeated 'kiep, kiep, kiep...' or 'wo-wo-wo-wo...' rising in scale. Sparsely but widely distributed in savanna woodland. 33-40 cm. **156**

1 AFRICAN GOSHAWK *Accipiter tachiro*. Rare. Exact status not established; sparsely recorded in the riverine and valley forests of eastern Botswana. A medium-sized goshawk with predominantly brown (not grey) colouring. Adult finely barred red-brown over entire underparts, eyes and cere yellow, legs dull orange-yellow. Immature heavily blotched black on underparts; cf. much smaller immature Little Sparrowhawk (p.127). Territorial male displays early mornings in high flight with bouts of fast wing-beats interspersed with glides during which it calls repeatedly 'krit' at two- or three-second intervals. Most active early mornings and evenings. 37-39 cm. **160**

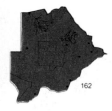

2 PALE CHANTING GOSHAWK *Melierax canorus*. Common resident. Large, pale grey goshawk with pink cere and legs; almost impossible to tell from the next species when perched except for slightly paler grey upperparts, but in flight shows much whiter upper-wings plus *white rump*. Immature of this and the next species indistinguishable. In early summer calls loudly and melodiously while perched, especially at dawn 'kleeeeuw, kleeeeuw, kleeeeuw, klu-klu-klu-klu.' Widely distributed, preferring more open habitat than the next species. Perches conspicuously with erect stance on a bush or roadside post. Alternatively walks about the ground in search of small prey, peering under rocks, logs and into rodent burrows. Seldom flies high, usually making low swoops from perch to perch. 53-63 cm. **162**

3 DARK CHANTING GOSHAWK *Melierax metabates*. Uncommon resident. Very similar to previous species but slightly darker on upperparts. In flight shows darker, more uniform upper-wings, the rump *finely barred* (not white). Immature as illustrated, cere and legs initially dull yellow becoming orange or coral-red while still in immature plumage; indistinguishable from immature of previous species. In early summer calls from a perch for long periods 'pha-leeoo-phwe-phwe-phwe-phwe-phwe...', the last sound being repeated up to 30 times. Frequents mature broadleafed woodland and savanna in the northern regions. Usually still-hunts for long periods from a prominent perch. 50-56 cm. **163**

128

158

1 BLACK SPARROWHAWK *Accipiter melanoleucus.* Rare, localised resident; recorded sparsely but known to breed in the southeast. Large black and white hawk, normally with white or partially white underparts (a), thighs and vent either speckled black and white or entirely black, eyes orange or red, cere and legs dull yellow. Melanistic form (b) has only throat white plus some white feathers on flanks. Immature buffy below streaked dark brown, sometimes more streaked than illustrated; cf. immature African Hawk Eagle (p.117) which is larger and has fully feathered legs. Usually silent. Singly or in pairs in well-developed woodland, riverine forests or stands of *Eucalyptus.* 46-58 cm. **158**

Harriers. Long-winged, longish-tailed, long-legged raptors which frequent marshlands or grasslands. Fly low with leisurely, buoyant action, head bent downwards and legs hanging slightly away from the body, bouts of flapping alternating with glides. Settle on the ground or perch on posts or mounds, seldom on trees. Silent birds.

168

2 BLACK HARRIER *Circus maurus.* Rare visitor. Adult appears entirely black when settled, but in flight has striking pied appearance produced by white flight feathers and white tail with black bars. Immature has buff underparts as illustrated; in flight wing pattern resembles that of African Marsh Harrier (p.133) but pale buff underbody diagnostic. Individuals at the northern extremity of their range occur occasionally in the extreme south-west; one record from Lake Ngami. When hunting flies low and hovers briefly before dropping to the ground. 48-53 cm. **168**

3 EUROPEAN MARSH HARRIER *Circus aeruginosus.* Exact status not established; no confirmed records. May occur occasionally in the Okavango Delta and Makgadikgadi Pans, having been recorded at scattered points elsewhere in southern Africa in recent years. Male differs from African Marsh Harrier (p.133) when settled in paler underparts and more streaky breast; in flight by striking whitish wings and tail plus rufous underwing coverts. Female dark, almost black, with diagnostic *buff crown and wing leading edges*, underwings all-dark. Frequents marshlands and waterways. 48-56 cm. **164**

1 AFRICAN MARSH HARRIER *Circus ranivorus.* Fairly common resident; commonest in the Linyanti-Okavango region. Adult differs from the rare European Marsh Harrier (p.131) and females of the next two species in overall darker colouring; in flight shows *white* on leading edges of inner-wings while old birds may show some white about the head. Immature has diagnostic pale breast-band plus white dappling on nape and mantle. Usually singly, flying low over marshlands, reedbeds and moist grasslands. 44-49 cm. **165**

2 PALLID HARRIER *Circus macrourus.* Rare summer visitor. White underparts and very white flight pattern of male diagnostic, upper-wings paler than those of next species; from above or below black primary feathers show as *narrow black wedges at wingtips.* Female told from female of next species only by pale ruff-collar behind ear coverts; females of both species differ from (1) in *white rump* and banded tail. Nomadic, flying low over grassland and semi-desert regions. 44-48 cm. **167**

3 MONTAGU'S HARRIER *Circus pygargus.* Rare summer visitor. Male told from male of previous species in darker grey colouring, belly white streaked brown; in flight by *entirely black* wingtips, upper wings with *black bar traversing the centre,* underwings with narrow black and rufous barring. Female hardly distinguishable from female of previous species but lacks the white ruff-collar; white rump and and well-barred tail preclude confusion with (1). Singly or in pairs flying low over grassland and semi-desert regions, often the grassy surrounds of pans. 40-47 cm. **166**

132

Miscellaneous raptors. The following three species are specialised raptors with no obvious affinities to other groups.

1 BAT HAWK *Macheiramphus alcinus.* Rare localised resident. A dark brown hawk with whitish eyes, white feet and a pale vent; at close range has a pale throat with a dark central streak. In flight looks black, wings sharply tapered. Immature has white underparts with a broad black band across the lower breast. Sometimes calls a high-pitched 'kik-kik-kik-kik-keee'. Singly or in pairs, by day perched in a tall, leafy tree, emerging to hunt bats and small birds at dusk or, in overcast weather, in the early morning. Frequents riverine forests, stands of tall trees and other well-wooded regions, often near water. Flight rapid when hunting. 45 cm. **129**

2 OSPREY (Family PANDIONIDAE) *Pandion haliaetus.* Rare summer visitor. Loosely crested head, masked appearance and white underparts identify this species at rest, the breast-band often vestigial, strongest in the immature. In flight appears large-winged, small-headed, underwings with bold, dark carpal patches and dark central bar, tail well banded. Normally silent. Singly on large, fish-rich waters but sparsely distributed and of irregular occurrence. Perches on a branch or dead tree in water or hunts by flying slowly over water with shallow, loose wing-beats; catches fish with shallow dive or steep plunge-dive. 55-63 cm. **170**

3 GYMNOGENE *Polyboroides typus.* Fairly common resident. Large grey raptor with black flight feathers and black tail with *bold white central band,* bare yellow face and legs. In flight appears broad-winged, white tail-bar distinctive; sometimes has dark carpal patches on upper wings. Young birds have two colour phases as illustrated; difficult to identify but long yellow slender legs and small head with loose neck feathers diagnostic. In flight may call 'peeeeeee', but normally silent. Occurs singly in a wide range of habitats with a preference for well-wooded conditions. Clambers about dead trees or rocks, inserting its long legs into cavities in search of lizards, bats and other small creatures. Also raids weaver, swift and woodpecker nests, eating the nestlings. 60-66 cm. **169**

Falcons. Small raptors characterised by pointed wings and, usually, prominent 'sideburns'. Females larger than males. Aerial hunters, typically seizing smaller birds in a rapid dive from above. Build no nests but use old nests of crows and other raptors, or nest on rock ledges. Characteristic calls are high-pitched 'kek-kek-kek-kek-kek' sounds when agitated. Kestrels, related to falcons, are more slender-bodied and eat many insects caught in the air with their feet, or small mammals and reptiles caught on the ground. Their flight is more leisurely than that of falcons while some species are highly gregarious.

1 PEREGRINE FALCON *Falco peregrinus.* Rare resident and possible summer visitor. Resident birds (a) with broad 'sideburns' and fine, close barring and spotting on underparts, visiting birds (b) with narrow 'sideburns' and whiter underparts lightly spotted, mostly on flanks; immatures streaked. At rest all differ from next species in dark (not rufous) crown plus more stocky appearance. In flight wings and tail appear shorter than those of (2) and less pointed than Hobby Falcon (3); tail usually held closed. Singly, often near cliffs when breeding, otherwise anywhere. Flies with rapid, shallow wing-beats followed by brief glide, but perches most of day. 34-38 cm. **171**

2 LANNER FALCON *Falco biarmicus.* Fairly common resident. Largest falcon, recognised at all ages by *rufous crown,* paler in immature which also has underparts more heavily blotched than immature of (1). In soaring flight the tail is fanned. Singly or in pairs in almost any habitat, including the more arid regions. More often seen in flight than (1), progressing with bouts of fast wing-flapping followed by circling glides. 40-45 cm. **172**

3 HOBBY FALCON *Falco subbuteo.* Uncommon summer visitor. A small falcon identified by heavily marked body, adult with rufous thighs and undertail coverts; in flight by long, pointed wings heavily marked on the underside. Singly or in small flocks in light woodland. Hunts mostly at dusk, flying rapidly and with agility in pursuit of swallows and bats, or more leisurely with much gliding when catching flying termites, which are seized with the feet. 30-35 cm. **173**

1 PYGMY FALCON *Polihierax semitorquatus.* Uncommon, localised resident. Identified by very small size, entirely white underparts, female with rufous mantle. In flight by speckled wings and white rump. Singly or in pairs in the arid south-west, usually seen in the vicinity of the nests of the Sociable Weaver (pp. 296-297) with which it lives in close association; see illustration. 19,5 cm. **186**

2 SOOTY FALCON *Falco concolor.* No Botswana records but possibly a rare summer vagrant since it has been twice recorded close to Botswana's western boundary. Adult all-grey with blackish face and pale yellow cere and legs, the folded wings extending beyond the tail when perched. Immature greyer than other small falcons with grey blotches on creamy underparts and *creamy hind collar*; no rufous colouring. Likely to occur in tall-tree woodland near water. Active mostly at dusk. 31 cm. **175**

3 REDNECKED FALCON *Falco chicquera.* Uncommon resident. Identified at all ages by rusty head-top and nape plus well-barred appearance. In flight displays sharply pointed wings and pale underparts with a bold black subterminal tail-bar. A falcon of the more arid regions, in the north usually seen in association with *Hyphaene* palm trees, in the central and western regions with Camelthorn trees. Perches in the crown of trees and hunts other birds in rapid, often sustained aerial pursuit. 30-36 cm. **178**

1 AFRICAN HOBBY FALCON *Falco cuvierii.* Rare. Exact status not established. The most rufous falcon in the region, differing from any rufous kestrel in dark upperparts and behaviour. Sparsely distributed and irregular, apparently preferring richer woodland. Flight shape and behaviour similar to visiting Hobby Falcon (pp.138-9). 28-30 cm. **174**

2 GREATER KESTREL *Falco rupicoloides.* Common resident. At rest differs from Rock or Lesser Kestrels (pp.142-143) in entirely tawny (not red-brown) plumage with blackish streaks, spots and bars all over, plus *whitish eyes*; in flight by white underwings. Immature closely similar. Singly or in pairs in grassland, desert and lightly wooded regions; more common in the arid central and western regions. Still-hunts from a thorn tree, low shrub or roadside post or forages in low flight, occasionally hovering for brief periods. Flight bouyant, wing-action leisurely with much wheeling, banking, rising and falling. 36 cm. **182**

3 DICKINSON'S KESTREL *Falco dickinsoni.* Uncommon, localised resident. Distinctive grey kestrel with almost white head and neck, plus very pale rump; cere, eye-ring and legs yellow. Immature rather browner on the underparts. Singly or in pairs in broadleafed woodland, palm savanna and in association with baobab trees. Still-hunts from a tree perch, gliding down to catch terrestrial prey or chases small birds in rapid pursuit. Mostly confined to the northern regions. 38-40 cm. **185**

1 ROCK KESTREL (COMMON KESTREL) *Falco tinnunculus*. Fairly common resident. Differs from Greater Kestrel (pp.140-141) in having entirely red-brown (not tawny) plumage lightly spotted with black, plus grey head; female duller, sometimes lacking grey head as margin illustration. Told from male of next species in spotting of upperparts, lack of contrast between upper and underparts, lack of grey on upperwings, plus behaviour. Immature duller, lacks grey head. Singly or in pairs in hilly country, arid woodland and savanna. Perches on cliffs, dead trees and roadside posts. Flies with rapid wingbeats, frequently turning into wind and *hovering for prolonged periods*; the only brown kestrel to do this regularly. 30-33 cm. **181**

2 LESSER KESTREL *Falco naumanni*. Uncommon to fairly common summer visitor. Both sexes differ from previous species in *paler underparts* (male with more grey on upperwings) and different behaviour. Gregarious, occurring in flocks, often hundreds, in grassland and Kalahari scrub, perching on roadside posts, power pylons and lines, and bushes, or wheeling in leisurely, graceful flight at no great height. Nomadic, flocks following rainstorms. 28-30 cm. **183**

3 EASTERN REDFOOTED KESTREL *Falco amurensis*. Uncommon to fairly common summer visitor. Small kestrel, both sexes distinctive. Male differs from male of next species in much paler underparts, *white underwings*; female in whitish (not rufous) underparts. Immature similar to that of next species, less rufous. Gregarious, flocks perching on roadside wires, power lines and dead trees or flying over grasslands and open savanna, sometimes in company with the previous or next species. Occurs sparsely, mostly in the east and north. 28-30 cm. **180**

4 WESTERN REDFOOTED KESTREL *Falco verspertinus*. Uncommon to fairly common summer visitor. Male differs from male of previous species in overall dark grey plumage *including underwings*, vent only rufous; female from female of previous species in rufous colouring of head, body and underwings. Immature more rufous than that of previous species. Gregarious. Flock behaviour same as previous species with which it sometimes mixes, but is more frequent. 28-30 cm. **179**

Sandgrouse. Family PTEROCLIDIDAE. Cryptically coloured, pigeon-like birds, males boldly patterned. Wings pointed, bills short, legs short, front of tarsus feathered to toes. Immatures duller than adults. Gait shuffling but flight swift and powerful, often covering considerable distances daily to reach water. Inhabit arid regions, gathering at favoured pools in large numbers morning or evening.

1 DOUBLEBANDED SANDGROUSE *Pterocles bicinctus.* Common resident. Male distinguished by black and white bars on forehead, both sexes by fine black bars on belly. Calls 'chuck-chuck'; flocks coming to drink after sunset make a call resembling 'Don't *weep* so Charlie'. Widespread in the north and east. Favours Mopane, broadleafed and *Acacia* woodland plus stony regions. 25 cm. **347**

2 BURCHELL'S SANDGROUSE (SPOTTED SANDGROUSE) *Pterocles burchelli.* Fairly common resident. Both sexes told from other sandgrouse by ochre colouring and all-over heavy white spotting, male with grey about face, ear coverts and throat, female with yellowish face and ochre barring on belly. If alarmed on the ground utters a 'gug-gug-gug' sound but in flight calls 'chock-lit, chock-lit, chock-lit'. Widespread, favouring sandy soils, and so very uncommon in the east. 25 cm. **345**

3 NAMAQUA SANDGROUSE *Pterocles namaqua.* Uncommon to fairly common resident. Best told from other sandgrouse by long, pointed tails in both sexes. Flight call resembles the words 'Look at YOU'. Widespread but mostly absent from the north-east. Visits waterholes early mornings. Appears to be as widespread as (2) but commoner in some areas, less so in others for no obvious reason. 28 cm. **344**

4 YELLOWTHROATED SANDGROUSE *Pterocles gutturalis.* Common resident, almost entirely confined to the north and north-east December-June. Larger than other sandgrouse, the male with bold black gorget, both sexes with clear, pale yellow throats and ear coverts, blackish bellies and underwings. In flight calls a harsh 'tweet-weet'; on arriving at a waterhole emits a hoarse 'golli, golli'. An intra-African migrant; some present all months. 30 cm. **346**

Pigeons and doves. Family COLUMBIDAE. The distinction between pigeons and doves is ill defined: larger species tend to be called pigeons, smaller ones doves. Young are dull, scruffy versions of the adults. All except the fruit-eating pigeons feed on the ground.

1 MOURNING DOVE *Streptopelia decipiens.* Common, localised resident. The only collared dove with a *totally grey head plus yellow eyes* and red eye-rings. The call is distinctive, a soft 'kur-kurr' repeated once or twice; also a soft, descending 'kur-r-r-r-r-r'. Occurs in well developed riverine forests on the larger rivers. 30 cm. **353**

2 REDEYED DOVE *Streptopelia semitorquata.* Common resident. Differs from the previous species in having grey *on top of the head* only, eye deep red with a purple-pink eye-ring, the breast a deep pink. The well-known call is 'coo-coo, coo-*koo*-cuk-coo' the accent on the fourth syllable, and interpreted as 'Coo-coo, why don't you work?' Also makes a wheezy 'hraire'. Occurs in riverine forests, well-developed woodland and suburbia. The largest of the ring-necked doves. 33-36 cm. **352**

3 CAPE TURTLE DOVE *Streptopelia capicola.* Very common resident. Head and underparts more or less uniform pale grey, eyes blackish, no eye-rings. On take-off shows similar upper tail pattern to the next species, but mantle and wing-coverts greyish (not cinnamon). The call is a harsh and much repeated 'work-*harder,* work-*harder*...', also 'kerr-cherooo, kerr-cherooo...' and a snarling 'kerrr' on landing. Widespread, occurring in a wide variety of habitats including the most arid regions. 28 cm. **354**

4 LAUGHING DOVE *Streptopelia senegalensis.* Very common resident. *Has no black collar.* Pinkish head and cinnamon breast with black spots plus rusty coloured upperparts diagnostic. On take-off shows similar tail pattern to the previous species but has rusty (not grey) mantle and wing-coverts. The call is a soft 'coo-coo-CUK-coo-coo'. Widespread in a variety of habitats, including suburbia, but less frequent than (3) in the arid regions. 25 cm. **355**

5 NAMAQUA DOVE *Oena capensis.* Common resident. At all ages identified by long tail, male with black patch from forehead to breast. In flight combination of brown flight feathers and long tail diagnostic. The call is a seldom heard, explosive 'twoo-hoo'. Widespread, preferring arid conditions: semi-desert, grasslands, fallow farmlands and thornveld. Usually in pairs or small flocks, perching on low bushes and fences, or flying at great speed. Nomadic when not breeding. 27 cm. **356**

146

1 EMERALDSPOTTED DOVE (GREENSPOTTED DOVE) *Turtur chalcospilos*. Common resident. A small dove with green wing-spots, dull pink bill and feet; in flight shows chestnut-brown upper-wings and two broad, black bands across its back but differs from the Namaqua Dove (p.147) in having a short tail. The call is a soft, descending cooing 'du, du...du-du...du...du...du-du-dudu-du-du-du...' tailing off at the end. Occurs in woodland and riverine forest, being absent from the arid regions. 20 cm. **358**

2 FERAL PIGEON (DOMESTIC or TOWN PIGEON) *Columbia livia*. Locally common resident. Very well known and variable in colour. A wild-living domestic breed descended from the Rock Dove of North Africa and Europe. Main colour forms shown but many combinations occur including pure white, white with dark head and dark grey with white head. Calls 'coo-roo-coo'. Dependent on human settlements, occurring in towns where very tame. 33 cm. **348**

3 GREEN PIGEON *Treron calva*. Fairly common localised resident. Told by bright green colouring, yellow on wings and leg-feathers plus red base to bill and red legs. Call an explosive, high-pitched yet melodious bubbling, descending in pitch. Occurs in the north and east. A fruit-eating pigeon, small flocks frequenting riverine forests and wooded hillsides where wild figs are fruiting. Remains still in the foliage of the tree canopy when approached, concealed by cryptic colouring, the flock then 'exploding' from the tree and flying off rapidly. 30 cm. **361**

4 ROCK PIGEON *Columbia guinea*. Common localised resident, occurring in the east and south-east. A large pigeon with reddish, white-spotted upperparts and red facial mask on grey head. The call is a loud cooing 'doo, doo, doo, doo...' rising in crescendo, then falling. Normally an inhabitant of rocky cliffs but has increased its range by adapting to man-made structures, roosting and nesting in buildings. Particularly common in Gaborone. 33 cm. **349**

1 NARINA TROGON. Family TROGONIDAE. *Apaloderma narina.* Rare summer visitor to the far north. Blue-green upperparts and brilliant red underparts (washed cinnamon in female) unmistakable. The call is 'hoot-hoot, hoot-hoot, hoot-hoot...' repeated slowly. Occurs sparsely and irregularly in well developed riverine forests. 29-34 cm. **427**

Parrots and lovebirds. Family PSITTACIDAE. A well-known group of colourful birds with stout, well-hooked beaks. Feed by clambering about the outer branches of trees in search of seeds and kernels, which are obtained by cracking the hard pericarps. Their calls are shrill shrieks.

2 MEYER'S PARROT *Poicephalus meyeri.* Common and widespread resident in the northern and eastern regions, absent in arid areas. A small, dark-headed parrot with yellow on the forehead, shoulders and thighs; in flight displays a blue-green rump and yellow underwing coverts. The immature lacks yellow on the head, very little on the shoulders. Pairs and small flocks are found in broadleafed woodland plus riverine and hillside woodland. Flight very rapid. 23 cm. **364**

3 CAPE PARROT *Poicephalus robustus.* Rare, exact status not established; likely to occur very sparsely in the far north. A large green parrot with greyish head, orange forehead, shoulders and thighs (these vestigial in immature birds). In pairs and small flocks in broadleafed and riverine forests. Mostly nomadic, their occurrence dictated by suitable food availability. 33-35 cm. **362**

150

Louries. Family MUSOPHAGIDAE. Large, arboreal, fruit-eating birds with crested heads, fairly long tails and an agile springing action when moving in trees. Numbers (2), (3) and (4) are beautifully coloured and have crimson wing-feathers that are strikingly revealed in flight. Immatures are dull versions of the adults. Sexes alike.

1 GREY LOURIE (GO-AWAY BIRD) *Corythaixoides concolor.* Common to very common resident but absent from the central and south-western regions. All grey with pronounced head-crest. The well-known call is 'kweh-h-h-h' or 'go-way-y-y', the latter giving rise to its alternative name. Pairs and small parties are found in any woodland, usually in the upper stratum and invariably noisy. Flies with heavy wing movements, mostly below tree-top height. 47-50 cm. **373**

2 KNYSNA LOURIE *Tauraco corythaix.* Very rare, status not established; few records from the Chobe/Linyanti systems. Differs from the next species in green head and body, the crest white-tipped, bill coral-red; race (b) appropriate to northern Botswana. Normal call a slow 'kerk, kerk, kerk, kerk, kawk-kawk-kawk-kawk...' or a heavy breathing sound 'hurrr, hurrrr, hurrrr'. When alarmed flies off calling a rapid, high-pitched 'kerk-kerk-kerk-kerk-kerk...'. Frequents mature riverine woodland. 47 cm. **370**

3 PURPLECRESTED LOURIE *Tauraco porphyreolophus.* Not recorded in Botswana but may occur in riverine forests and well-wooded valleys of the extreme east. Differs from the previous species in dark blue crest with a purple sheen, more blue on the folded wings and tail, ochre-washed breast and black bill. The call is a long sequence of notes starting quietly and reaching a crescendo 'kerker-kerkerkerk kok-kok-kok-kok-kok...', the last sound repeated about 20 times, becoming more deliberate and spaced out. 47 cm. **371**

4 ROSS'S LOURIE (LADY ROSS'S TAURACO) *Musophaga rossae.* Very rare, exact status not established; the very few records are from the upper Okavango Delta. The only dark blue, yellow-faced lourie in the region. Several birds usually call in unison, a loud cackling, cooing. 47-50 cm. **372**

Cuckoos and coucals. Family CUCULIDAE. Cuckoos are brood parasites, laying their eggs in the nests of other birds. The related coucals are larger, more robust and mainly sedentary birds which build their own nests and rear young in the conventional manner. Most members of the family are inconspicuous birds but have diagnostic calls. In most species the immatures resemble the adults.

385

1 KLAAS'S CUCKOO *Chrysococcyx klaas.* Uncommon summer resident, a few may be present all year. Male differs from next species in white mark *behind* eye only and lack of any white wing markings; also *dark eye* (not red) and *green bill.* Female from female of (3) by *white mark behind eye*, greener upperparts and reduced barring of underparts. The call is a mournful 'hueet-jie' repeated five or six times. Usually singly in a variety of well-wooded habitats though apparently absent from otherwise suitable regions. Secretive, heard more often than seen. Known to parasitise sunbirds. 17 cm. **385**

386

2 DIEDERIK CUCKOO *Chrysococcyx caprius.* Fairly common to common summer resident. Both sexes differ from male of previous species in having white marks *before and behind* the eye, a white central stripe over the crown, *multiple white marks* on the folded wings, red eyes (browner in female) and black bill; female usually more coppery on the upperparts. Immature has *coral-red bill, blue eyes* and spotted underparts. Male calls a plaintive, far-carrying 'dee-dee-deederik'; female 'deea-*deea*-DEEA'. Usually singly or in pairs in thornveld, riverine bush and suburbia. Hosts are weavers and bishop birds among others. 18,5 cm. **386**

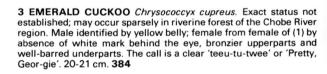

3 EMERALD CUCKOO *Chrysococcyx cupreus.* Exact status not established; may occur sparsely in riverine forest of the Chobe River region. Male identified by yellow belly; female from female of (1) by absence of white mark behind the eye, bronzier upperparts and well-barred underparts. The call is a clear 'teeu-tu-twee' or 'Pretty, Geor-gie'. 20-21 cm. **384**

381

4 STRIPED CUCKOO *Clamator levaillantii.* Fairly common summer resident. Differs from the white form of the next species in larger size and heavily streaked throat and breast. The call is 'klew, klew, klew, klew' followed by a long warbling 'chiriririririri...' and other shrill warbling sounds. Occurs in pairs or small parties in broadleafed, *Acacia* and riverine woodland. Hosts are Arrowmarked Babbler, possibly Pied Babbler. 38-40 cm. **381**

382

5 JACOBIN CUCKOO *Clamator jacobinus.* Fairly common summer resident. Two forms: (a) with clear white underparts (cf. previous species) and (b) totally black except for white wing-bar. The call is a shrill, flute-like 'kleeuw, pewp-pewp, kleeuw, pewp-pewp...'. Usually in pairs in any woodland, riverine forest or valley bush. A noisy and conspicuous species. Normally parasitises Blackeyed and Redeyed Bulbuls. 33-34 cm. **382**

1 REDCHESTED CUCKOO *Cuculus solitarius.* Uncommon, localised summer resident; very few records from the northern region. Differs from the next two species in *broad* russet upper breast (although this is reduced to russet pectoral-patches in some individuals), and characteristic call. Immature has entire head and upperparts charcoal-grey, all feathers edged white as illustrated. The well-known and far-carrying call of the male is 'Wip-wip-weeu' resembling the Afrikaans name 'Piet-my-vrou', repeated for long periods throughout the day and even the night; the female calls, less often, a loud 'pik-pik-pik-pik'. Occurs in well-wooded habitats, particularly around hills, the male calling from a high tree or in flight. Flight hawk-like. Parasitises mostly robins. 28 cm. **377**

2 EUROPEAN CUCKOO *Cuculus canorus.* Rare summer visitor. Female (a) told from the previous species in generally much fainter russet collar extending obscurely onto nape and ear coverts. Male lacks russet colouring and is closely similar to the next species with which it can be easily confused. In both sexes the bill is black with a yellow or greenish-yellow *base* (see small illustration), the gape less conspicuous than in (3), the undertail barred in the male, spotted in the female. In one race the upperparts, especially the head, are a paler grey while the female also occurs in a rare brown form (b). Flight pattern hawk-like. Silent in Africa. Occurs in any woodland, but is inconspicuous. 30-33 cm. **374**

3 AFRICAN CUCKOO *Cuculus gularis.* Uncommon to fairly common summer resident. Scarcely different from male of previous species but bill has *black tip only* (see small illustration), yellow gape more conspicuous. Female also occurs in rare brown form. Immature brownish on upperparts, throat and breast, upperparts barred and spotted white, underparts barred blackish. Best identified by calls, heard September-January, male makes a melancholy 'hoop-hoop' or 'coo-cuck', second note slightly higher, female calls a loud 'pik-ik-ik-ik-ik'. Singly in any woodland. Known host is Forktailed Drongo. 32 cm. **375**

1 GREAT SPOTTED CUCKOO *Clamator glandarius*. Uncommon summer resident. Distinguished by white-spotted upperparts, grey crested head and creamy-white underparts. Immature similar but cap blackish, less crested, primary wing-feathers showing chestnut-brown in flight. Male calls a rapid, rasping 'keeow, keeow, keeow...' in strophes of about eight, or 'keeow, keeow, krikrikrikrikri...'; female calls a bubbling 'burroo-burroo'. Widespread, usually singly, in woodland and *Acacia* savanna. Parasitises crows and starlings. 38-40 cm. **380**

2 THICKBILLED CUCKOO *Pachycoccyx audeberti*. Very rare, exact status not established; recorded once only on Khwai River, Okavango; known to occur across the border in Zimbabwe. Adults distinguished by plain grey-brown upperparts, entirely white underparts, a long, graduated tail with white-tipped feathers and heavy bill, the lower mandible yellow or pink. Immature characterised by white-spotted upperparts and almost entirely white head. Has a loud querulous call 'chwee-cher-cher', or 'were-wik' and a rippling 'Oui-yes-yes'. A restless, elusive, hawk-like cuckoo with slow, deliberate movements. Parasitises the Redbilled Helmetshrike. 34 cm. **383**

3 BLACK CUCKOO *Cuculus clamosus*. Fairly common summer resident. Entirely black or with indistinct brown barring on the underparts. Immature browner. Male has a much repeated, monotonous call 'whoo-whoo, wheee' or 'I'm so, sick', rising on the last syllable; also an excitable 'yowyowyowyowyowyowyowyow' rising to a crescendo then dying away. Singly in wooded regions, perching for long periods in one place when calling. Hosts are boubou shrikes. 30 cm. **378**

4 BLACK COUCAL *Centropus bengalensis*. Rare, status not established; occurs very sparsely in the northern wetlands. Adult in breeding plumage (breeding not confirmed in Botswana) distinctive as illustrated, non-breeding adult browner on upperparts with buff barring and creamy streaking similar to immature (see illustration), underparts deep buff with some spotting on neck and breast; darker than immature at all times. Female larger. The call starts with the bird in a hunched, head-lowered posture, when a low 'ooom, ooom, ooom,' is uttered, then, with the head raised, it makes a 'pop-pop' sound; when excited also makes a 'kwik-kwik-kwik' sound. Prefers long, rank grass and thickets in marshes. May also perch openly in taller trees. 30-37 cm. **388**

Note: The three coucals on this plate are difficult to differentiate by call since the sounds are almost identical, a deep bubbling 'doo-doo-doo-doo-doo...' up to 20 times, descending then ascending like the sound of liquid pouring from a bottle. They also have deep 'kurrr' alarm calls. Secretive, seldom perching openly.

1 SENEGAL COUCAL *Centropus senegalensis.* Locally common resident. Distinguished from the next species by smaller size, more rufous upperparts, shorter tail with *green* iridescence and less heavy bill; from (3a) by plain, *unbarred rump and upper tail coverts.* Immature has white streaking on head, dark brown barring on upperparts and *barred upper tail coverts*; probably indistinguishable from immature of (3). Frequents the lower stratum of dense riverine vegetation, reedbeds and thickets in thornveld and woodland. 41 cm. **390**

2 COPPERYTAILED COUCAL *Centropus cupreicaudus.* Locally common resident. Distinguished from (1) and (3) by larger size, darker upperparts, purple-black cap and mantle, very heavy bill and long tail with a coppery sheen; upper tail coverts faintly barred tawny. Occurs in reed and papyrus beds and adjacent riverine bush of the Chobe-Linyanti-Okavango region. 44-50 cm. **389**

3 BURCHELL'S COUCAL (WHITEBROWED COUCAL) *Centropus superciliosus.* Fairly common resident. Southern race (a) recognised by smaller size and *blue-black* head and tail, northern race (b) by white eyebrows plus streaked head and mantle; *both races with barred upper tail coverts and rump.* Immature of both races has white eyebrows, white-streaked head and mantle and upperparts well barred in dark brown. Secretive in reeds, dense thickets and tall rank grass, but will perch conspicuously after rain. 38-44 cm. **391**

Owls. Families TYTONIDAE and STRIGIDAE. Nocturnal, erect-standing birds of prey characterised by large, rounded heads and large forward-facing eyes set in a flattened face; all (with the exception of Pel's Fishing Owl) have feathered legs. Some have feather adornments on their heads which resemble ears. Immatures are fluffier than adults.

1 MARSH OWL *Asio capensis.* Uncommon resident. Medium-sized, dark brown owl with small 'ear' tufts, brownish face and dark eyes; shows russet wings in flight. Sometimes calls 'krzzk' in flight. Singly or in pairs in long grass in dry grassland, marshy ground and moist valleys. Often active early mornings and late afternoons, flying low or perched on some low prominence. When flushed from grass during the day flies around above the intruder before resettling. 36 cm. **395**

2 WOOD OWL *Strix woodfordii.* Uncommon, localised resident. Told by lack of 'ears', large, pale, spectacle-like eye-orbits and barred underparts. Immature darker, underparts fluffier, creamy. Both sexes call a rapid 'HU-hu, hu-HU-hu-hu, hu-hu', the female in higher pitch than the male, or male makes call and female replies with a single high-pitched 'hoo'. Pairs and family groups in well-developed riverine forests and broadleafed woodland. During the day roosts in large trees, close to the trunks. 30-36 cm. **394**

3 BARN OWL *Tyto alba.* Fairly common resident. A pale, slimly built owl with distinctive heart-shaped facial disc and whitish underparts. The normal call is an eerie, wavering screech 'hreeeeeeee'. Singly or in pairs in a variety of habitats, including the arid central and south-west, roosting and breeding in cavities in large trees, caves, buildings and Hamerkop nests (p.43). Widespread throughout the country, including suburbia. 30-33 cm. **392**

162

1 SCOPS OWL *Otus senegalensis*. Fairly common resident. The plumage resembles tree-bark, the grey form (a) being commoner than the brown (b). The only very small owl with 'ear' tufts. Calls mostly at night, sometimes by day, a soft 'prrrrp' repeated at about ten second intervals. Occurs in any woodland and dry savanna but unaccountably absent from some suitable areas. By day perches close to a tree-trunk where its cryptic colouring makes detection difficult. This camouflage is further enhanced by its habit of depressing its feathers to appear long and thin, and of raising its 'ear' tufts and half closing its eyes, creating the illusion of a tree stump; see (a). 15-18 cm. **396**

2 WHITEFACED OWL *Otus leucotis*. Uncommon to fairly common resident. Largest of the small owls. Predominantly grey with *orange eyes*, a distinct *black facial disc* and 'ear' tufts. The call, heard only at night, is an explosive, bubbling 'b-b-b-b-b-bhooo'. Widespread. Singly or in pairs in riverine forests, woodland and arid savanna. 25-28 cm. **397**

3 PEARLSPOTTED OWL *Glaucidium perlatum*. Common resident. Very small 'earless' owl, upperparts brown with small white spots, underparts white streaked with brown with pearl-like white spots. Has two black spots on its nape giving the appearance of eyes when viewed from the rear. The call, often heard by day, is a series of ascending notes 'tee-tee-tee-tee-tee-tee-tee-tee...' followed by a brief pause, then a series of descending notes 'teeew, teeew, tew, tew, tew, tew, tew...'. Widespread in broadleafed woodland (including Mopane), riverine forest and *Acacia* savanna. Frequently seen by day and is often mobbed by other small birds. 15-18 cm. **398**

4 BARRED OWL *Glaucidium capense*. Fairly common resident. Slightly larger than the previous species, the upperparts finely barred, the wings with a row of bold white spots reaching the shoulder, underparts white with brown spots arranged in rows. The call is an urgent 'kerrooo-kerrooo-krrooo-krooo-krooo-krooo-krooo-krooo' or 'krrooo-trrooo, krrooo-trooo...', either sequence repeated many times. Found mostly in well-developed riverine forests and large-tree woodland; roosts in dense thickets. Less often seen by day than the previous species. 20 cm. **399**

1 GIANT EAGLE OWL *Bubo lacteus*. Uncommon to fairly common resident. Large grey owl with 'ear'-tufts, dark brown eyes and *pink eyelids* at all ages. Voice a series of deep grunts 'hu-hu-hu, hu-hu'; female and immature make a long, drawn-out whistle which may be repeated for long periods. Widespread. Usually seen singly in large trees, especially along rivers and watercourses. 60-65 cm. **402**

2 CAPE EAGLE OWL *Bubo capensis*. Not recorded in Botswana, but occurs in adjacent Motobo Hills of Zimbabwe. Could occur in the extreme east. Large brown owl of stocky proportions. Easily confused with the next species but differs in combination of larger size, orange-yellow eyes (orange in young birds) and heavily blotched underparts with *bold* barring; feet and talons larger. Calls a deep hooting 'hu-hooooo' or 'hooooo-hu' and 'hu-hooooo-hu'. Pairs frequent valleys with cliffs or rocks at the higher end, or grassland with rock outcrops and trees. 48-55 cm. **400**

3 SPOTTED EAGLE OWL *Bubo africanus*. Fairly common resident. Fairly large, grey-brown owl, easily confused with the previous species from which it differs in smaller size, pale yellow eyes, lightly blotched underparts with *fine barring*, smaller feet and talons. A rufous form (b) with orange-yellow eyes also occurs, though less commonly; this can be told from (2) by the fine barring on the underparts. Male calls 'hu-hooo' lower on the second note, female calls 'hoo-hu-hoo' the second note hardly discernible; pairs also call to each other. Usually in pairs in a wide range of habitats; rocky regions, woodland, savanna, arid thornveld and suburbia. Habitually sit on roads at night and are frequently killed by cars. 43-50 cm. **401**

1 PEL'S FISHING OWL *Scotopelia peli.* Fairly common, localised resident. A very large, distinctive owl, differing from other large owls in rufous-brown upperparts and cinnamon underparts. The usual calls are resonant nasal hoots by both sexes 'uhg-hwoom-HWOOM', the first two sounds are uttered by the male, the first almost inaudible, the second with increasing inflection; the third sound, uttered by the female, is of much lower tone with decreasing inflection. Other calls are 'uh-uh-uhu' by the male building up to a higher 'hwoom', the female replying with the deeper 'HWOOM'. Various high-pitched screams and wails are made by the young when soliciting for food. Pairs or single birds are found in the riverine forests of the Linyanti and Okavango Rivers and in the Okavango Delta. Roosts by day in some large waterside tree with dense foliage or creepers, fishes at night from a branch over a river pool or backwater. If flushed by day flies a short distance and resettles in another tree from where it watches the intruder. 63-65 cm. **403**

Nightjars. Family CAPRIMULGIDAE. Nocturnal, insectivorous birds with soft, cryptically coloured plumage, short beaks, wide gapes surrounded by stiff bristles, large eyes and short, weak legs. Immatures duller. Feed by hawking flying insects. By day they roost on a horizontal branch or on the ground, flushing reluctantly. Habitually settle on roads at night. All species are so alike as to be nearly indistinguishable, but can be identified by their characteristic calls. In the hand can be identified by wing and tail formulae, illustrated opposite and on pages 171-173.

2 NATAL NIGHTJAR *Caprimulgus natalensis.* Uncommon, localised resident. Male has entire outer web of the outermost tail-feathers and half the outer web of the adjoining tail-feathers white; wing-spots as illustrated. The female has wing and tail markings buff-coloured. From the ground calls a fairly slow and continuous 'chook-chook-chook-chook...' or a bubbling 'poipoipoipoipoipoi...', both sequences less rapid than the similar call of the Mozambique Nightjar (pp. 170-171). Occurs in the Chobe-Linyanti River region and throughout the Okavango Delta in grassy locations near water, roosting in grass, often near palm trees. 23 cm. **407**

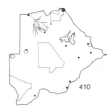

1 PENNANTWINGED NIGHTJAR *Macrodipteryx vexillaria*. Rare, status not established; very few records. Male with long wing-pennants unmistakable; female lacks any white in wings or tail. The call, made from some low prominence, is a continuous, high-pitched, ringing 'titititititititi...', not unlike the sound of a cricket. Is found in broadleafed woodland, especially on hillsides in stony or sandy terrain. Roosts on the ground. 25-28 cm (excluding male's wing-pennants). **410**

2 RUFOUSCHEEKED NIGHTJAR *Caprimulgus rufigena*. Fairly common to common summer resident. Upperparts pale in colour; see pp. 172-173 for wing and tail formulae. Calls from the ground 'ke-wook, ke-wook, ke-wook' followed by a sustained, mechanical churring 'trrrrrrrrrr...' *without variation*; may also call 'ke-wook, ke-wook' in flight. Widespread in a variety of habitats including arid regions. Roosts on the ground in the shade of a tree but if flushed may settle in a tree temporarily. 23-24 cm. **406**

3 EUROPEAN NIGHTJAR *Caprimulgus europaeus*. Rare summer visitor. A large, dark-coloured nightjar; see pp. 172-173 for wing and tail formulae. Mostly silent in Africa but sometimes calls 'coo-ic' in flight and 'quick-quick-quick' from the ground. Occurs singly in woodland and riverine forests, preferring large trees where it roosts by day *lengthwise along a horizontal branch*; perches on branches more often than any resident nightjar. 25-28 cm. **404**

4 FIERYNECKED NIGHTJAR *Caprimulgus pectoralis*. Common resident. Has extensive rufous colouring about the neck, head and upper breast; see pp. 172-173 for wing and tail formulae. Has a characteristic quavering call resembling the words 'Good Lord, deliver us.' Widespread in most wooded regions but sparsely recorded outside the north and east. Roosts on the ground. 23-25 cm. **405**

5 MOZAMBIQUE NIGHTJAR *Caprimulgus fossii*. Uncommon to fairly common resident. No distinctive colouring apart from wing and tail formulae: see pp.172-173. Makes a prolonged, engine-like gurgling sound which *varies in pitch and frequency*, becoming louder or quieter, faster or slower. Prefers sandy ground in savanna or riverine bush, roosting on the ground. 23-24 cm. **409**

6 FRECKLED NIGHTJAR *Caprimulgus tristigma*. Uncommon localised resident. Has *dark freckling* overall with few distinct markings, resembling weathered granite; see pp. 172-173 for wing and tail formulae. The call is a sharply repeated 'wheeoo-wheeoo' or 'poor-will', like the distant yapping of a small dog. Found in rocky hills and granite outcrops in woodland, roosting by day on shaded rocks where its plumage pattern closely matches the rock surface. 27-28 cm. **408**

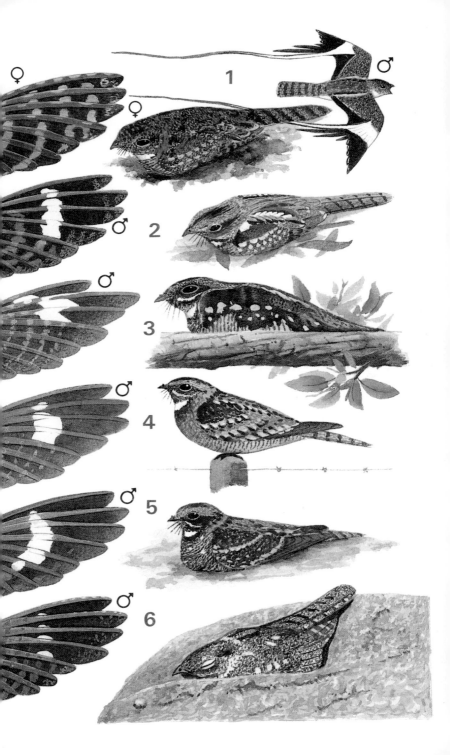

DIAGRAMMATIC ILLUSTRATIONS

These illustrations show the major wing-feathers and outer tail-feathers with the outer webs of each blackened for clarity. The position of the wing emarginations or 'kinks' in relation to the wing-spots, the format and colouring of the wing-spots (if present) plus the

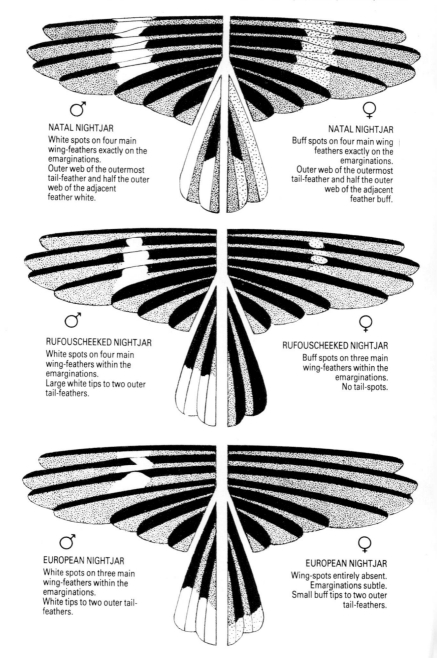

♂

NATAL NIGHTJAR

White spots on four main wing-feathers exactly on the emarginations.
Outer web of the outermost tail-feather and half the outer web of the adjacent feather white.

♀

NATAL NIGHTJAR

Buff spots on four main wing feathers exactly on the emarginations.
Outer web of the outermost tail-feather and half the outer web of the adjacent feather buff.

♂

RUFOUSCHEEKED NIGHTJAR

White spots on four main wing-feathers within the emarginations.
Large white tips to two outer tail-feathers.

♀

RUFOUSCHEEKED NIGHTJAR

Buff spots on three main wing-feathers within the emarginations.
No tail-spots.

♂

EUROPEAN NIGHTJAR

White spots on three main wing-feathers within the emarginations.
White tips to two outer tail-feathers.

♀

EUROPEAN NIGHTJAR

Wing-spots entirely absent.
Emarginations subtle.
Small buff tips to two outer tail-feathers.

OF NIGHTJAR WINGS AND TAILS

presence or absence of bold tail markings are diagnostic for each species. The normal, irregular buff patterning present on nightjar feathers has been omitted. This diagram is intended to aid identification of nightjar road kills.

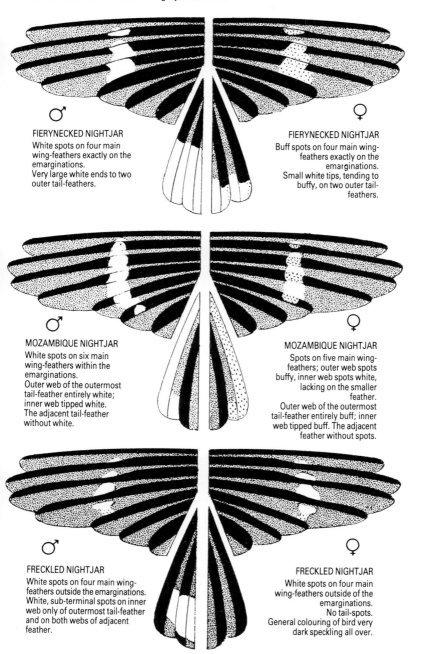

♂

FIERYNECKED NIGHTJAR
White spots on four main wing-feathers exactly on the emarginations.
Very large white ends to two outer tail-feathers.

♀

FIERYNECKED NIGHTJAR
Buff spots on four main wing-feathers exactly on the emarginations.
Small white tips, tending to buffy, on two outer tail-feathers.

♂

MOZAMBIQUE NIGHTJAR
White spots on six main wing-feathers within the emarginations.
Outer web of the outermost tail-feather entirely white; inner web tipped white.
The adjacent tail-feather without white.

♀

MOZAMBIQUE NIGHTJAR
Spots on five main wing-feathers; outer web spots buffy, inner web spots white, lacking on the smaller feather.
Outer web of the outermost tail-feather entirely buff; inner web tipped buff. The adjacent feather without spots.

♂

FRECKLED NIGHTJAR
White spots on four main wing-feathers outside the emarginations.
White, sub-terminal spots on inner web only of outermost tail-feather and on both webs of adjacent feather.

♀

FRECKLED NIGHTJAR
White spots on four main wing-feathers outside of the emarginations.
No tail-spots.
General colouring of bird very dark speckling all over.

Swallows and martins. Family HIRUNDINIDAE. Small, long-winged, aerial-feeding birds, swallows with upperparts mostly glossy blue (some with rufous caps), underparts whitish, rufous or streaked; exceptions are the blackish saw-winged swallows (pp. 178-179) which have rough, saw-like leading edges to their primary feathers (not apparent in the field). The closely related martins are mostly brown above, white or brownish below and have square (not forked) tails, except the House Martin which resembles a swallow. In all species immatures are duller than adults. They build nests with mud or burrow tunnels in earth, drink and bathe in flight by skimming the surface of still waters and perch to rest. See comparison between these and swifts on pp. 182-183.

1 REDBREASTED SWALLOW *Hirundo semirufa*. Fairly common summer resident. Identified by large size, blue cap extending to below the eyes and covering the ear coverts, and entirely orange-chestnut underparts. In flight differs from the next species by rufous (not white) underwing coverts and longer tail-shafts. Immature is duller, browner above and paler below, tail-shafts shorter but differs from the next species in dark cap covering ear coverts. The call is a soft warbling. Pairs are usually found in the vicinity of their nest sites; road culverts, causeways and antbear holes. Their flight is low and slow, with much leisurely gliding. 24 cm. **524**

2 MOSQUE SWALLOW *Hirundo senegalensis*. Rare, status not established; occurs sparsely in the far north. Differs from the previous species in white throat and upper breast; in flight by *white* underwing coverts and shorter tail-shafts. Makes a nasal, tin trumpet-like 'harrrp', occasionally a guttural chuckling. Pairs and small flocks occur in large-treed woodland, often near water. The flight is usually at some height, with bursts of fluttering flight followed by a glide. Frequently skims across water or perches on leafless branches. 23 cm. **525**

3 GREATER STRIPED SWALLOW *Hirundo cucullata*. Fairly common summer resident; a few birds all months in the north. Identified by chestnut cap, pale chestnut rump and *lightly streaked underparts*. Rump and underparts can appear almost white in flight; cf. next species. The call, uttered in flight, is a soft 'chissik'. In pairs when breeding otherwise small flocks flying over woodland, riverine forests or grassland, often near human habitation. Flies with much gliding and perches frequently on trees or wires. 20 cm. **526**

4 LESSER STRIPED SWALLOW *Hirundo abyssinica*. Common resident and summer visitor. Differs from the previous species in orange cap extending *over the ear coverts* and more heavily streaked underparts which appear very dark in the field; cf. previous species. Flight call a characteristic descending series of four notes 'eh-eh-eh-eh'. Pairs and small flocks are found near bridges, road culverts, permanent camps and various woodland and savanna regions. Flies more actively than (3), with less gliding. Perches frequently on bare twigs and wires. 16 cm. **527**

174

1

2

3

4

1 EUROPEAN SWALLOW *Hirundo rustica.* Abundant summer visitor. Told by dark chin and throat; moulting birds (November-January) often *without long tail shafts*; young birds common October-December. Flocks make a soft twittering sound, especially when settled. Widespread and gregarious at all times, outnumbering all other swallows in summer and mixing freely in flight with other swallows and with swifts. Flocks perch on telephone wires or on roads while very large flocks gather at dusk to roost in reedbeds. 18 cm. **518**

2 WIRETAILED SWALLOW *Hirundo smithii.* Fairly common localised resident. Told by *full* orange cap, entirely white underparts and *wire-like* tail-streamers. Usually silent, may utter a double chirp. Pairs, sometimes small groups, are found near river bridges, dam walls and buildings near water in the northern regions. Perches on dead trees, bridge and jetty rails. 13 cm. **522**

3 PEARLBREASTED SWALLOW *Hirundo dimidiata.* Uncommon resident and winter visitor. Identified by entirely blue upperparts including cap, entirely white underparts and lack of tail-streamers. Has a short, chittering song. Pairs and small flocks frequent woodland, human settlements and Kalahari scrub in the north, east and south-east, but sparsely distributed and nomadic when not breeding. Perches on the upper twigs of dead trees; flight fast and agile. 14 cm. **523**

4 GREYRUMPED SWALLOW *Pseudhirundo griseopyga.* Uncommon to locally fairly common resident. Grey-brown cap and pale grey rump are diagnostic, but cap not easily seen in flight and rump may appear almost white, then told from House Martin (pp. 180-181) by more deeply forked tail. Makes a grating 'chaa' in flight. In flocks, usually over grassland, riverbanks or edges of pans where they nest in ground burrows. Occurs in the far north, occasionally in the east and south-east. 14 cm. **531**

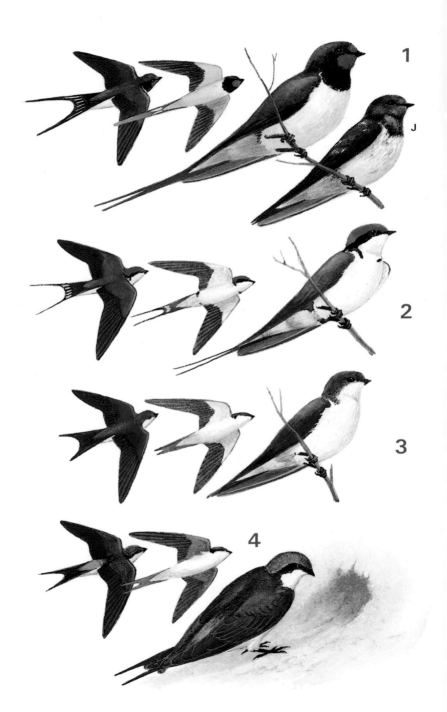

1 SOUTH AFRICAN CLIFF SWALLOW *Hirundo spilodera*. Rare, exact status not determined. In Botswana this species is seen as a passage migrant between South Africa and Zaïre during August and April at which time it could occur anywhere but is seen most regularly in the south-east. Square-tailed with mottled chin and throat; like European Swallow (pp. 176-177) but with more robust appearance and pale throat. Immature browner, duller on upperparts. Has a three- or four-syllable call 'chor-chor-chor-choor'. There are no breeding records for the country. 15 cm. **528**

2 WHITETHROATED SWALLOW *Hirundo albigularis*. Fairly common, localised summer resident and visitor. Told from the European Swallow (pp.176-177) by clear white underparts with black breast-band. Utters a soft twittering and has a warbling song. When breeding (summer) occurs in pairs near nest site under rock overhang, bridge, culvert or building close to water, at other times singly or in small groups near riverine forests and adjacent woodland. Commonest on early and late summer passage with fewer records in between. 17 cm. **520**

3 BLACK SAW-WING SWALLOW *Psalidoprocne holomelas*. Rare, exact status not established. Recorded only in the extreme north-west. All-black, fork-tailed swallow. In flight told from swifts by slower wing-beats and steadier flight with much gliding. Normally flies in pairs and small parties at low altitude. 15 cm. **536**

4 EUROPEAN SAND MARTIN *Riparia riparia*. Uncommon summer visitor. A small martin with white underparts and brown band across upper breast; told from the larger Banded Martin (pp.180-181) by small size and, in flight, by *brown* (not white) underwings. The call is a weak twittering. Usually occurs near large waters and over grasslands but may occur anywhere with other swallows. 12 cm. **532**

178

1 HOUSE MARTIN *Delichon urbica.* Fairly common summer visitor. Differs from the Greyrumped Swallow (pp.176-177) in *blue* cap (not grey-brown) and *white* rump, the tail only slightly forked, but the two species can be easily confused in flight. Makes a distinctive, single 'chirrup' call. Occurs in nomadic flocks, sometimes many hundreds, October-April mainly in the east and far north. Often associates with the European Swallow (pp. 176-177) when it can be separated in flight by more compact appearance, squarer tail and white rump. 14 cm. **530**

2 BROWNTHROATED MARTIN (AFRICAN SAND MARTIN) *Riparia paludicola.* Fairly common resident. A small, almost entirely brown martin except for white belly. Is sometimes seen with entirely brown underparts, then differs from (4) in notched tail without white 'windows', more slender appearance. The call is a weak twittering. Occurs in flocks usually near water, especially near rivers with sandy banks (where it breeds June-September). Nomadic when not breeding. 13 cm. **533**

3 BANDED MARTIN *Riparia cincta.* Fairly common resident. Recorded mostly in the north and Makgadikgadi Pans, sporadically in the south-east. Differs from the European Sand Martin (pp.178-179) in larger size, *broad* breastband, white eyebrows, square tail and *white underwing coverts.* Makes a chippering sound in flight and has a pleasant, subdued warbling song when perched. Pairs and flocks frequent grasslands near water, seasonal ponds or river banks (where they breed). Flight slow and leisurely, the birds alighting frequently to rest on a bare branch or fence. 17 cm. **534**

4 ROCK MARTIN *Hirundo fuligula.* Fairly common localised resident. A small, all-brown martin identified by broad wings and a square tail which has white 'windows' visible when fanned; appears very stocky in flight. Makes a melodious twittering in the air. Pairs and small groups frequent the vicinity of cliffs or rocky screes along sand rivers, occasionally man-made structures such as bridges, dam walls and tall buildings. Flight slow with much gliding, twisting and turning. Occurs mostly in the east. 15 cm. **529**

1

2

3

4

Swallows and martins have wider, comparatively more rounded wings than swifts.

Swallows are blue on their upperparts, white or orange, sometimes spotted on their underparts.

Swallows may have orange caps, foreheads or throats, and buff or orange-coloured rumps.

Martins are brown, the underparts usually paler. The House Martin is the exception, since it has the appearance of a swallow.

Martins have squarish tails with white 'windows' in them, visible when the tail is fanned.

Swallows have forked tails, often with long streamers on the outer feathers, and frequently have 'windows' in the tail.

Swallows glide frequently between bouts of flapping flight.

Swallows and martins can perch.

COMPARED WITH SWIFTS

The wings of a swift are slender, scimitar-like and appear to sweep straight back from the body with little bend at the carpal joint.

Swifts are dark grey-brown, blackish or ash-brown, and mostly appear all dark in flight.

Swifts may have whitish throats and white rumps, but no bright colours.

Swifts may have square or forked tails; in our region only the Palm Swift has tail streamers.

Only the large Alpine Swift and the small Batlike Spinetail have white on the belly.

Swifts sometimes fly with their wings steeply angled upwards.

Most swifts fly very rapidly with only brief gliding spells.

Swifts cannot perch.

Swifts. Family APODIDAE. All-dark, blackish-brown in appearance, some with white throat and rump, one with white throat and belly. Unrelated to swallows. Entirely aerial in habits, feeding on airborne insects and never intentionally settling on the ground. Flight powerful and rapid with complete mastery of the air. Unable to perch but cling to vertical surfaces. Their calls are high-pitched screams. See pp. 182-183 for comparison with swallows.

1 PALM SWIFT *Cypsiurus parvus.* Common resident. Most frequent in the northern palm belt, more localised in the east but fairly common in Gaborone. The most slender, long-tailed swift; paler than most other swifts, being entirely grey-brown. Usually in small flocks, flying rapidly around tall palms where they roost and nest, rarely under bridges and eaves of buildings. May mix briefly with other swifts when feeding, but slim build diagnostic. 17 cm. **421**

2 LITTLE SWIFT *Apus affinis.* Fairly common localised resident; regular only in the east and south-east. Told from all other local swifts by large white rump which *curls around the sides of the body*, and square tail; wings rather less pointed than in other swifts. Often glides, tail fanned. A noisy species. Frequently associates with urban areas, roosting and breeding under eaves and bridges, but may feed well away from the roost, mixing with other swifts and swallows. 14 cm. **417**

3 WHITERUMPED SWIFT *Apus caffer.* Fairly common localised summer resident. Most easily confused with the next species but has slimmer build, more deeply forked tail and *thin white crescent shape on the rump* which does *not* extend over the sides of the body. Pairs and flocks may occur anywhere in the east and south-east, often associated with man-made structures. 15 cm. **415**

4 HORUS SWIFT *Apus horus.* Rare; exact status not established; very few records for Botswana. Differs from the previous species in stouter appearance (more like (3) with a forked tail), less deeply forked tail and large white rump-patch which extends to the sides of the body. Elsewhere in southern Africa occurs in small flocks near river banks, quarries and cuttings where they breed and roost in holes in the banks, ranging more widely during the day. 17 cm. **416**

5 ALPINE SWIFT *Apus melba.* Rare visitor, possibly localised resident but breeding not confirmed for Botswana. Large size plus white throat and belly distinguish this from all other swifts. Fast-flying and wide-ranging, occurring occasionally in small numbers in the east and south-east, often at great height and feeding with other swifts. 22 cm. **418**

1 EURASIAN SWIFT (EUROPEAN SWIFT) *Apus apus*. Fairly common summer visitor. European race all blackish, differing from the previous species in *uniform upperparts* (no contrast between inner secondaries and body); from below closely similar to (2) but tail more deeply forked; darker than (3). The Asian race (frequent in western regions) is *browner*, from above has *pale inner secondaries contrast with darker wing coverts and body;* cf. (2) which is blacker. Occurs in flocks anywhere November-February, always flying, often following thunderstorms; no known roosting places. 18 cm. **411**

2 BLACK SWIFT *Apus barbatus*. Rare visitor and possible resident but breeding not confirmed for Botswana. Fairly large, mostly black swift, easily mistaken for the previous species. When seen from above has *marked contrast between upper wings and body* (cf. brown Asian race of (1)); from below is uniformly blackish-brown with whitish throat like (1) but tail is less deeply forked. Elsewhere in southern Africa flocks frequent the vicinity of mountain cliffs, at other times range more widely and fly high. Very few records for Botswana, all easterly. 19 cm. **412**

3 BRADFIELD'S SWIFT *Apus bradfieldi*. Exact status not established; no confirmed records for Botswana. Similar in size to the previous two species but body and underwing coverts paler, contrasting with darker primaries, secondaries and tail, apparent when seen in company with (1) and (2). Single birds or small flocks may occasionally occur in the extreme south. 18 cm. **413**

4 BOHM'S SPINETAIL (BATLIKE SPINETAIL) *Neafrapus boehmi*. Rare, exact status not established; only one confirmed record for Botswana. A small, distinctive swift with white underparts, white rump and *tailless appearance*. Pairs and small parties may occur in the far north. Outside Botswana found in broadleafed woodland near water and often in association with baobab trees in which they are known to breed. Flight fluttering, bat-like and erratic. 9-10 cm. **423**

Mousebirds. Family COLIIDAE. Frugivorous birds with crested heads, soft, hair-like plumage and long stiff tails. Usually in parties of up to twenty birds which maintain contact by call. When feeding they clamber, mouse-like, about trees. Young birds resemble adults, but are duller, shorter-tailed.

1 SPECKLED MOUSEBIRD *Colius striatus*. Uncommon resident. Identified by dull brown colouring and bill with black upper mandible, white lower mandible. The call is a rasping 'zwit-wit'. Flocks frequent dense bush, scrub and tangled thickets, flying from bush to bush in straggling order. Occurs sparsely in the east. 30-35 cm. **424**

2 WHITEBACKED MOUSEBIRD *Colius colius*. Uncommon to locally fairly common resident. Identified by pale grey upperparts, buff underparts, white back (visible in flight only) and *whitish bill with black tip* to upper mandible. The call is 'zwee, wewit'. Singly or in small flocks in thornveld, dry riverine bush and suburbia. 30-34 cm. **425**

3 REDFACED MOUSEBIRD *Colius indicus*. Common resident. Identified by red facial mask. The call is a descending whistle 'tree-ree-ree', frequently repeated and uttered both in flight and while feeding. Flocks fly in compact groups. Widespread in all wooded habitats, including arid regions and in suburban gardens. 32-34 cm. **426**

Bee-eaters. Family MEROPIDAE. Highly coloured, aerial-feeding birds with long curved bills, many with elongated tail-feathers. Immature birds are dull versions of the adults but lack elongated tail-feathers. Mostly in flocks, catching flying insects while twisting and turning in graceful aerial manoeuvres or by hawking them from a perch in brief aerial sallies, usually returning to the same perch to eat their prey. Breed colonially in tunnels in earth banks, nomadic at other times.

4 SWALLOWTAILED BEE-EATER *Merops hirundineus*. Fairly common to locally common resident. A small bee-eater, adults distinguished by *forked tail*; immature has *throat pale green, tail unforked*. Calls a soft 'kweet-kwit' or 'kweep kweepy bzzz'. Singly, in pairs or in small groups in a variety of wooded habitats. 20-22 cm. **445**

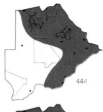

1 LITTLE BEE-EATER *Merops pusillus*. Common resident. Identified by small size, yellow-ochre underparts and squarish tail. Immature lacks the black collar, has lower neck to belly green and has a shorter bill. The call is a quiet 'chip, chip, trree-trree-trree'. In pairs or groups near rivers, open areas in woodland and savanna, usually perching on some low branch or reed from where they hawk; common in the Okavango Delta. 17 cm. **444**

2 CARMINE BEE-EATER *Merops nubicoides*. Locally common summer resident in the north, a passage migrant in the east and southeast. Adult unmistakable. Immature has brown upperparts, cinnamon underparts. The call is a deep 'turk, turk' or, in flocks, 'turk-a-turkturkturk...'. In the north flocks occur near large rivers (where they breed in the banks), in riverine and broadleafed woodland and on roadside telephone wires. 33-38 cm. **441**

3 EUROPEAN BEE-EATER *Merops apiaster*. Common summer visitor. Identified by golden-brown mantle, turquoise-blue forehead and underparts and yellow throat. The call in flight is diagnostic, a clear, liquid 'quilp' or 'kwirry'. Flocks occur anywhere apart from the more arid areas, often mixing with other bee-eaters and frequently hawking from roadside telephone wires. 25-29 cm. **438**

4 WHITEFRONTED BEE-EATER *Merops bullockoides*. Fairly common localised resident. Identified by white forehead and upper throat, plus red lower throat; lacks elongated tail-feathers. The call is a querulous 'quirk', 'kwair' or 'quirk-k-k-k''. Occurs in flocks near rivers and is more sedentary than other bee-eaters, roosting in nest-tunnels even when not breeding. 22-24 cm. **443**

5 BLUECHEEKED BEE-EATER *Merops persicus*. Fairly common to locally common summer visitor. A large, greenish bee-eater differing from (6) in blue forehead, eyebrows, cheeks and *under-belly, plus yellow throat* and brown upper breast. Immature has a dark olive-green cap and *lacks a yellow throat; cf. next species*. The short, liquid call is 'prruik' or 'prree-oo, prree-oo'. Usually in small flocks near rivers, flood pans and marshes where they hawk from a dead tree in water, but also in arid regions far from water. 27-33 cm. **440**

6 OLIVE BEE-EATER *Merops superciliosus*. Rare, exact status not established; very few records from the far north only. Distinguished from the previous species by *olive-brown cap*, all-brown throat (chin *may* show yellow tinge) and uniform pale green underparts; *cf. immature of previous species which also has a brownish cap and with which it can be readily confused*. The call is a twittering 'twip, twee-tittle-tirr'. Should be watched for in the Chobe River region. 29-33 cm. **439**

Kingfishers. Family HALCYONIDAE. Colourful, short-legged, dagger-billed fish or insect-eating birds. The fish-eating species plunge-dive for their food from a perch or, in some cases, while hovering, the insectivorous species hunt from a low branch, watching for and seizing insects on the ground. Fish are taken to a perch or on the ground and beaten into immobility before being swallowed. Their flight is rapid and direct. They breed in holes in river banks or trees. Young kingfishers resemble adults but are duller.

1 GIANT KINGFISHER *Ceryle maxima*. Fairly common localised resident. The largest kingfisher, much larger than the next species, the male with a chestnut breast, the female with a chestnut belly. The usual call is a raucous 'kek-kek-kek-kek-kek'. Occurs singly, sometimes in pairs, on wooded rivers or dams, the loud call often being the first indication of its presence. Perches inconspicuously on a low branch overhanging deep water. Occasionally hovers briefly before plunging but not regularly, nor is the hovering ever sustained as in the next species. Is found at water points in the north and east, absent from the dry interior. 43-46 cm. **429**

2 PIED KINGFISHER *Ceryle rudis*. Common resident. Smaller than the previous species, entirely black and white, the male with a double breast-band, the female with two black pectoral patches as illustrated. The call is a frequent high-pitched twittering, often by two or more birds at the same time. Pairs and small family groups are found on rivers, dams, sewage ponds, marsh pools and pans, being particularly common in the northern water systems. Habitually hovers conspicuously over water while fishing, bill pointed down-wards as small illustration, then plunge-dives to seize its prey; sometimes fishes from a perch. 28-29 cm. **428**

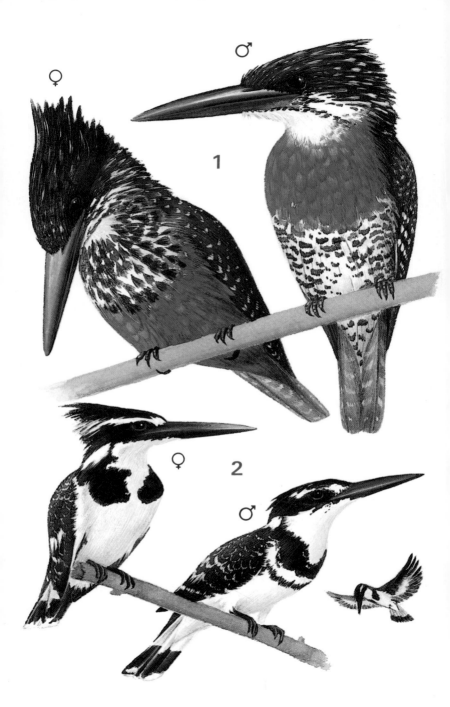

1 WOODLAND KINGFISHER *Halcyon senegalensis.* Fairly common summer resident. A distinctive, insectivorous kingfisher distinguished by very white appearance, turquoise-blue upperparts plus red and black bill. The immature has a *red bill with a small black tip.* The male calls continuously through much of the period October-February, a loud, far-carrying 'yimp-trrrrrrrrrrrrrrrr', the last part drawn out and descending. Frequents broadleafed, riverine and well developed *Acacia* woodland; also suburban gardens, catching insects on the ground by still-hunting from a perch. Breeding pairs greet each other with outspread wings. 23-24 cm. **433**

2 GREYHOODED KINGFISHER (CHESTNUTBELLIED KINGFISHER) *Halcyon leucocephala.* Uncommon summer resident. Identified by grey head and mantle plus *chestnut belly.* Not very vocal, the call a weak, descending 'chi-chi-chi-chi'. An insectivorous kingfisher, usually found singly in riverine woodland or savanna, seldom far from water. Hunts by watching the ground from a branch. Occasionally bathes by plunging into water. 20 cm. **436**

3 STRIPED KINGFISHER *Halcyon chelicuti.* Fairly common resident. Differs from Brownhooded Kingfisher (pp.196-197) in smaller size, streaked head, two-coloured bill, bold black eye-stripe extending to the nape and white collar encircling the neck. In flight shows blue upper tail coverts only, male with darker underwings than female. The call is 'tirrrrrr, *deeeoo-deeeoo-deeeoo*', frequently a pair calling in duet while performing a wing-opening display. Most often heard in the evenings when several individuals may call from scattered points. Usually in pairs in woodland and savanna, perched high on an outer branch from where insects are caught on the ground. Widely distributed and entirely independent of water. 18-19 cm. **437**

1 BROWNHOODED KINGFISHER *Halcyon albiventris*. Fairly common resident. Differs from the Striped Kingfisher (pp.194-195) in *larger size*, lack of bold streaking on cap, absence of a white collar and red bill darker only at base and tip; also has ochre wash on breast. Male has black, female brown wings and shoulders (see illustrations); in flight shows *bright blue back and rump*. The call is a loud 'KIK-kik-kik-kik-kik' repeated several times. Usually singly in woodland, savanna or suburbia. Still-hunts for insects, lizards and other small animal life from a low branch, but often nests in river bank tunnels. 23-24 cm. **435**

2 PYGMY KINGFISHER *Ispidina picta*. Rare, exact status not established; of sparse occurrence in the east and north. Very like the Malachite Kingfisher (4) but has mauve wash on ear coverts, crown colour same blue as rest of upperparts (not turquoise) and *does not reach the eyes*. Makes a 'chip' sound in flight. Single birds frequent broadleafed woodland, thickets in dry riverbeds and savanna, usually away from water. 13 cm. **432**

3 HALFCOLLARED KINGFISHER *Alcedo semitorquata*. Rare; status not established. Identified by black bill (cf. the smaller, immature of next species), entirely bright blue upperparts and cinnamon-coloured lower breast and belly. Calls a shrill 'teep' or 'seek-seek'. Singly on well-wooded rivers and streams. Fishes from a low perch. Although breeding was recorded from Gaborone in the early 1970s, this species has not been found in the region since. 20 cm. **430**

4 MALACHITE KINGFISHER *Alcedo cristata*. Fairly common to locally common resident. Differs from the Pygmy Kingfisher (2) in having a turquoise cap which *reaches the eyes*, no mauve on the ear coverts. The immature has a *black bill*, differing from the previous species in smaller size, blackish back and less extensive white on throat. When flushed utters a shrill 'peep-peep'. Singly on almost any waters with fringing vegetation, fishing from a low reed, grass, branch or rock perch. 14 cm. **431**

196

Rollers. Family CORACIIDAE. Colourful, heavy-billed birds with brilliant blue wing-feathers and harsh, croaking voices. Spend much of the day hunting from a convenient perch, flying down to seize large insects, reptiles and other small prey on the ground. They breed in holes in trees and have active display flights which involve aerial manoeuvres with much harsh calling.

1 RACKET-TAILED ROLLER *Coracias spatulata.* Rare; status not established. Identified by plain blue underparts and spatulate tips to the tail-shafts; cf. (3) and (4). The immature lacks elongated tail-feathers, more lilac on cheeks and sides of breast, but differs from immature of (4) in deep blue primary wing coverts (not greenish-blue) and generally browner upperparts. Has a high-pitched cackling call. Singly in dense, well-developed broadleafed woodland in the far north where sparse and irregular. 36 cm. **448**

2 BROADBILLED ROLLER (CINNAMON ROLLER) *Eurystomus glaucurus.* Uncommon summer resident. Told by small size, bright yellow bill, cinnamon upperparts and purple underparts. Immature has duller brown upperparts streaked black, dull, rusty underparts. Makes various harsh, croaking and cackling sounds, 'keow, keow, keow-r-r-r-r...' Singly or in pairs in well-developed riverine forests and broadleafed woodland in the north and north-east. Hunts from a high perch, catching insects on the wing. 27 cm. **450**

3 LILACBREASTED ROLLER *Coracias caudata.* Common resident. The only roller with lilac throat and breast and blue belly, vent and tail; tail-shafts straight (not spatulate as in (1)), often absent when moulting. The immature is duller, browner, tail-shafts shorter or absent. Normally silent but makes various harsh rattling sounds when displaying. Singly or in pairs in open woodland or savanna, preferring less densely wooded regions than (1). Perches in an exposed position, frequently on roadside telephone wires from where it catches large insects, reptiles and other small animal life on the ground. 36 cm. **447**

4 EUROPEAN ROLLER *Coracias garrulus.* Common summer visitor. Differs from (1) and (3) in lacking tail-shafts. Pale blue over entire head and underparts, upperparts brown but shows electric-blue wings in flight. Mostly silent but sometimes makes a harsh 'rack-kack, kacker'. Singly in woodland savanna or grassland. Perches low down on a branch or palm frond, often on roadside telephone wires, catching large insects, frogs and lizards on the ground. 30-31 cm. **446**

5 PURPLE ROLLER *Coracias naevia.* Fairly common resident. A large, heavily built roller with a square tail, upperparts olive-green, underparts deep reddish-brown heavily streaked white. Immature duller. Makes various harsh cackling and cawing sounds and, when displaying, a continuous 'ka-raa-ka-raa-ka-raa...' as it flies up. Singly in woodland and savanna. Perches low down and is normally less active than other rollers. Has a rocking display flight in which the wings appear to beat independently, calling as described above. Widespread but with seasonal movements. 36-40 cm. **449**

Woodhoopoes and scimitarbill. Family PHOENICULIDAE. Glossy, dark blue-green birds with long graduated tails, long curved bills and short legs. They clamber about tree trunks and branches probing with their bills in search of insects and their larvae. Also investigate the nests of weavers and sparrows in their search for insects and may throw out eggs and small chicks while so doing. Woodhoopoes nest in tree cavities.

1 REDBILLED WOODHOOPOE *Phoeniculus purpureus.* Fairly common resident. Larger than the next species and with red (not black) bill and feet plus more white in the tail; the immature does have a black bill, but less curved than that of (2). The characteristic call is a high-pitched cackling started by one and taken up by others to produce a cacophony of hysterical laughter similar to, but more musical, less mechanical-sounding than the call of the Arrowmarked Babbler (pp. 236-237). Occurs in parties of three to eight or more in any woodland or well-wooded suburbia. Fly from tree to tree in straggling procession, settling low down on the trunk and working their way to the top before flying off again to the next tree. Largely absent from the dry interior. 30-36 cm. **452**

2 SCIMITARBILLED WOODHOOPOE *Phoeniculus cyanomelas.* Fairly common resident. Smaller than the previous species, the bill black (not red) and more curved. The female and immature have the throat and breast dark brown, upperparts less glossy. The normal call, heard in summer, is 'pwep-pwep-pwep-pwep-pwep...' repeated about ten times at half-second intervals. Singly or in pairs in dry, broadleafed woodland, savanna and thornveld. Feeds in the larger trees, clambering about the outer branches and twigs. Quieter, less conspicuous than the previous species. Widespread, being more common in the arid regions. 24-28 cm. **454**

Hoopoe. Family UPUPIDAE. One species throughout Europe, Africa and Asia to Japan. Characterised by well-crested head, long, curved bill, cinnamon colouring and black and white wings. Feeds on the ground, nests in cavities in trees, rocks or walls.

3 HOOPOE *Upupa epops.* Fairly common to common resident. The crest is usually depressed, being raised only when the bird is attentive or alarmed. Female and immature duller than male. The call is 'hoop-hoop, hoop-hoop-hoop' frequently repeated (cf. call of African Cuckoo, pp. 156-157); young birds being fed by adults call 'sweet, sweet'. Occurs singly or in pairs in any woodland, Kalahari thornveld and suburbia, widespread in all regions but nomadic. Walks about probing the ground with its bill. Has an undulating, butterfly-like flight, black and white wings then conspicuous. 27 cm. **451**

Hornbills. Family BUCEROTIDAE. Insectivorous and frugivorous birds with heavy-looking, curved bills, sometimes with a horny casque on the upper mandible. Arboreal or terrestrial feeders, or both; most nest in holes in trees and, in many species, the female seals herself in during incubation and early chick development. Their flight is heavy and undulating with periods of gliding.

1 BRADFIELD'S HORNBILL *Tockus bradfieldi.* Fairly common to locally common resident. Differs from (3) in grey-brown head, brown upperparts and *orange* bill. The call is a series of piping whistles with the bill directed upwards 'pi-pi-pi-pi-pi-pi-pi-pi-peeeeeu'. Occurs in pairs or small flocks in the northern broadleafed woodland, feeding in the tree canopies during the wet season, on the ground during the dry season. Subject to local movements. 50-57 cm. **461**

2 YELLOWBILLED HORNBILL *Tockus flavirostris.* Common to very common resident. Large yellow bill (smaller in female) diagnostic. The immature has a duller yellow bill with a reddish base, the size of bill then serving to distinguish it from the next species. The call is 'wurk, wurk, wurk, wurk, wurk, wurk, wukwukak, wukwukak, wukak, wukak, wurk, wurk, wurk...' the sound rising to a crescendo then fading away, often two birds calling together with a wing-opening, head-bowing display. Pairs and small groups in any woodland, savanna and thornveld including the arid regions. Spends much time feeding on the ground as well as in trees. 48-60 cm. **459**

3 REDBILLED HORNBILL *Tockus erythrorhynchus.* Fairly common to common resident. Identified by combination of red bill and black-and-white checkered upperparts; cf. next species which has plain brown upperparts. The immature has a shorter bill, the upperparts with buff spots. The call is similar to that of the previous species but is uttered more rapidly, 'wha, wha, wha, wha, wha, wha, kawacha, wacha, wacha, wacha, wacha, wacha...' rising to a crescendo then fading. Pairs and small flocks frequent any woodland in the north and east, but are absent from the arid interior. Forages mostly on open ground and probes actively with its bill. 42-50 cm. **458**

4 GREY HORNBILL *Tockus nasutus.* Common to very common resident. The small, dark bill of the male is diagnostic, the female has a smaller casque, that and the upper mandible creamy, tip red; cf. Bradfield's Hornbill (pp.204-205). Immature duller, bill similar to that of female. The call is a thin, piping, plaintive series of notes ascending and descending the scale, 'phe, phephee, pheephee, pheeoo, phew, pheeoo-pheeoo...'. Pairs or flocks of up to about 30 in woodland and savanna in all regions. Mainly arboreal. 43-48 cm. **457**

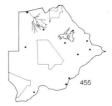

1 TRUMPETER HORNBILL *Bycanistes bucinator.* Uncommon, localised resident of the Chobe River region and Kasane Forest Reserve. Distinguished by large size, pied appearance and very heavy bill with prominent casque, larger in male than in female. The characteristic call, heard mostly early mornings and evenings, resembles the crying of a baby 'waaaa-aaa-aaa-aaa-aaaaaa' often uttered by several birds at once, plus various braying calls. Small flocks frequent riverine forests and adjacent woodland, feeding in the canopies of the larger fruiting trees. 58-65 cm. **455**

2 GROUND HORNBILL *Bucorvus leadbeateri.* Fairly common resident. Turkey-sized black bird, male with red face and throat-pouch, female with a blue central patch on the pouch; in flight show white wing-feathers. Immature with yellow facial skin and throat pouch. The call, heard mostly early mornings, is a deep booming 'oomph, oomph-oomph' frequently repeated. Usually seen in family groups of four to ten individuals in woodland or savanna. Mainly terrestrial, groups walking slowly in loose array in search of food. If disturbed all take off in low flight and settle temporarily in trees; also roost in trees. Extends its range in years of good rains. 90 cm. **463**

Barbets. Family CAPITONIDAE. Stout-billed, robust and often colourful relatives of the woodpeckers with loud, characteristic calls. They feed on fruit and insects and excavate nest-holes in trees. The smaller species are called tinker barbets from the likeness of their calls to the sound of a hammer on metal. Young birds are dull versions of the adults.

1 YELLOWFRONTED TINKER BARBET *Pogoniulus chrysoconus*. Uncommon to locally fairly common resident. Forehead may be yellow or *orange*, underparts very pale yellow; immature has little or no yellow on forehead. The call is a monotonous 'phoo-phoo-phoo-phoo-phoo...' uttered for long periods during the heat of the day; also calls 'dit-dit-dit...' in rapid morse-like sequences or 'trroooo, troooo, troooo'. Occurs in the northern broadleafed woodland including riparian woodland, and in mixed woodland in the south-east. Feeds in the canopies of the larger fruiting trees. 12 cm. **470**

2 PIED BARBET *Lybius leucomelas*. Common resident. Recognised by red forehead, pied upperparts and white underparts. Immature has a black forehead. The call is a loud, nasal 'peh-peh', less frequently a hoopoe-like 'poop-poop'. Widespread, occurring singly or in pairs in a wide range of drier habitats. 17-18 cm. **465**

3 BLACKCOLLARED BARBET *Lybius torquatus*. Uncommon to fairly common resident. The only local bird with bright red forehead, face and foreneck and heavy black bill. Immature has red speckling on black. The call is a loud duet, starting with a whirring 'kerrr-kerrr-kerrr' (one bird) and then (both birds) 'too-puddely-too-puddely-too-puddely...' about eight times, the calling usually accompanied by wing-quivering, swaying or bowing; also calls 'snaar'. Occurs in pairs or small groups in any woodland and well-wooded suburbia. Most common in the north, often associated with hills in the south-east. 19-20 cm. **464**

4 CRESTED BARBET *Trachyphonus vaillantii*. Common resident. Unmistakable yellow, black and red bird with heavy, yellow bill and crested head; immature duller, bill more dusky. The call is a distinctive trilling like a muffled alarm clock 'trrrrrrrrrr...' continuing sometimes for long periods; louder, slower and of higher pitch when agitated 'kekekekekekek...'. Usually singly in moist, well-wooded regions, including suburbia. 23 cm. **473**

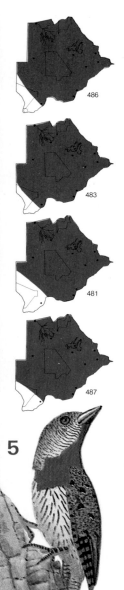

Woodpeckers. Family PICIDAE. Small, robust birds with straight, pointed bills, stiff tails and zygodactylous feet in which the outer toe may be directed backward or foreward. They glean insects and their larvae from within crevices in trees and from beneath bark by tapping with their bills to loosen or chip the wood and by inserting their long sticky tongues. While feeding the tail is used as a prop. They normally occur in pairs and excavate holes in trees for nesting, these frequently being used in turn by other hole-nesting species. Territorial pairs tap loud drumming signals with their bills on dead tree trunks. Many woodpeckers are very similar in appearance and are best identified by head and breast markings plus call.

1 CARDINAL WOODPECKER *Dendropicos fuscescens.* Fairly common resident. Identified by small size, *streaked* breast, black moustachial stripes and brown forehead in both sexes; male with crimson crown, female with black crown. The call is a shrill chittering 'tritritritritrit'. Pairs are found in any woodland, often in quite small trees or bushes where it taps quietly. Widespread. 14-16 cm. **486**

2 GOLDENTAILED WOODPECKER *Campethera abingoni.* Fairly common resident. Streaky-breasted but larger than the previous species, male with moustachial streak and entire crown red, spotted black, female with crown black spotted white, nape red. (The golden tail, being common to most woodpeckers, is not diagnostic). The call is a single, nasal 'waaa'. Singly or in pairs in any woodland or bush fringing dry riverbeds. 20-23 cm. **483**

3 BENNETT'S WOODPECKER *Campethera bennettii.* Uncommon resident. Has *spotted underparts*, male identified by entirely red crown and moustachial streaks, female by *brown facial and throat-patches.* The call is an excitable, high-pitched chattering, sometimes by two or three birds together and accompanied by wing-flapping 'whirrwhirrwhirrwhir-it-whir-it-whir-it-wrrrrrrrrrr...'. Singly, in pairs or small groups in well-developed woodland, foraging much of the time *on the ground.* Widespread but sporadic. 22-24 cm. **481**

4 BEARDED WOODPECKER *Thripias namaquus.* Fairly common resident. A large, long-billed species with *banded* underparts, bold black moustachial streaks and ear-patches; male with top of crown red, female with crown black, both with black, white-spotted foreheads. The call is a loud 'wickwickwickwickwick-wick-wick'. Has a particularly loud and far-carrying drumming 'trrrrrrr-tap-tap-tap-tap'. Usually in pairs in any well-developed woodland and riverine forest, feeding high in large trees. 23-25 cm. **487**

Wrynecks. Fåmily JYNGIDAE.

5 REDTHROATED WRYNECK *Jynx ruficollis.* Exact status not established; no confirmed sightings in Botswana but is known to occur in adjacent Transvaal. Identified by rust-brown patch on throat and upper breast, plus brown-speckled upperparts with blackish broken line from crown to mantle. The call, uttered frequently, is a high-pitched 'kek-kek-kek-kek'. Singly or in pairs in woodland or in suburbia where it favours wattle trees (Australian *Acacia* spp.). Perches or clings to tree trunks like a woodpecker or hops on the ground with tail raised. 18 cm. **489**

Honeyguides. Family INDICATORIDAE. Small, drab birds which show *white outer tail-feathers in flight*. Some species have distinctive calls and regular call-sites, others have weak, sibilant calls that are seldom heard. Their food is mostly insects but a few species have a liking for beeswax and bee larvae. These have developed the habit, in remoter areas, of leading man to bees' nests by continually chattering and fluttering conspicuously in the desired direction in the hope that the nest will be broken open. Like cuckoos honeyguides build no nest but parasitise various other small birds. Young birds are dull versions of the adults.

1 SHARPBILLED HONEYGUIDE *Prodotiscus regulus*. Rare resident. Differs from the Slenderbilled Honeyguide (3) by *brown* (not greenish) upperparts, *white rump* and white throat. Has a thin, tinkling call resembling a weaker version of that of the Crested Barbet 'trrrrrrrrrrrr' of three to four second duration; also calls 'zeeet, zeeet, zeeet'. Individuals are sparsely distributed in woodland and suburbia. Usually perches on top of a tree and *peers slowly from side to side while bobbing its head up and down*. Makes aerial sallies to hawk insects or catch them on the ground. Also makes high display flights in which the white tail-feathers are displayed, or chases other individuals in similar manner while calling 'zeeet'. Restless, seldom remaining in one place for long. Does not guide. Parasitises various warblers. 13 cm. **478**

2 LESSER HONEYGUIDE *Indicator minor*. Uncommon resident. Identified by thick bill with pale patch at base of upper mandible, plus yellow edges to flight feathers. Calls 'klew, klew, klew ...', 30-40 calls at a time, from a regular call-site. Found singly in any woodland. Does not guide. Parasitises hole-nesting species, especially barbets and woodpeckers. 15 cm. **476**

3 SLENDERBILLED HONEYGUIDE *Prodotiscus zambesiae*. Rare, status not established; two records only for the far north-west. Told from the Sharpbilled Honeyguide (1) by *greenish* (not brown) upperparts, the flight feathers yellow-edged, throat dark, finely streaked white. The call is a harsh, repetitive 'skeee-aa' during an undulating flight high above the trees in which the white outer tail-feathers are displayed conspicuously. Frequents the canopy of broadleafed woodland. Does not guide. Parasitises white-eyes. 11,5 cm. **479**

4 GREATER HONEYGUIDE *Indicator indicator*. Fairly common resident. In both sexes the yellow shoulder-patch is frequently vestigial or absent, dark throat of male often incomplete, thus adults may appear as nondescript, bulbul-sized birds but always have *white outer tail-feathers*. Immature distinctive as illustrated. From a regularly used call-site the male calls for long periods during summer 'VIC-terrr, VIC-terrr...' or 'WHIT-purr, WHIT-purr...' up to eleven times. Guides humans to bees' nests, the call then a high-pitched chattering like a box of matches being rattled, the bird fluttering in an agitated manner. Occurs singly in woodland and savanna. Usually inconspicuous, but the male sometimes performs a swooping display with spread tail while making mechanical 'whirring' sounds with its wings. Parasitises hole-nesting species: kingfishers, bee-eaters, woodhoopoes, swallows, starlings, etc. 19-20 cm. **474**

1 AFRICAN BROADBILL *Smithornis capensis*. Family EURY-LAIMIDAE. Status not established; recorded once in nothern Okavango. Broad bill, dumpy appearance, black crown and heavily streaked underparts diagnostic. In display flies in small circles with its back feathers puffed out while uttering a frog-like 'purrrup' rising in pitch. Perches low down in dense woodland and thickets where it hawks insects like a flycatcher. 14 cm. **490**

Larks. Family ALAUDIDAE. Small, sombrely coloured terrestrial birds with confusingly similar, nondescript brownish plumage patterns. Many species show regional plumage variations, palest in the west. Young resemble adults but are usually more speckled. Larks are best identified by the male's call plus behaviour and habitat preference. Their flight is usually of a dipping nature and of brief duration.

2 SPIKEHEELED LARK *Chersomanes albofasciata*. Fairly common to locally common resident; found mainly in the southern and central regions. Characterised by erect stance, *long slender bill and short tail with white terminal bar*; the hind claw is long and straight. Makes a rapid, mellow trill in flight. Occurs singly or in small, loose parties in grassland and Kalahari scrub. Largely terrestrial in habits, running quickly between bouts of feeding. Flies reluctantly but with undulating action and fanned tail, calling as described above; perches briefly on low, scrubby vegetation. Widespread except for the north-western woodlands. 15-16 cm. **506**

3 FLAPPET LARK *Mirafra rufocinnamomea*. Uncommon resident. Very similar to the next species, the rufous form (a) mostly in the east, the grey form (b) in drier regions. Best identified by display behaviour and mainly exclusive distribution. Usually seen singly in savanna and hilly grassland fringing woodland. Unobtrusive April-September but, during summer, the male performs a high aerial cruise, making bursts of audible wing-claps, the sound a muffled 'purrit-purrit-purrit' followed by an almost inaudible, reedy 'chik-chik-a-wee', repeated after a short pause; see illustration. May ascend into wind to some height then descend almost vertically before flying parallel to the ground prior to settling. 16 cm. **496**

4 CLAPPER LARK *Mirafra apiata*. Fairly common to locally common resident. Very similar to the previous species but distribution mostly exclusive, behaviour and habitat preference markedly different. May call from the ground, often mimicking the songs of other birds, but more noticeable while displaying October-March. The male flies upwards a few metres, hovers briefly and claps its wings, then drops steeply while uttering a long, drawn-out 'fooeeeeeeee' as illustrated. Widespread and common in grassland and Kalahari scrub, but unobtrusive in the non-breeding season. 16-17 cm. **495**

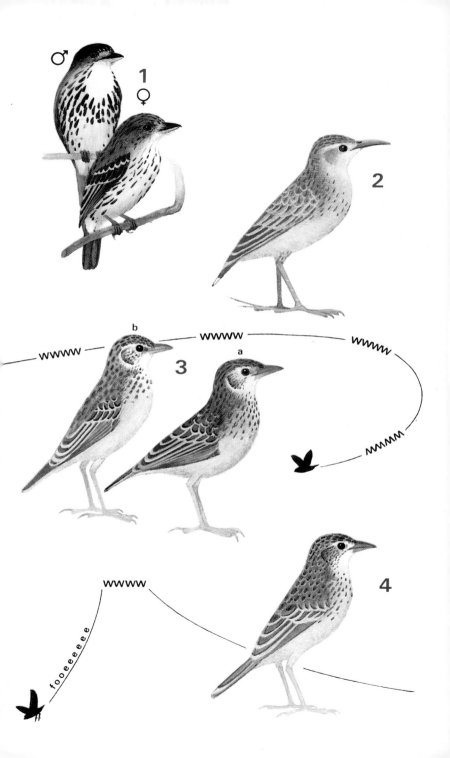

1 MELODIOUS LARK (SINGING BUSH LARK) *Mirafra cheniana*. Rare; exact status not established; one confirmed record only from grassland near Lake Ngami. Distinguished from the next two species only with difficulty, upperparts and lateral breast more heavily marked, underparts frequently whiter than shown, buffy on flanks, throat and outer tail-feathers *white*. In flight shows rufous wings. In early summer utters a lively song comprised of imitations of other birds, while perched on top of a tree *or in flight*. Outside Botswana associated with edaphic rooigrass. 14 cm. **492**

2 MONOTONOUS LARK *Mirafra passerina*. Locally and seasonally common resident. Differs from the previous species in duller appearance, less clearly defined markings on upperparts and breast, indistinct eyebrows and buff outer tail feathers; wings show rufous in flight. Easily overlooked unless singing. Flocks arrive in an area after the first summer rains and all males immediately start calling, a monotonous and much-repeated 'corrr-weeooo' through much of the day, often at night, the call uttered from the ground or a low bush or in brief, fluttering flight with plumage fluffed. Inhabits savanna with stony ground and sparse grass cover or Kalahari scrub. Annual occurrence in any region unpredictable; highly nomadic when not breeding. 14 cm. **493**

3 SABOTA LARK *Mirafra sabota*. Common resident. Plumage variable; brownest in the east (a), palest in the west (b) with intermediate grades elsewhere. Upperparts boldy mottled, eyebrows, throat and belly clear white (these features diagnostic), breast well spotted, outer tail-feathers pale buff; *no rufous wing-edges*. Has a mellow and variable song involving imitations of other birds, *usually uttered from the top of a bush*, occasionally in hovering flight. Singly in dry savanna with stony ground, open woodland and thornveld; less commonly in Kalahari scrub. Perches in trees when disturbed. 15 cm. **498**

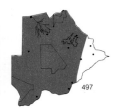

4 FAWNCOLOURED LARK *Mirafra africanoides*. Common resident. Told by reddish-fawn (a) to distinctly fawn upperparts (b) (palest in the west) with dark streaking, white underparts sometimes streaked brown on breast, white outer tail-feathers and, in flight, reddish wings. The song, uttered from the top of a bush or in flight, is an urgent-sounding 'te-e-e-tee-ree-tee-ree-tee-ree-chee' with variations. Occurs in thornveld and semi-desert scrub, mostly on Kalahari sands. Feeds on open ground but perches on bushes when disturbed. Widespread, less frequent in the north. 16 cm. **497**

214

1 REDCAPPED LARK *Calandrella cinerea*. Fairly common to locally common resident. Rust-brown crown and pectoral patches diagnostic. The crest is raised only when the bird is agitated or hot. The immature has dark brown upperparts, breast speckled blackish. The normal call is a brief 'cheep', 'chirrup' or 'cheeree'; during flight display has a sibilant, trilling song ending in a harsh '...tcheet, tcheet, tchrreet'. In pairs or small, loose flocks when breeding, at other times in larger flocks in favoured habitat. Occurs in short, overgrazed grassland, grassy fringes of pans, bare ground, dry riverbeds and airstrips; widespread and more common in arid regions. Territorial birds execute an aerial cruise while singing; see above. Walks rapidly while feeding or makes short runs, flies short distances (displaying white outer tail feathers) then drops down. Disturbed flocks take off as a cohesive unit, twist and turn briefly, then resettle abruptly. 15 cm. **507**

2 RUFOUSNAPED LARK *Mirafra africana*. Fairly common to locally common resident. Distinguished by rufous crown and *wing-feather edges* which show as a rufous patch on the folded wing. Eastern birds (a) have rich rufous upperparts and rufous wash on underparts, western birds (b) with upperparts much greyer, white edges to feathers, underparts faintly tinged buff on breast. The call, a good recognition feature in summer, is a melancholy 'tseep-tseeooo', repeated at about eight second intervals; also has a rambling song-flight when it imitates other bird songs. Usually singly in open grassland or with scattered bushes, savanna and Kalahari scrub. During summer male calls for long periods from prominent perch on bush, anthill or post, shuffling its wings and raising its crest frequently, often many birds within sight of each other. Widespread but unobtrusive when not calling. 18-19 cm. **494**

3 DUSKY LARK *Pinarocorys nigricans*. Uncommon summer visitor. Dark colouring and bold markings of face and breast distinctive; resembles Groundscraper Thrush (pp.238-239) but upperparts darker, bill more robust. Has a soft 'wek-wek-wek...' call in flight. On passage can occur in flocks in dry woodland and savanna, otherwise usually seen singly. Runs while foraging and perches in trees frequently. Flies with marked dipping action. Sparse and irregular. 19 cm. **505**

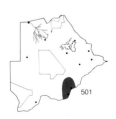

4 SHORTCLAWED LARK *Mirafra chuana*. Common but very localised resident; occurs only in the south-east. Shape and stance reminiscent of Buffy Pipit (p.221) with longish, slender bill and tail, very streaked upperparts with no rufous on crown or wings, but rusty colour on rump. The call is a shrill 'phew-pheeoo-pheeoo, phew-pheeoo-pheeoo, pheeeeeoo, pheeeit...' with variations including several clear trills, usually uttered from the top of a bush. Also has a display flight in which it rises and then drops steeply calling a long, drawn-out 'foooeeee'; cf. Clapper Lark (pp. 212-213). Found in dry grassland with scattered bushes and *Acacia* savanna, being particularly common in the Pitsane and Diabo grasslands. 17-18 cm. **501**

216

1 STARK'S LARK *Alauda starki*. Rare, exact status not established; recorded sporadically in Kalahari grasslands and pans. A small, very pale lark with a small crest and pale bill; long feathers of crown give a peaked appearance to the head. Has a melodious song of trilling notes 'prrt, prrt, preee, preee, prrr, prrr...'. Occurs in small flocks which, when disturbed, take off and fly in a wide arc before re-settling. Nomadic, numbers fluctuating. 13 cm. **511**

2 PINKBILLED LARK *Spizocorys conirostris*. Uncommon localised resident; occurrence seems to centre on the grasslands surrounding the Makgadikgadi Pans and the Pitsane region of the south-east. A small lark with stout, *conical pink bill* and pale rufous underparts. The call is 'chi*zic*' or 'twee-twee-twee' on the ground or in flight. Usually in loose, scattered flocks foraging in grassland, but easily overlooked in tall grass. Nomadic, numbers fluctuating. 12 cm. **508**

Finchlarks. Small, sparrow-like larks with white, conical bills and marked sexual plumage differences, males predominantly black. Occur in flocks and are highly nomadic.

3 CHESTNUTBACKED FINCHLARK *Eremopterix leucotis*. Fairly common to seasonally common resident. Both sexes differ from other finchlarks in having chestnut wing coverts and grey under-wings, female with small white collar. Has a sharp, rattling call 'chip-chee-w' and a pretty song in fluttering flight. Flocks occur in dry, open flats, bare ground around pans, in dry riverbeds, on tracks, airstrips and cultivated lands, usually with bushes nearby. Makes off in low irregular flight when disturbed, then suddenly resettles. Widespread except for the more arid regions. 12-13 cm. **515**

4 BLACKEARED FINCHLARK *Eremopterix australis*. Rare, loca-lised summer resident. Male has no white plumage; upperparts of both sexes rufous, belly of female *white* (not black). Calls a buzzing 'zht-zht-zht' in flight. Sparse and irregular, occurring when breeding conditions are right in the red Kalahari sands of the extreme south-west. 12-13 cm. **517**

5 GREYBACKED FINCHLARK *Eremopterix verticalis*. Fairly common to seasonally common resident. Both sexes distinguished by grey upperparts, male with *white patch on crown,* female pale, no rufous on upperparts. A shrill chirp is made when the birds are feeding and a sharp 'chik, chik, chik' in flight. Flocks, frequently many hundreds, occur in arid, short-grass plains, Kalahari scrub, dry pans and riverbeds and overgrazed areas, less commonly on cul-tivated lands; less dependent on bushes than (3). Widespread but more sporadic in the north and east. 12-13 cm. **516**

Pipits, longclaws and wagtails. Family MOTACILLIDAE. Small, insectivorous terrestrial birds, the wagtails water-associated. Sexes alike or closely similar, all with white or buff outer tail-feathers. Many pipits are so similar as to make field identification difficult, they utter a 'chissik' call on take-off and have flight of a dipping nature, while most bob their tails to some degree. Longclaws are large, colourful pipits while wagtails, also colourful or striking, are mostly well known because of their confiding and friendly behaviour, and their habit of constantly bobbing their tails.

1 RICHARD'S PIPIT *Anthus novaeseelandiae.* Fairly common resident. Bold facial markings, boldly marked breast and *white* (not buff) *outer tail-feathers* distinguish this from other similar pipits. April-August plumage duller, mantle less mottled, paler edges to flight feathers. When disturbed takes off with a 'chissik' call and characteristic dipping flight, resettling on the ground nearby or on a low bush. Calls in flight 'chree-chree-chree-chree-chree' during each dip. Widespread in grassland and savanna; runs a short distance then stops and dips its tail two or three times. 16 cm. **716**

2 MOUNTAIN PIPIT *Anthus* species. Rare, status not established; four specimens collected near Francistown in October. Possible passage migrant. Similar to (1) but slightly larger, upperparts darker, breast markings generally bolder, base of bill pink or yellow, outer tail-feathers *buff.* Call like (1) but slightly deeper, slower. Could occur anywhere during spring and autumn passage. 17-19 cm. **901**

3 LONGBILLED PIPIT (NICHOLSON'S PIPIT) *Anthus similis.* Uncommon resident. Build more robust, upperparts darker, more *grey-brown* than previous species, moustacial streak prominent, the breast lightly blotched, margins of outer tail-feathers buff (not white), bill slightly longer than others on this plate. Calls from mound or bush a repeated 'chreep, chroop' and on take-off, a clear metallic 'kilink'. Usually solitary in undulating, stony terrain, lightly bushed regions with sparse grass cover or lightly grassed broadleafed woodland where it readily perches in trees. Is attracted to burnt areas. Has an erect, full-chested stance. Appears to be widespread and may be commoner than is thought since it is easily overlooked. 18 cm. **717**

4 PLAINBACKED PIPIT *Anthus leucophrys.* Uncommon resident. Distinguished by lack of distinct markings on dark mantle. Moustacial streak faint; breast markings faint or absent, edges of outer tail-feathers buff. From the ground calls a rather slow, sparrow-like 'jhreet-jeroot'. Has similar dipping flight to (1) during which it calls a quiet 'tsip-tsip'. Singly or in small flocks in grassland, preferring overgrazed or burnt conditions, and tilled lands. Occurs in the southeast and north. 17 cm. **718**

5 BUFFY PIPIT *Anthus vaalensis.* Fairly common resident. Generally more buff-coloured than the previous three pipits; moustachial streaks not pronounced, breast-streaking variable, often indistinct, edges of outer tail-feathers pale buff. Slightly larger, stockier than previous species. In flight makes an occasional soft 'chissik' call. Occurs singly in sparsely grassed conditions, overgrazed cattle areas, airstrips and in Kalahari scrub with patchy grass and scattered calcrete mounds. Has the habit of running a short distance then standing erect with chest thrust out; cf. (1) and (3) which tend to keep their bodies more horizontal. Also bobs its hind quarters more often than other pipits. Appears to be widespread but records lacking for some apparently suitable regions. 19 cm. **719**

1 ORANGETHROATED LONGCLAW *Macronyx capensis.* Uncommon localised resident. Orange throat with black surround diagnostic; immature may have throat same colour as underparts. Normal call a mewing 'me-yew' from ground or in flight; also a far-reaching whistle 'dweeeet'. Solitary or in pairs in grassland. Walks *over* grass with big strides and often stands momentarily with erect stance on tuft, stone or termite mound. When disturbed takes off in stiff-winged flight for a short distance uttering its characteristic call. Occurs in the extreme south-eastern grasslands. 20 cm. **727**

2 PINKTHROATED LONGCLAW *Macronyx ameliae.* Uncommon resident. Reddish throat and underparts diagnostic; immature has throat more buffy, black gorget vestigial. The call is a repeated 'tee-yer, tee-yer, tee-yer, tee-yer, trip, trip, trip, trip'. Singly or in pairs in marshes and flooded grasslands. More secretive than the previous species, but behaviour similar. Lies low when approached, then makes off for a short distance *when white wing-bars and dark back markings can be seen.* Occurs sparsely from the Okavango Delta northwards. 20 cm. **730**

3 TREE PIPIT *Anthus trivialis.* Rare summer visitor; sparsely recorded in the north-east. Identified by short bill, black moustacial streak, white throat and breast with tear-shaped spots. Flight call 'teez', from the ground 'seea'. Singly or in small groups in woodland or savanna. Walks in crouched posture, bobs tail up and down when pausing. Flies into trees when disturbed. 16 cm. **722**

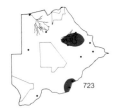

4 BUSHVELD PIPIT *Anthus caffer.* Uncommon resident; occurs sparsely in the east and south-east. Small, inconspicuous pipit with distinctly streaky appearance; upperparts brown with bold streaking, underparts smoky-buff, breast boldly streaked. Sings from a tree-top 'skeer-trurp, skeer-trurp, skeer-trurp-skee-skee...'; from the ground calls 'tshweep'. Feeds on the ground in broadleafed woodland and savanna. Makes off in erratic flight when disturbed. 13,5 cm. **723**

5 STRIPED PIPIT *Anthus lineiventris.* Rare resident; occurs sparsely in the east and south-east. Distinguished by bright yellow-edged wing-feathers and white underparts with profuse black streaking. Has a loud, whistling, thrush-like song. Usually solitary on stony wooded hillsides or rocky banks of small rivers. Walks about with horizontal stance and large strides and perches in a tree *lengthwise* along a branch when disturbed. Occurs sparsely in the east. 18 cm. **720**

1 CAPE WAGTAIL *Motacilla capensis*. Fairly common resident. Greyer than other local wagtails, northern races with breast-band absent or vestigial; see (b). The call is a loud, cheerful 'tsee-eep' or 'steep'. Singly or in pairs near water, especially slow-flowing rivers and muddy pools, or on lawns. Struts about feeding on the ground, occasionally bobbing its tail. If disturbed flies briefly to a tree or building, but normally tame and confiding. Widespread except in arid areas. 18 cm. **713**

2 AFRICAN PIED WAGTAIL *Motacilla aguimp*. Uncommon, localised resident. Differs from other wagtails in striking pied plumage, upperparts *black*. The call is a loud 'tu-weee' and 'twee twee twee'. Singly, in pairs or family groups near large, rock-strewn rivers with sandbanks, lagoons with grass fringes and on lawns. Habits similar to those of the previous species but less widespread, mostly confined to major waters. 20 cm. **711**

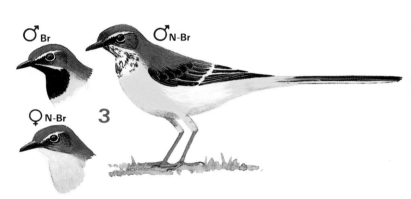

3 GREY WAGTAIL *Motacilla cinerea*. Very rare summer visitor; recorded once in the north. Distinguished from the following species by white eyebrows, *grey* (not green) upperparts from head to mantle, *yellow rump*, dark shoulder patch and *white* or *speckled throat* (black throat of breeding plumage unlikely in southern Africa). Underparts yellow and white or with faint brownish smudges. Call a sharp 'tseet' or 'stee-eet'; in flight repeats a high-pitched 'tsiit'. Prefers rocky streams in woodland. 18 cm. **715**

4 YELLOW WAGTAIL *Motacilla flava*. Uncommon summer visitor to the north; occasional in the south-east. Many races occur, each with different head patterns; (a) and (c) most common in this region but (b) also known. Told from the previous species by shorter tail, *yellow throat* and greener upperparts, including the rump. Calls 'tsee-eep', similar to other wagtails. Occurs in moist, grassy situations: marshes, grassy edges of pans and sewage pans, either singly or in small, loose groups. 18 cm. **714**

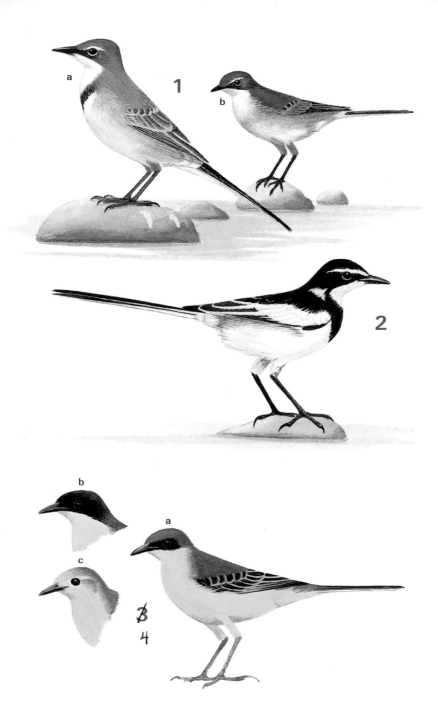

Similar black birds. The three species on this plate are unrelated but are similar in appearance, behaviour and habitat preferences, and are grouped here for ease of comparison.

1 FORKTAILED DRONGO *Dicrurus adsimilis.* Family DICRURI-DAE. Common resident. Differs from the next two species in having a prominent *forked tail*, the outer feathers curved outwards; cf. (2) and (3). Immature as illustrated. Has a variety of unmusical twanging notes interspersed with imitations of other bird calls, especially those of owls and other birds of prey. Singly or in pairs in almost any wooded habitat and savanna. Perches on a prominent low branch from where it hawks insects in erratic aerial manoeuvres, or seizes them on the ground. Noisy and aggressive. 25 cm. **541**

2 BLACK FLYCATCHER *Melaenornis pammelaina.* Family MUSCI-CAPIDAE. (See also pp. 266-271.) Locally fairly common resident; rather uncommon in the east and south-east. The tail has a *small indentation* at the tip (not a distinct fork) while the outer tail-feathers are straight (not splayed); cf. previous species. Immature as illustrated. Not very vocal, makes various quiet sibilant sounds 'swee', swee, swee-ur'. Singly or in pairs in any woodland. Catches insects on the ground, flying down from a perch in typical flycatcher fashion and often occurs alongside the previous species but, by contrast, is unobtrusive. 19-22 cm. **694**

Cuckooshrikes. Family CAMPEPHAGIDAE. Insectivorous, heavy-billed birds, some of cuckoo-like appearance, found in the larger trees of well-developed woodland and riverine forests. See also pp. 228-229.

3 BLACK CUCKOOSHRIKE *Campephaga flava.* Uncommon summer resident. Male differs from previous two species in *rounded tail* and prominent orange gape; may have a yellow shoulder-patch (a) or lack this entirely (b). Female strikingly different, cuckoo-like as illustrated. Immature like female, young male with increasing areas of black with age. The call is a high-pitched, prolonged trill 'trrrr-rrrrr...'. Occurs singly or in pairs in moist woodland, especially in dense vegetation, where it feeds unobtrusively; absent in the more arid regions. 22 cm. **538**

1 WHITEBREASTED CUCKOOSHRIKE *Coracina pectoralis.* Rare resident. Distinctive, sexes differing as illustrated. Immature barred with dark grey and white on upperparts, spotted dark grey below, outer tail-feathers pointed. Male makes a softly whistled 'duid-duid', female a long trilling 'ch-e-e-e-e-e-e-e'. Usually seen singly in canopies of large trees in broadleafed woodland and riparian forest. Moves from branch to branch with long hops, peering closely at leaves in search of insects, or makes short aerial sallies. 27 cm. **539**

Crows. Family CORVIDAE. Large, mainly glossy-black, omnivorous scavenging birds. Sexes are alike and young similar to adults. All have loud cawing calls. Bold and opportunistic.

2 PIED CROW *Corvus albus.* Common resident. Distinguished by white breast and collar. The call is a loud 'kwaak'. A widespread, bold species often found in association with human settlements where it gleans food scraps, especially on refuse dumps, highways and at cattle posts. Usually in loose flocks. Less common than (2) in the central Kalahari and absent from the south-west. 46-52 cm. **548**

3 BLACK CROW (CAPE ROOK) *Corvus capensis.* Common resident. Entirely glossy black; bill more slender than in (2). The normal call is a loud, high-pitched 'kraaa', but also makes various 'gollop' sounds and similar guttural noises. Single birds, pairs and flocks frequent human settlements, farmlands, cattle ranges, grasslands and semi-desert, outnumbering (1) in the more arid regions. 48-53 cm. **547**

4 WHITENECKED RAVEN *Corvus albicollis.* Status not established; no confirmed records. Occurs in the montane regions of Zimbabwe but forages widely, therefore may occur occasionally in the north-east of Botswana. Has a white hind collar only, otherwise glossy black with a very heavy bill. The call is a falsetto 'kraak', although deeper notes are sometimes uttered. 50-54 cm. **550**

Orioles. Family ORIOLIDAE. Predominantly yellow, pink-billed, frugivorous and insectivorous birds with clear, liquid-sounding calls. They feed mostly in the canopies of large broadleafed trees.

1 EUROPEAN GOLDEN ORIOLE *Oriolus oriolus*. Uncommon to common summer visitor. The male differs from the male of the next species in black wings and black spot *before eye* only; female resembles the immature illustrated but is less streaked on underparts. The call is a ringing 'weela-weeoo' plus a churring alarm note common to all orioles. Singly in any woodland, preferring broadleafed and riverine woodland. Sparse but widespread, occurring occasionally even in the arid regions. Unobtrusive when feeding in the canopies, unless calling, but distinctive in its rapid, undulating flight. 24 cm. **543**

2 AFRICAN GOLDEN ORIOLE *Oriolus auratus*. Uncommon resident. The male is the yellowest of orioles with a distinct *black line through the eyes to the ear coverts*, this present also in the immature. The female is less bright than the male, upperparts greener, underparts duller. The calls are liquid whistles 'wee-er-er-wul' or 'fee-yoo-fee-yoo-fee-yoo', longer than the calls of the next species. Occurs in well-developed woodland and riverine forests, feeding unobtrusively in the canopies of fruiting trees. Absent from the more arid regions. 24 cm. **544**

3 BLACKHEADED ORIOLE *Oriolus larvatus*. Fairly common resident. Distinguished by black head; cf. Masked Weaver (pp.300-301) which is smaller with a black bill. Immature as illustrated. The usual call is a loud, liquid 'pheeoo' or 'pheea-pheeoo' plus a 'churr' alarm note. Singly or in pairs in a wide variety of wooded habitats including exotic plantations and suburbia where it feeds in the canopies of fruiting trees; absent from the drier regions. A noisy, conspicuous species. 25 cm. **545**

Bulbuls. Family PYCNONOTIDAE. Frugivorous and insectivorous birds, many with clear, melodious calls. In Botswana they frequent evergreen bush, riverine forests, broadleafed woodland and arid thornveld according to species, some being largely terrestrial. Sexes are alike, immatures duller.

1 BLACKEYED BULBUL *Pycnonotus barbatus*. Common resident. Differs from the next species in *dark eye and lack of a distinctive eye-ring*, otherwise known by its dark, crested head and yellow vent. Has several cheerful, mellow call phrases sounding like 'Wake-up, Gregory' and a much repeated 'chit, chit' chit...' alarm call. Fairly gregarious, either in pairs or small groups in moist, well-bushed regions and woodland, riverine forests and suburban gardens in the east and north, overlapping with that of the next species in many regions but outnumbering it in the north. 20-22 cm. **568**

2 REDEYED BULBUL *Pycnonotus nigricans*. Common resident. Differs from the previous species in having an *orange-red eye and eye-ring*, otherwise closely similar. Has a variety of cheerful, chattering calls similar to (1) and is very much like it most other ways. Widespread. Found in similar habitats to (1) but extends into the arid regions of the country where (1) does not occur. 19-21 cm. **567**

3 YELLOWSPOTTED NICATOR *Nicator gularis*. Not recorded in Botswana; may occur in the Chobe River region. Identified by heavy bill, greenish upperparts with yellow-spotted wing-feathers, yellow-tipped tail plus yellow vent and under-belly. The call is a series of mellow trills and warbles. Highly secretive in dense riverine thickets, easily overlooked unless calling. 23 cm. **575**

4 YELLOWBELLIED BULBUL *Chlorocichla flaviventris*. Uncommon to locally fairly common resident. Identified by olive-green upperparts and bright yellow underparts, *including the underwings*, plus reddish eyes with conspicuous *white eyelids*. Noisy at times, the call a loud 'pur, pur, pur, pur, peh, peh, peh, peh...' often several calling at once. Singly or in pairs in well-developed riverine forests and thickets; frequents established camps and the grounds of rural hotels. Spends much time foraging on the ground or in the mid-stratum. 20-23 cm. **574**

5 TERRESTRIAL BULBUL *Phyllastrephus terrestris*. Uncommon to locally fairly common resident. A very drab brown species, apart from white throat, the underparts barely paler than the upperparts; at close range a yellowish gape is discernible. Feeding parties maintain a quiet chuckling or murmuring 'wuk, wuk, wukka, wak, wukkle, wukkle...'. In small parties in dense riverside thickets, always scratching about in ground debris and seldom ascending above the lower stratum; often tame in the gardens of rural hotels and permanent bush-camps. Easily overlooked unless heard. 21-22 cm. **569**

Tits. Families REMIZIDAE (penduline tits) and PARIDAE (true tits). Small insectivorous and frugivorous arboreal birds with short, stout beaks, the nostrils obscured by bristles. Habitually forage in the tree canopies, clambering about the branches in agile fashion, often feeding in the inverted position. Restless little birds with rasping calls. True tits nest in holes, penduline tits make purse-like nests.

1 CAPE PENDULINE TIT *Anthoscopus minutus.* Fairly common resident. Distinguished by very small size, black forehead and yellow underparts; may be greyer on upperparts than illustrated. Makes a sibilant 'swee-swee-swee-swee, tree-tree-tree'. Usually in groups of two to eight, widespread in *Acacia* savanna and Kalahari scrub. Feeds in the outer canopies of trees, constantly on the move, flitting one after another from tree to tree. 9-10 cm. **557**

2 GREY PENDULINE TIT *Anthoscopus caroli.* Uncommon resident. Told by very small size, the underparts more buff or yellowish than the previous species, throat and breast pale grey. Makes a weak 'cheep' and has a squeaky, two-syllable song 'tshweewhee', first note highest. Occurs in small parties in broadleafed woodland; habits much the same as (1). 8-9 cm. **558**

3 RUFOUSBELLIED TIT *Parus rufiventris.* Rare, status not established; sparsely recorded in the extreme north-west. Entirely black head, cream-coloured eyes and rufous underparts distinctive. Immature duller, eyes brown, wing-feathers edged yellowish. Has a rasping call-note plus a repeated 'chick-wee, chick-wee...'. Frequents well-developed broadleafed woodland where it feeds in the mid- and upper strata. 15 cm. **556**

4 ASHY TIT (ACACIA GREY TIT) *Parus cinerascens.* Fairly common resident. Differs from the next species in *blue-grey* mantle and underparts; no tawny wash. The song is 'trewet-treet-treet-treet, tretretretretretretre' plus a prolonged rattling sound. Singly or in pairs in thornveld, *Acacia* savanna and Kalahari scrub. Widespread. Often in bird parties. 14 cm. **552**

5 SOUTHERN GREY TIT *Parus afer.* Not recorded in Botswana but its presence in the extreme east of Namibia is well documented; may therefore occur in the extreme west. Distinguished from the previous species by *grey-brown* (not blue-grey) mantle and back, tawny underparts, shorter tail. The call is a rapid 'tsitsi-kr-kr-kr-kr', the song a shrill 'chee ree ree, chee ree ree, chee ree ree chip...teree teree teree, pee-peeoo pee-peeoo pee-peeoo...' with variations. Frequents small trees and bushes in arid thornveld and scrub. 13 cm. **551**

6 SOUTHERN BLACK TIT *Parus niger.* Fairly common to locally common resident. A small black bird with white edges to the wing-feathers; female and immature greyer. The call is a harsh and rasping 'twiddy, zeet-zeet-zeet' or 'zeu-zeu-zeu-twit'. The song, less often heard, is a shrill 'tiroo, tiroo, tiroo, peeit-woo, peeit-woo, peeit-woo, pee-wirrit, pee-wirrit, pee-wirrit...' with variations and interspersed with harsh grating sounds. Usually in pairs, often in mixed bird parties in a wide variety of woodland habitats in the east and north. 16 cm. **554**

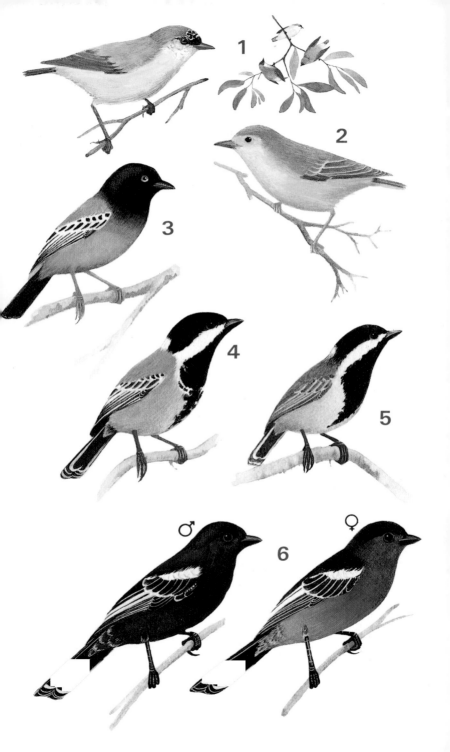

Babblers. Family TIMALIIDAE. Insectivorous and partially frugivorous, noisy thrush-like birds of gregarious habits and with distinctive babbling calls. Feed mostly in the lower stratum of woodland or on the ground. The sexes are alike.

1 ARROWMARKED BABBLER *Turdoides jardineii*. Common resident. Identified by whitish, *arrow-like streaks* on the head, mantle and underparts (cf. Whiterumped Babbler (3) which has scale-like markings plus white rump and vent). The immature lacks arrow-marks (see illustration) but has *dark spotting on the upper breast*, differing mainly in this from the immature of the next species. The call is a noisy, excitable whirring started by one bird and taken up by the entire party until it resembles hysterical giggling, 'scurrurrur-rururrurrurr...': harsher, more mechanical-sounding than that of the Redbilled Woodhoopoe (pp.200-201) and of lower pitch than the calls of the next two species. Noisy, conspicuous parties of six to ten occur in woodland, riverine forests and hillside thickets in the north and east. 23-25 cm. **560**

2 PIED BABBLER *Turdoides bicolor*. Common resident. Entirely white except for black wings and tail; immature closely similar to that of previous species but *lacks dark breast-spots*; accompanying adults should clarify. The call is a high-pitched babbling, one bird beginning 'sk-sk-sk-sk-skerr-skerr-skerr-skerr...' and all others in the party joining in; shriller than that of (1). Parties frequent dry thornveld, dry woodland and Kalahari scrub, being widespread and present in most regions. 26 cm. **563**

3 WHITERUMPED BABBLER *Turdoides leucopygius*. Common, localised resident. Differs from (1) in having a white rump, underbelly and vent, the head, mantle and breast have all feathers pale-edged, giving a scaly appearance; the immature has a paler throat. The call is a noisy, high-pitched babbling 'kwekwekwekwekwekwekwe...' or 'papapapapapapapapa...' similar to that of the next species. Parties occur in mature riverine forests, reeds and papyrus of the Chobe-Linyanti-Okavango River systems. Habits much the same as other babblers. 26 cm. **562**

4 BLACKFACED BABBLER *Turdoides melanops*. Uncommon, localised resident. Black mask and yellow eyes diagnostic. The call is similar to that of the previous species, a shrill 'papapapapa-papapapa...' by many birds in a party. Small groups occur in grass and thickets within both broadleafed and *Acacia* savanna in the extreme north-west. Shy and secretive, usually keeping within dense cover. 28 cm. **561**

236

Thrushes, chats and robins. Family TURDIDAE. Arboreal, terrestrial-feeding, insectivorous or frugivorous birds. Many are good songsters, the songs of some robins rating as the finest in southern Africa. Sexes alike unless otherwise stated; all have spotted young.

1 GROUNDSCRAPER THRUSH *Turdus litsitsirupa.* Fairly common resident. Grey-brown upperparts and white, spotted underparts distinctive; cf. Dusky Lark (pp.216-217) which has a stouter bill and darker upperparts; in flight the wings look distinctly orange. The immature has buff tips to the feathers of the upperparts plus *orange flanks*; cf.immature of next species. Has a chuckling call note and a brisk, fairly shrill song 'trrooee-tli-tli-trrooee, troo-troo, tweet-tweet-chichiruchee-tru-chitrroo...' the phrases continually varied, with pauses between. Widespread, frequenting broadleafed and *Acacia* savanna, Kalahari scrub and overgrazed areas around cattle posts. Feeds on the ground, scratching about in leaf debris but resorts to trees when alarmed and to sing. 22 cm. **580**

2 OLIVE THRUSH *Turdus olivaceus.* Rare, very localised resident; occurs only in the south-east. Much duller than the next species, differing in *speckled throat* (see enlarged head illustration) and lack of white on the belly. Immature speckled blackish below. On the ground or in flight calls 'wheet'; from a tree sings a mellow 'trootee-trootee-trootee-trootee, treetrrroo...' in spring and autumn. Singly or in pairs in riverine bush, but mainly in suburban gardens. Males display by walking with drooped wings and fanned tail dragging on the ground. 24 cm. **577**

3 KURRICHANE THRUSH *Turdus libonyana.* Common resident. Normally told from the previous species by brighter colours, white eyebrows and distinct black and white throat-markings; see enlarged head illustration. However, a dark morph of this species occurs locally, when confusion with (2) is possible. Immature with spotted breast as illustrated; cf. Groundscraper Thrush (1). Calls a loud 'peet-peeoo, peet-peeoo', the song a mellow series of trills and warbles in short outbursts. Singly or in pairs in various wooded habitats, including suburbia, throughout the north and east. 22 cm. **576**

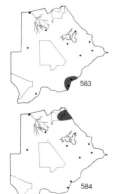

4 SHORT-TOED ROCK THRUSH *Monticola brevipes.* Uncommon, localised resident. Male distinguished by blue-grey head and *mantle*, the crown *sometimes* paler but race *M.b.pretoriae* in Botswana does *not* have pale crown; female by *whitish central throat* and dark brown upper tail. Immature spotted blackish above and below. Has a clear, whistled song, details not recorded. Singly or in pairs in bush-covered, rock-strewn hills of the south-east. 18 cm. **583**

5 MIOMBO ROCK THRUSH (ANGOLA ROCK THRUSH) *Monticola angolensis.* Rare and localised, possibly resident; recorded very sparsely in *Brachystegia* (Miombo) woodland in the extreme north-east. Male distinguished by grey upperparts speckled black, orange breast and white belly, female by brown upperparts speckled and streaked black, plus whitish underparts with orange breast. Immature like female but speckled on underparts. Has a sweet and varied song 'pe-pe-per-pee-pew, per-per, pee-pew...' Forages on the ground; is *not* associated with rocky habitats. 18 cm. **584**

1 ANTEATING CHAT *Myrmecocichla formicivora.* Common to locally very common resident. Entirely dull brown, the white shoulder patch frequently absent; pale wing feathers look translucent in flight. The immature has plumage washed rusty. The call is a loud 'peeek' given frequently; the song a slow series of mellow notes 'prreeet-chu, prreeet-chu, chirri-chu, chirri-chu, preee, preee, preee, pru, pirri-preee...'. Singly, in pairs or small groups in grasslands, *Acacia* savanna, open regions in woodland, airstrips, road verges and Kalahari scrub. Mainly terrestrial in habit, feeding in grass, perching on termite mounds, low bushes and fences, and making brief, fluttering flights. 18 cm. **595**

2 MOCKING CHAT *Thamnolaea cinnamomeiventris.* Uncommon, localised resident found in the east and south-east. Sexes differ as illustrated; immature like female. Has various mellow calls and an attractive, rambling song, mostly involving imitations of other bird calls. Occurs in pairs on rocky hills with bushes. A cheerful, lively species that habitually raises its rear end after settling. 20-23 cm. **593**

3 BOULDER CHAT *Pinarornis plumosus.* Fairly common, localised resident. Sooty-brown except for white in the wings and tail; immature similar. Makes a monotonous squeaking 'ink, ink, wink, wink' like an unoiled wheel, plus a clear whistle and a pleasant warbling with the bill held vertically. This species is confined to the well-wooded lower slopes of hills with granite boulders in the north-east. Usually in pairs or small family groups. Lively and agile, hopping and bounding over rocks and raising and lowering its tail when stopping. 23-27 cm. **610**

1 (EUROPEAN) WHEATEAR *Oenanthe oenanthe*. Status not established; may prove to be a very rare summer visitor. Non-breeding plumages illustrated. Both sexes have striking T-shaped tail pattern, displayed in flight and when characteristically bowing with tail raised high; *cf. immature of next species*. Generally silent in Africa and very rare anywhere in southern Africa. Usually solitary in open, dry terrain with sparse grass or stony ground. 16 cm. **585**

2 MOUNTAIN CHAT *Oenanthe monticola*. Exact status not established; recorded once in the extreme south-west. May occur more regularly along the Molopo and Nossob valleys. Male variable as illustrated (a) and (b), *may even be white from lower breast to tail*, but white rump and under-tail coverts diagnostic; white shoulder patches sometimes absent. Immature like female. Usually silent, but male has a rich, fluty song of jumbled notes. Frequents sandy valleys with scrub and rocks, or dry watercourses. Stands conspicuously on rocks, termite mounds or low bushes; may fly upwards a short distance, drop down and fly off low to another perch. Bold and confiding. 17-20 cm. **586**

586

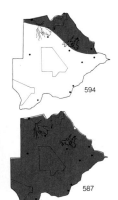

3 ARNOT'S CHAT *Thamnolaea arnoti*. Fairly common resident. Superficially resembles the previous species but their distributions are mutually exclusive. Black birds, male with white cap, female with white throat, both with white shoulders. The song involves a musical 'feeeeee' ascending and descending the scale. Pairs and small parties in the northern *Mopane* woodlands. Hops about the trunks, on fallen trees and on the ground; lively and conspicuous. 18 cm. **594**

594

587

4 CAPPED WHEATEAR *Oenanthe pileata*. Common resident. Adult unmistakable. At all ages has striking T-shape on upper tail. Immature lacks the black crown, mask and breast-band, eyebrows barely discernible, underparts smoky-brown, breast spotted causing misidentification of (1); *see illustration and cf. female of (1)*. Sings from some low prominence or while fluttering above ground, the song variable with imitations of other birds. Singly or in loose groups on arid, open ground, dry riverbeds and stony plains. Walks about with much wing-flicking and tail-bobbing, perches conspicuously on rocks, termite hills or low bushes and makes exaggerated bows, displaying tail. Widespread. 18 cm. **587**

4

J

The following four species are very alike in appearance and habits. All frequent open ground, perch conspicuously and flick their wings. All have races showing plumage colour variations, darkest in the eastern and palest in the western forms with graduations between the extremes. Most make quiet 'chak-chak' sounds. Identity best confirmed by colours of tails and upper tail-coverts.

1 SICKLEWINGED CHAT *Cercomela sinuata.* Rare, localised visitor; occasional in the extreme south. Closely resembles the next species but dumpier, wing feathers more distinctly edged rufous, legs longer and eye-wattle more accentuated; upper tail dark with buff outer edges forming a *dark triangle* in flight, only upper tail-coverts rufous. Immature as illustrated, tail pattern as adult. Occurs in sparse grassland and similar semi-arid conditions. 15 cm. **591**

2 FAMILIAR CHAT *Cercomela familiaris.* Fairly common resident. Very similar to the previous species but slimmer, less dumpy-looking, buffy edges to wing feathers less obvious, upper tail *rich rusty-rufous* with dark central feathers and subterminal band giving *dark T-shape* in flight. Tail pattern only way to distinguish immatures of this and (1). Occurs singly or in pairs on rocky, wooded hillsides, in dry woodland, *Acacia* savanna and Kalahari scrub. Tame and confiding near human habitations. Perches on fences, posts, bushes, termite mounds etc. flicking its wings more frequently than other chats. 15 cm. **589**

3 TRACTRAC CHAT *Cercomela tractrac.* Exact status not established. Occurs sparsely in the Kalahari Gemsbok National Park and individuals probably enter Botswana at this point occasionally. Slightly smaller, plumper than other similar chats, underparts much paler, whitish, upper tail pattern shows *broad white area with dark terminal triangle*. When alarmed calls a sharp 'trac-trac'. Singly or in small, loose groups in arid grassland and shrubby patches in desert and semi-desert, runs on ground or perches on some low prominence, flicks wings and jerks its tail. 14-15 cm. **590**

4 KAROO CHAT *Cercomela schlegelii.* Exact status not established. May occur sparsely at the western end of the Molopo River, this being the northern extremity of its Cape range. Larger, more robust than other similar chats, greyer in general colour, especially underparts, the *tail dark with white outer tail feathers only*, rump grey. The call is a rattling 'tirr-tit-tat'. Singly or in pairs in calcrete flats and slopes with sparse scrub cover in semi-desert. Perches on some low prominence, fluttering its wings on landing, drops to the ground to feed. 15-18 cm. **592**

1 STONECHAT *Saxicola torquata*. Fairly common resident but uncommon winter visitor to the south-east. Male conspicuous and unmistakable. Female best told by white lateral rump, often visible at rest, but some females show a white eyebrow, this making for confusion with (2). In flight both sexes told by *broad white rump and wing patches*. Immature like female but more spotted. Makes a grating 'tsak, tsak' like two stones being clapped together, or 'seep-tsak-tsak' and has a short, shrill, warbling song. Usually in pairs in a variety of open habitats, stony grass shores of dams, pans, sewage ponds and rivers, fallow lands, road verges; in the northern wetlands in reed and papyrus islands. Perches on some low bush, weed or post and watches the ground for insects. 14 cm. **596**

2 WHINCHAT *Saxicola rubetra*. Very rare summer vagrant; recorded twice in the Okavango Delta. Non-breeding male resembles female, but may occur in either plumage. Both sexes told from previous species by *white eyebrows in combination with white malar streak* plus heavily streaked upperparts. In flight shows white wing patches and white *tail-base* (not rump). Habits and preferred habitats much the same as for the previous species. 13-14 cm. **597**

3 WHITETHROATED ROBIN *Cossypha humeralis*. Uncommon to fairly common resident. Distinguished by white breast and white wing bar; the immature is well spotted like all young robins. Early mornings calls repeatedly 'swee-swer, swee-swer...'; alarm note a quiet 'tseep, tseep, tseep...'. Also has a pretty, subdued song. Singly or in pairs in thickets in dense woodland and riverine bush, gardens or at the base of rocky, wooded hills and termitaria. Stays mostly within cover, foraging on the ground. 16-18 cm. **602**

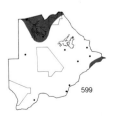

4 HEUGLIN'S ROBIN *Cossypha heuglini*. Fairly common localised resident. Identified by entirely rich orange underparts and black cap with prominent white eye-stripes. Immature duller, spotted. An accomplished songster having various rich, melodious phrases which start quietly and work up to a crescendo 'pip-pip-uree, pip-pip-uree...' or 'don't-you-do-it, don't-you-do-it, don't-you-DO-IT' ending ubruptly, or 'tirrootirree, tirrootirree, tirrootirree...' each phrase repeated up to 16 times. Sings mostly at dawn and dusk, often two birds in duet. Generally inhabits dense thickets in riverine forests, singing from within cover. In the Okavango, Linyanti and Limpopo systems spends much time in the mid-stratum of mature riverine forest, from where it sings conspicuously. 19-20 cm. **599**

1 WHITEBROWED ROBIN (WHITEBROWED SCRUB ROBIN) *Erythropygia leucophrys*. Common resident. A small, brownish robin with white eyebrows and wing markings plus well-streaked breast. When flying the fanned tail shows white tips; see small illustration. Immature similar but upperparts mottled. Sings for long periods in the heat of the day, various loud phrases repeated almost without pause, 'pirit-pirit, tertwee . . . pirit-pirit, tertwee . . . chee, chee, choochu-it-chu-it . . . chiroo-chu, chu-chiroo . . . perpwee, perpwee, tirrittirrit . . .' Usually singly in broadleafed woodland and *Acacia* savanna; avoids the more arid regions. Sings from an exposed bush-top, otherwise secretive and largely terrestrial. 15 cm. **613**

2 KALAHARI ROBIN *Erythropygia paena*. Common resident. A pale, sandy-looking robin with conspicuous rufous tail having a black subterminal band and white tips; see illustration. Immature has lightly spotted underparts. Often perches on a bush calling 'twee' intermittently for long periods. The song is a repeated sequence of high-pitched phrases 'seeoo-seeoo, tweetoo-tweetootweetoo, seetoo-seetoo, tritritritritri . . .'. Singly or in pairs in *Acacia* savanna and Kalahari scrub. Feeds on open ground but enters thorn thickets when alarmed. Widespread even in the more arid regions. 16-17 cm. **615**

3 BEARDED ROBIN *Erythropygia quadrivirgata*. Rare localised resident. Identified by white eyebrows with black lines above and below, plus white throat with black moustacial streaks and dull, pale orange breast. Immature more spotted and scaled above and below. The song is loud and clear, a series of pleasant phrases each repeated three or four times with brief pauses 'pee-pee-pee, terrtree, chiroo-chiroo-chiroo, witchoo-witchoo-witchoo, pee-pee-peepee, chu-it, chu-it, chu-it . . .', some phrases rising in crescendo. Largely terrestrial unless singing. 16-18 cm. **617**

4 COLLARED PALM THRUSH *Cichladusa arquata*. Not recorded in Botswana but occurs in the Zambezi valley close to the Chobe River. Identified by rufous colouring of upperparts plus yellow throat with distinctive black gorget and yellow eyes. Immature mottled below, black gorget vestigial. Has a melodious, liquid song heard most mornings and evenings. Pairs and small parties are found where *Hyphaene* palms occur. Lively and conspicuous, spends much time foraging on the ground. When perched on a branch droops its wings and raises and lowers its tail continuously. 19 cm. **603**

Warblers. Family SYLVIIDAE. Small, insectivorous birds of mostly sombre colouring. Several species visit southern Africa from Europe during summer, and many have attractive warbling songs which are an aid to identification. Sexes alike in all species.

1 WILLOW WARBLER *Phylloscopus trochilus.* Common summer visitor. The yellow form illustrated becomes much paler, less yellow in mid-summer, while an entirely brown form with whitish underparts also occurs. Best identified at all times by *distinct eyebrows and scalloped tail-tip*, plus call and behaviour; smaller than the next species, never as yellow. While feeding calls a querulous, quiet 'foo-wee', rising on the last syllable. Sings, usually early mornings September-November and February-March, a pleasant, descending jumble of notes repeated every 10-15 seconds 'tee-tee-tee-tee-tu-tu-tu-twee-twee-sweet-sweet-sweet-sweet...' Widespread in almost any wooded habitat, including suburbia, and is very common in the better developed woodland. An active leaf-gleaner that works its way busily through the canopy and mid-stratum, occasionally darting out to seize a flying insect. 12 cm. **643**

2 ICTERINE WARBLER *Hippolais icterina.* Common summer visitor. Larger than the previous species, usually more yellow with clearly yellow-edged wing coverts, sharply sloping forehead, orange lower mandible and *non-scalloped* tail-tip. Sings a repetitive, vehement jumble of warbled notes, some pleasant, others harsh. Widespread. Usually singly but can be found in some numbers in *Acacia* thornveld and savanna where it feeds and sings while hopping about actively in the tree canopies. 14-15 cm. **625**

3 GARDEN WARBLER *Sylvia borin.* Rare summer visitor. A plain-coloured warbler with no distinctive markings. Usually located by song, a quiet warbling of rather monotonous quality uttered from the depth of a bush. Always singly in dense bush thickets, especially along watercourses and in gardens. Secretive, widespread but sparse. 15 cm. **619**

4 THRUSH NIGHTINGALE *Luscinia luscinia.* Rare mid-summer visitor. Normally a visitor to central Africa where it arrives in December; records for northern Botswana indicate overshoot, but a few may occur more regularly. Tail- and wing-feather margins rich rufous, underparts whitish with *mottled breast.* The song is a rich melody of variable notes, some sweet, some harsh. Returns to the same thicket each year, often in riverine bush, where it sings from a low perch, but very secretive. 16-18 cm. **609**

5 OLIVETREE WARBLER *Hippolais olivetorum.* Rare summer visitor. A comparatively large warbler with white eyebrows, sharply sloping forehead, large two-coloured bill and pale outer edges to wing feathers and tail-tip. Song louder and deeper than most warblers, a grating jumble of notes with sharp 'tch-tch' sounds interspersed; similar to the song of the Great Reed Warbler (pp.252-253). Singly in riverine bush and *Acacia* savanna. Feeds and sings from within the foliage of the mid-stratum. A scarce visitor but probably regular in small numbers, having been recorded at widely scattered points. 16-18 cm. **626**

1 WHITETHROAT *Sylvia communis*. Uncommon summer visitor. Identified by white throat contrasting with pale buff breast, pale eye-ring, *prominent rufous wing-feather edges* and white outer tail feathers. The crown feathers are frequently raised and impart a *peaked appearance to the head*. Has a sharp 'tacc-tacc' call, a conversational 'wheet, wheet, whit-whit-whit-whit' and a brisk, scratchy warble. A restless, lively species found in thickets, particularly in thornveld and Kalahari scrub. Widespread, frequenting *Acacia* tree canopies and small, scrubby bushes. If disturbed darts off at speed, the white outer tail feathers prominent. 15 cm. **620**

2 RIVER WARBLER *Locustella fluviatilis*. Very rare summer visitor; one confirmed record from Francistown. Difficult to identify (or even see) in the field. White chin radiates in streaks onto throat, breast faintly blotched, tail rounded, *large undertail coverts* with pale edges to feather-tips. Makes an intermittent, cricket-like 'zer, zer, zer, zer...'. Highly secretive in dense thickets, reedbeds and other herbage near rivers, creeping about low down; when alarmed drops to the ground and *runs* away. Easily overlooked. 13 cm. **627**

3 TITBABBLER *Parisoma subcaeruleum*. Common resident. A small greyish bird with bright whitish eyes, boldly streaked breast and *rufous vent*. Immature similar but lacks breast-streaking. Calls frequently, a variety of clear, ringing, quickly rendered notes, typically 'cheriktiktik' or 'chuu-ti, chuu-ti chuu chuu'. Widespread in a variety of wooded habitats, preferring dry thornveld, riverine bush and scrub. Highly active and mobile, feeding and calling from the tree canopies. 15 cm. **621**

4 GREAT REED WARBLER *Acrocephalus arundinaceus*. Uncommon summer visitor. Best known by very large size (for a warbler) and characteristic song; a slow, harsh warble 'gurk-gurk, twee-twee, gurk-gurk, trrit-trrit, gackle, kurra-kurra...' Occurs singly in reedbeds, waterside thickets or dense bush away from water. Usually detected by call but is less secretive, more inquisitive than most reed warblers, occasionally perching conspicuously, its movements heavy. 19 cm. **628**

5 GREATER SWAMP WARBLER *Acrocephalus rufescens*. Uncommon, localised resident. A fairly large warbler with prominent, slender bill, dark upperparts, dusky underparts and dark legs; no eyebrows. Has a loud song with guttural notes 'churr-churr, chirrup, chuckle', shivering its tail while singing; also makes an occasional 'churr' or 'chirr-up' sound. Found in permanent papyrus and reedbeds of the Okavango Delta, but secretive. Best located by song. 18 cm. **636**

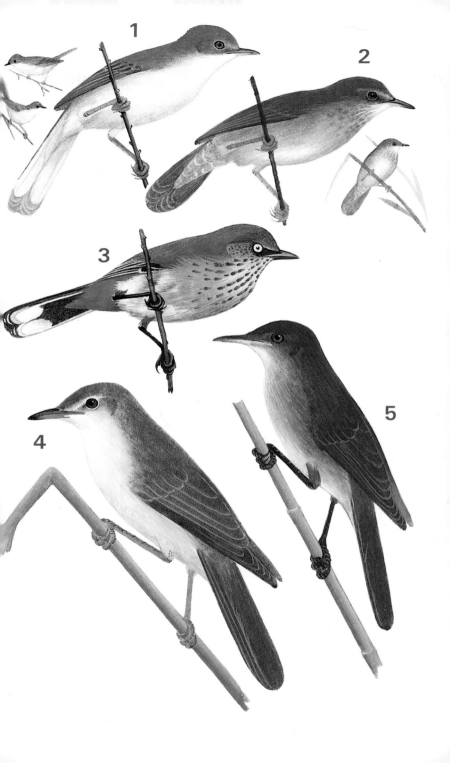

1 EUROPEAN SEDGE WARBLER *Acrocephalus schoenobaenus.* Uncommon summer visitor. Recognised by boldly marked upperparts, especially eye-stripes, streaked crown and faintly blotched breast. Feeding call a quiet 'tick, tick...', alarm call a harsh, rasping 'churrr'. Has a loud, hurried song with little repetition, chattering, trilling and sweet passages mixed with imitations of other birds. Singly or in small groups in dense riverine vegetation, reedbeds, marsh fringes and thickets *away from water.* Creeps about at low level. 13 cm. **634**

2 AFRICAN MARSH WARBLER *Acrocephalus baeticatus.* Fairly common localised resident. No distinctive eyebrows (cf.next species), underparts predominantly white, legs purple-brown. Makes a sharp 'tik' while creeping about in thick cover, plus a harsh, rachet-like 'churrr' when alarmed. Song a nasal warbling of slow tempo 'churr-churr-churr-chirruc-chirruc-chirruc-pui-pui-pui...' for long periods with few imitations; cf. (6). In reeds and other dense herbage near water or away from water in tall grass and thickets. Remains well hidden but moves about constantly, disturbing the foliage as it does so. 13 cm. **631**

3 CAPE REED WARBLER *Acrocephalus gracilirostris.* Fairly common resident. Larger than the previous species but similar, differing in *white eyebrows,* dark brown legs. The song is a melodious 'chir-roo, chirroo, tiririri, chirroorirroochoo-chooo-chooo-chirroee', slowly at first, then fast; does not sing continuously like some other warblers. Singly or in pairs *always near water,* in reeds or other waterside herbage. Bold and inquisitive. 17 cm. **635**

4 AFRICAN SEDGE WARBLER *Bradypterus baboecala.* Fairly common but localised resident. Upperparts dark, *tail broad and rounded,* definite eye-stripe plus faint markings on the upper breast. Call a loud, distinctive 'cruk, cruk, cruk, crukcrukcrukcrukcrukcrukcruk' like a stick being drawn across a railing, this followed by wing-snapping. Singly or in pairs in dense vegetation *over water.* Secretive, mostly in the lower stratum. 17 cm. **638**

5 EUROPEAN MARSH WARBLER *Acrocephalus palustris.* Uncommon summer visitor. Eyebrows indistinct, underparts (except throat) lightly washed yellow-buff, upperparts including rump uniformly olivaceous-brown. Makes a frequent 'tcchh' while creeping about in cover; cf. (2). Has a pleasant, liquid chattering song involving mostly imitations of other bird songs; heard mid-summer until departure in March or early April. Singly in thickets in woodland, stands of tangled grass, dense canopies of *Acacia* trees and reeds, but mostly found away from water. Sings for long periods while moving about *within cover.* 12 cm. **633**

6 EUROPEAN REED WARBLER *Acrocephalus scirpaceus.* Very rare summer visitor; recorded once in northern Botswana. Only three records in total for southern Africa. Very similar to previous species but has rufous tinge to rump and upper tail coverts, legs dark brown. The song is inseparable from that of (2). Frequents reedbeds or dense cover away from water. 13 cm. **630**

1 BARTHROATED APALIS *Apalis thoracica.* Uncommon resident. Pale eyes and black throat-bar separating white throat from pale yellow underparts diagnostic; female may have narrow throat-bar or none. Has a loud, distinctive call 'pilly-pilly-pilly...'; often in duet, the female calling much faster than the male. In pairs in dense woodland on hillsides, in valleys and along streams in the eastern regions, but sparse. Lively, noisy little birds. 12-13 cm. **645**

2 YELLOWBREASTED APALIS *Apalis flavida.* Uncommon resident. Very small warbler with greenish upperparts, grey cap (variable in extent) and yellow breast on white underparts, male with a small black bar on central breast. The normal call is 'skee skee skee chizzick chizzick chizzick...' to which the mate replies 'krik krik krik...'. Usually in pairs in riverine forest, thornveld and mixed woodland. A highly active leaf-gleaner, foraging in the outer canopy of small trees and bushes. 10-12,5 cm. **648**

3 LONGBILLED CROMBEC *Sylvietta rufescens.* Fairly common resident. Tailless appearance diagnostic, the immature similar. The call is a loud, urgent-sounding 'tree-cheer, tree-cheer, tree-cheer...'. Singly or in pairs in dry thornveld, mixed woodland and savanna, often in mixed bird parties. Gleans insects busily from twigs and branches, often low down, then darts off in undulating flight to the next tree. Widespread and common in arid regions. 10-12 cm. **651**

4 BURNTNECKED EREMOMELA *Eremomela usticollis.* Uncommon resident. Told by small size, blue-grey upperparts, yellow-buff underparts, rusty-brown markings on ear coverts and throat plus pale eyes with brown eye-rings. Immature lacks brown markings on ear coverts and throat, has dark eyes. The call is a rapid, high-pitched 'teeup, titititititi...' followed by a short trill. In groups of two to five in *Acacia* savanna and mixed woodland, feeding in the thorn canopies and often mixing with other small warblers. Widespread but sparse in the northern, eastern and south-eastern regions. 12 cm. **656**

5 YELLOWBELLIED EREMOMELA *Eremomela icteropygialis.* Fairly common resident. Distinguished by grey-brown upperparts, dark line through eyes, off-white breast and yellow ventral region from lower breast to vent. Compared to Cape Penduline Tit (pp. 234-235) is larger, has darker upperparts and yellow on belly only. Has a lively song 'chirri-chee-chee-choo' or 'How are you two?'. Usually singly or in pairs, often in mixed bird parties, in *Acacia* savanna, mixed woodland and Kalahari scrub. Widespread but particularly common in the arid regions. Forages in the outer and lower branches of small trees and bushes. 9-10 cm. **653**

6 GREENCAPPED EREMOMELA *Eremomela scotops.* Rare resident. Told by dark green upperparts, pale yellow underparts, grey lores and *yellow eyes with red eye-rings.* Makes a rapid, excitable chattering 'tru tru tru trrutrrutrrutrrutrrutrretrreetrreetree...' usually by two or more birds simultaneously and accompanied by audible wing-snaps. Occurs in broadleafed woodland in the north, usually in small, active parties which forage in the canopies and indulge in much chasing between individuals. 12 cm. **655**

1 BLEATING WARBLER *Camaroptera brachyura*. Fairly common resident. Told by very small size, call and behaviour. Upperparts grey in summer, ashy-brown in winter, wings and tail olive-green. Best detected by characteristic bleating alarm note 'bzeeeb' or, in summer, a loud clapping call continued for long periods 'chirrup, chirrup, chirrup...' or 'chivvit, chivvit, chivvit...' from fairly high in a bush. Occurs in dense thickets in thornveld, woodland, bush-covered termitaria and hillsides in the less arid regions. Secretive when not calling, creeping about in tangled undergrowth near the ground with tail raised beyond the vertical. 12 cm. **657**

2 BARRED WARBLER *Cameroptera fasciolata*. Fairly common resident. Breeding male more buffy below than (3), with dark-banded overlay, breast brown, face mottled, eyes grey; female and non-breeding male entirely buff below, darkly barred face to vent. Normal call 'brrzeeet-brrzeeet-brrzeeet-brrzeeet' uttered in bursts of three to five, or 'trree-ti-ti-ti-ti-ti' repeated. In pairs in well-developed *Acacia*, *Mopane* and dry riverine woodland. Secretive, creeps about in dense thickets, gradually working its way to the top before flitting to the next, the tail held raised when alarmed. However often noisy. Range overlaps with (3) apparently only around Francistown. 13-15 cm. **658**

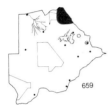

3 STIERLING'S BARRED WARBLER *Cameroptera stierlingi*. Rare resident. Whiter, more clearly barred below at all times than (2), tail shorter, eyes orange-brown; sexes alike. Has a far-carrying, much repeated call 'birribit-birribit-birribit' in sequences of three to five. Occurs in the northern regions frequenting broadleafed woodland, often in bush-covered termitaria. Behaviour much like (2) but, when alarmed, flies into the tree canopy. 11,5-13 cm. **659**

Cisticolas. Small, closely similar, brown grass warblers. Breeding and non-breeding plumages often differ markedly as do tail-lengths and, frequently, the sexes, but best identified by song, habitat preference and behaviour.

4 FANTAILED CISTICOLA *Cisticola juncidis*. Fairly common resident. Female resembles non-breeding male. Conspicuous only in summer when male cruises at a height of about 30 m with dipping flight, calling 'tink, tink, tink, tink...' at two second intervals, each note synchronising with a dip; this call also made while perched. Found in grassland, marshes, pans and fallow lands. When alarmed perches on a grass stem and flicks its tail sideways. Flight jerky with fanned tail cocked upwards. 10-12 cm. **664**

5 DESERT CISTICOLA *Cisticola aridula*. Fairly common resident. Similar to the previous species but less boldly marked. In summer male sings during display flight or when perched, a high-pitched 'zink ... zink ... zink ...'; when alarmed darts about erratically calling 'tuc ... tuc ...' accompanied by wing-snaps. Occurs in similar habitat to (4) but extends into arid grassland, especially near salt pans. Breeding male displays with erratic, zig-zagging flight above grass, calling as above. 10-12 cm. **665**

6 PALECROWNED CISTICOLA *Cisticola brunnescens*. Not illustrated. Exact status not established. Recorded once only on the edge of the Okavango Delta. In summer male distinguished by *pale crown*. Both sexes have black spot between bill and eyes, otherwise almost inseparable on appearances in the field from previous two species. Male calls in flight or from a perch a quietly repeated 'siep-siep-siep ...' followed by almost inaudible notes 'wee-twee-twee-ti-ti-ti-ti-ti-ti-ti-ti-tsee-tsee'. Occurs in short, moist grassland but inconspicuous. 9-11 cm. **668**

1 BLACKBACKED CISTICOLA *Cisticola galactotes.* Common, localised resident. Distinguished by *boldly marked, blackish back and habitat.* Similar to the next species but has discrete distribution; the only black-backed cisticola in the north. Immature has underparts sulphur-yellow; see illustrations. Calls a rasping 'zreeee' or 'rraaare' often interspersed with various 'chirps' or 'chit-chit-chit' or 'trrrp-trrrp-trrrp'. When alarmed calls a loud, deliberate 'PRRRIT-PRRRIT-PRRRIT...'. Occurs in the Okavango and Linyanti waterways, frequenting papyrus and reedbeds. Noticeable when breeding, otherwise unobtrusive. 12-13 cm. **675**

2 LEVAILLANT'S CISTICOLA *Cisticola tinniens.* Rare, exact status not established. Recorded once near Lobatse in July. Similar to the previous species but distribution discrete; the only black-backed cisticola in the south-east. Immature duller, rustier, the face (occasionally the breast) lightly sulphured. Calls 'chi-chi-chirrueee', the first two notes nearly inaudible, final phrase loud; alarm call 'tsing, tsing, tsing...'. Frequents reeds, grasses and sedges bordering streams, dams and marshes, also rank grass away from water. Perches and calls conspicuously when breeding. 11-15 cm. **677**

3 RATTLING CISTICOLA *Cisticola chiniana.* Common resident. A robust cisticola with few distinguishing features; rusty crown may be plain or streaked, seasonal differences slight. Immature duller, rustier. The characteristic song is loud with a distinct rattling quality 'chi-chi-chi-chrrrrrr'; when agitated calls 'chee-chee-chee...'. Frequents *Acacia* savanna, mixed dry woodland and Kalahari scrub, foraging low down in the lower stratum of tangled grass and bush. Widespread and conspicuous in the less arid regions, calling for much of the year from the top of a bush. 11-15 cm. **672**

4 TINKLING CISTICOLA *Cisticola rufilata.* Fairly common resident. Best identified by reddish head markings, white eyebrows, long orange-brown tail and distinctive call. Similar in size to the previous species, but altogether more rufous. Immature duller. The song is a series of tinkling bell-like notes uttered while perched on a shrub or tree, 'tweee, tweee, tweee', the alarm call a twittering 'dee-du-du-e-e-e'. Inhabits dry Kalahari scrub, stunted *Acacia* savanna and secondary growth fringing dry broadleafed woodland. Widespread but secretive, best located by call. 12-13 cm. **671**

5 CHIRPING CISTICOLA *Cisticola pipiens.* Common, localised resident. Non-breeding plumage illustrated; breeding plumage (during rains) less rufous about face and underparts, greyer on mantle, tail shorter; appears rufous at all times. Immature whiter below. The song, in hovering flight or while perched, is four twanging notes repeated 'trrrit-trrrit-trree-trreeeeee...'. Occurs alongside (1) in the Okavango Delta and Linyanti Swamp inhabiting papyrus and reeds in water, or bushes and grasses on shoreline. Makes a hovering flight above the reeds while calling with fanned tail flirted side to side as though loose. 13-15 cm. **676**

1 LAZY CISTICOLA *Cisticola aberrans*. Rare localised resident. Appears plain-backed; non-breeding plumage (April-October) generally warmer rufous on upperparts, underparts more strongly suffused with ochre, tail-length constant. Immature more rusty. The song is a series of fairly loud metallic notes 'tu-hwee-tu-hwee-tu-hwee...' reaching a crescendo; the alarm call a loud 'breeerp' or 'tu-hweeee' usually uttered with the long tail cocked vertically. Frequents bushy granitic hillsides with rocks and long grass, often at the foot of the hill near a stream. Hops about on rocks and flirts its tail upwards like a prinia. 14-16 cm. **679**

2 REDFACED CISTICOLA *Cisticola erythrops*. Rare localised resident of the Chobe and Limpopo systems. A plain-backed cisticola, crown concolorous with rest of upperparts in all seasons, lores, eyebrows and ear coverts washed reddish, most strongly when not breeding. The call, loud and arresting, is 'wink-*wink*-WINK' getting louder with successive notes, or a series of eight to ten notes 'weep, weep, weep...' in a crescendo. Inhabits waterside vegetation. Secretive but calls frequently. 12-13 cm. **674**

3 CROAKING CISTICOLA *Cisticola natalensis*. Rare, exact status not established; one record for the extreme north-east. A large, heavy-bodied, thick-billed cisticola with well-streaked upperparts and lacking a rufous crown. Seasonal differences as illustrated; female smaller than male. Immature like non-breeding adult but bright sulphur below. When breeding the male cruises about a few metres above the ground with a loose wing action, uttering a harsh 'cru-cru-cru-cru-cru...'; also calls from a low bush, a harsh 'CHEE-FRO' or 'chip-MUNK'. Alarm call a frog-like 'tee-YRRR'. Frequents rank grass with scattered bushes, or grassy clearings in woodland, often feeding on the ground. Very active and conspicuous November-March. 13-17 cm. **678**

1 NEDDICKY (PIPING CISTICOLA) *Cisticola fulvicapilla*. Fairly common resident. A small, *plain-backed* cisticola with an unmarked rufous crown; immature similar, duller. Sings mostly in the summer for long periods 'chirrup-chirrup-chirrup-chirrup . . .'. The alarm call is a rapid ticking, often by several birds while flitting about in low scrub 'ticki-ticki-ticki-ticki-tickety-tickety-tickety . . .'. Pairs and small parties in grassy broadleafed woodland and thornveld in the less arid areas. The male sings from a high perch but otherwise frequents the lower stratum of tangled grass and bush. 10-11 cm.**681**

Prinia ?

2 RUFOUSEARED WARBLER *Malcorus pectoralis*. Uncommon resident. A prinia-like bird with black chest-band (width varies) and rufous ear patches. Characterised also by streaky upperparts and straggly tail-end; cf. prinia tails which are more usually square-ended. Has a loud, penetrating call 'tee tee tee tee' plus a quiet 'chit'. Frequents the drier western and southern regions in low Kalahari scrub, often near salt pans and along dry watercourses. Singly or in pairs; spends much time on the ground, often preferring to run than fly. The tail is usually held upright. 14-16 cm. **688**

3 BLACKCHESTED PRINIA *Prinia flavicans*. Common resident. Distinctive in summer when breeding; at other times the black breast-band is either absent or vestigial, the underparts more yellow. The immature resembles the non-breeding adult. The call, from the top of a small bush or weed, is a loud, much repeated and fairly rapid 'chip-chip-chip . . .' (closely similar to the call of the next species) plus an occasional 'zrrrrt zrrrrt zrrrrt' alarm note. Pairs and small parties forage in the lower stratum of *Acacia* savanna, Kalahari scrub, tangled thickets in woodland and along watercourses in grassland. The long tail is frequently held in the vertical position. Widespread, preferring more arid regions than (4) but overlapping with it in the east. 13-15 cm. **685**

4 TAWNYFLANKED PRINIA *Prinia subflava*. Fairly common to locally common resident. Told by clear white underparts, *rufous flanks* and red-brown wing edges. The immature has the underparts washed yellow. When disturbed makes a characteristic weeping sound 'sbeeeee-sbeeeee . . .'; the normal call is a loud, continuous 'przzt-przzt-przzt . . .' or 'trit-trit-trit . . .' similar to that of (1). Noisy and conspicuous, usually in parties of four to six in riverine vegetation, rank grass, tangled thorn thickets and suburban gardens, preferring moister regions than the previous species, but behaviour much the same, tail held vertically much of the time. 10-15 cm. **683**

Flycatchers. Family MUSCICAPIDAE. Small, insectivorous birds with prominent bristles protruding from the base of their bills. Many of the soberly coloured species catch insects on the ground or in flight while watching (still-hunting) from a low perch, while others, especially the colourful and ornate species, are leaf-gleaners in addition to hawking insects in short aerial sallies.

1 CHAT FLYCATCHER *Melaenornis infuscatus.* Fairly common resident. Superficially similar to the Familiar Chat (pp. 244-245) and the Marico Flycatcher (2) but larger, pale wing-feather edges more prominent with buffy underparts and uniformly brown tail. Confusion also possible with smaller Mousecoloured Flycatcher (pp. 268-269), but distributions mutually exclusive. The immature is heavily speckled as illustrated but markings of underparts less heavy than those of the immature of the next species. Not very voca, but calls 'chirr, chirr, cheep, chirr, chirr . . .'. A species of arid regions. Commonly perches on tops of bushes in open savanna, from where it flies to the ground to seize insects. Does not favour low perches like the next species. 20 cm. **697**

697

2 MARICO FLYCATCHER *Melaenornis mariquensis.* Common resident. Differs from similar flycatchers in *white underparts which contrast sharply with brown upperparts.* The immature is spotted whitish above, streaked dark on white below as illustrated, the streaking heavier than in immature of previous species. Calls a soft 'chew-week' or 'chreep-chiu'. Widespread in *Acacia* savanna, perching prominently on the outer branch of a bush, often quite low down, from where it watches for insects on the ground. 18 cm. **695**

695

3 MOUSECOLOURED FLYCATCHER (PALLID FLYCATCHER) *Melaenornis pallidus.* Uncommon resident; only recorded in the northern region. A dull-coloured, featureless bird, the underparts scarcely paler than the upperparts. Smaller than the Chat Flycatcher (1) and ecologically separated. Immature similar to immatures of (1) and (2) but feather edges of upperparts more buffy. Mostly quiet but has a jumbled song 'trree trree trroo trrip trroo trrrippy trroo trree . . .'. Usually in pairs, sometimes small groups, in broadleafed woodland. Still-hunts from a low branch. 15-17 cm. **696**

696

4 FISCAL FLYCATCHER *Sigelus silens.* Fairly common localised resident, mainly in the south-east with extensions of range in winter. Told from the similar Fiscal Shrike (pp. 274-275) in less robust bill, white 'windows' in the tail and white wing-bars extending only halfway along the folded wing, *not* to the shoulder. Female brown (not black) on upperparts; immature has underparts less boldly spotted than previous three immatures. Has a sibilant, rather weak song 'swee-swee-ur, see-swee-sippy-see . . .' in prolonged sequences. In pairs in light woodland and savanna where it perches prominently on a branch or post and flies to the ground to seize insects. 17-20 cm. **698**

698

1 SPOTTED FLYCATCHER *Muscicapa striata*. Fairly common summer visitor. Distinguished by dark-streaked crown and white underparts, faintly streaked greyish on breast and flanks. Occasionally makes a thin, sibilant, two-syllabled 'tze-ee' while flicking its wings. Occurs singly in both *Acacia* and broadleafed woodland, savanna and well-wooded suburbia. Still-hunts from a low branch beneath a tree canopy frequently returning to the same perch after catching an insect, flicking its wings after settling. An inconspicuous but widespread species, being equally common in both moist and arid woodland October-April. 14-15 cm. **689**

2 BLACK FLYCATCHER *Melaenornis pammelaina*. For full description and comparison with other all-black birds of similar size see pp.226-227.

3 FANTAILED FLYCATCHER *Myioparus plumbeus*. Uncommon resident. Differs from the next species mainly in behaviour plus *white outer tail feathers*. The immature is spotted brownish. The call is a loud, cheerful 'teeee-reeee', the second syllable lower than the first. Occurs singly or in pairs in broadleafed woodland, savanna and riverine forests. Calls frequently and *fans its tail while raising and lowering it,* constantly moving through the mid-stratum; cf. habits of the next species. Often joins bird parties. 14 cm. **693**

4 BLUEGREY FLYCATCHER *Muscicapa caerulescens*. Fairly common resident. Differs from the previous species in behaviour and lack of any white in the tail. Immature like that of (3) but lacking white in the tail. Calls 'tsip-tsip-tsip-tsip-tse-tslipip', though mostly silent. Usually singly in riverine forests and broadleafed woodland. Perches in the mid-stratum, remaining motionless for long periods while watching the ground for insects; also hawks flying insects, returning to the same perch. A quiet, inconspicuous species. 14-15 cm. **691**

1 PRIRIT BATIS *Batis pririt.* Common resident. Male almost in-distinguishable from male of Chinspot Batis (3) but usually has black flecks on flanks; female and immature lack the clear brown breast-band of (3), being washed orange-buff over throat, breast and flanks, eyebrows buff (not white). The call is a long, descending sequence of notes 'peep, peep, peep, peep ... choo, choo, choo, choo ...' as many as 100 times or more during the breeding season. Usually in pairs in dry *Acacia* savanna, thickets along watercourses and around pans, the distribution being mainly west of that of (3). Forages mostly in the mid- and lower strata. 12 cm. **703**

2 PARADISE FLYCATCHER *Terpsiphone viridis.* Fairly common summer resident. The only small flycatcher with orange-brown upper-parts, blue-grey head and underparts; male unmistakable, female sometimes with slightly elongated central tail feathers. Immature like female, duller. The call is a sharp 'zwee-zwer', the song a lively, trilling 'wee-te-tiddly, wit-wit'. Highly active and vociferous little birds found among large trees in riverine forests, broadleafed wood-land, well-wooded hills and suburbia. Catches flying insects in agile sallies from a perch, seldom returning to the same perch. Calls frequently. ♂ :41 cm. ♀ :23 cm. **710**

3 CHINSPOT BATIS *Batis molitor.* Common resident. Male almost indistinguishable from the male of (1) but lacks any black spotting on flanks; female has clearly defined, rich rufous chin-spot and breast-band. Immature like female, upperparts washed rusty. Has several calls, the most characteristic a descending series of three notes 'choi-choi-choi', sounding like 'Three blind mice'. Also calls 'chi-chirr' or 'chee-chir-chir'. Pairs are found in broadleafed woodland and savanna, often in bird parties, feeding in the mid- and lower strata. Ranges mostly to the north and east of the Pririt Batis (1). 12-13 cm. **701**

4 FAIRY FLYCATCHER *Stenostira scita.* Uncommon winter visitor. Very small grey and black bird with conspicuous white wing-bar and outer tail feathers, the pink central belly inconspicuous in the field. The call is a short, sibilant trill 'kisskisskisskiss'. Singly and sparsely in well-developed *Acacia* savanna, riverine woodland and suburbia. Highly active, feeding within bushes or the outer canopy of trees, frequently fanning and bobbing its tail. 12 cm. **706**

True shrikes. Family LANIIDAE and allies. Insectivorous or partially carnivorous birds with stout, hooked or slightly hooked bills. Members of the various genera are illustrated according to plumage similarity.

1 LONGTAILED SHRIKE *Corvinella melanoleuca.* Common resident. A distinctive, long-tailed, pied bird. Female may have white on flanks and have shorter tail; immature bronze-brown with grey rump. The call is a sqeakily whistled 'prooit-preeoo, prooit-preeoo-preeoo' the first sound descending, the second and third ascending. Small groups occur in thornveld, *Acacia* savanna and mixed bush communities, preferring lightly wooded and well-grassed regions where they hunt while perched on outer branch of a bush or tree. Widespread in all regions except the extreme south-west. 40-50 cm. **735**

2 REDBACKED SHRIKE *Lanius collurio.* Common to locally very common summer visitor. Sexes differ as illustrated. Female differs from immature Fiscal Shrike (pp.274-275) in more rufous upperparts and lack of white wing-bars. Rarely male may occur with white wing-bars, then resembles Sousa's Shrike (pp.276-277) but differs in clear grey crown and nape plus more rufous, unbarred mantle. Mostly silent, sometimes makes a harsh 'chak, chak'. Singly in a variety of wooded habitats. Still-hunts conspicuously from a fence, low branch or small bush. 18 cm. **733**

3 WHITECROWNED SHRIKE *Eurocephalus anguitimens.* Common resident. Distinguished by white crown, throat and breast, and black mask plus large size. Immature mottled and scaled brownish on upperparts, white on ear coverts, underparts entirely brownish. Makes a curious, babbling 'kwep-kerk-kererk, kwep-kerr-kerr-kerr-kerr . . .'. Singly or in scattered groups, widespread in woodland and savanna. Perches conspicuously, still-hunting from an outer branch or roadside telephone wire. 23-25 cm. **756**

4 LESSER GREY SHRIKE *Lanius minor.* Common summer visitor. Distinctive shrike with grey and black upperparts, white underparts, the full black mask (a) often absent November to January, then appears as (b). Has a harsh, twittering song but is normally silent in southern Africa; occasionally makes a harsh 'chek' sound. Widespread in a variety of open and lightly wooded habitats, being particularly common in the Kalahari region, frequently in loose association with (2) but favouring more open habitat. Still-hunts conspicuously from top of a bush, outer branch of a tree or a fence, remaining in one place for long periods. 20-22 cm. **731**

272

1 FISCAL SHRIKE *Lanius collaris*. Uncommon resident. Locally more common in the south, otherwise widely but sparsely distributed. Pied, heavy-headed, heavy-billed bird with white wing-bar *extending to the shoulder*, female with rufous flanks; cf. thinner-billed Fiscal Flycatcher (pp. 266-267) in which wing-bar does *not* reach the shoulder. In eastern individuals (a) white eyebrow may be absent. Immature has ash-brown upperparts, greyish underparts with fine barring; cf. Sousa's Shrike (pp.276-277). The call is a harsh 'gercha, gercha . . .' or 'skiza, skiza . . .', also has a rambling song incorporating sweet notes and the characteristic 'gercha' sound. Occurs singly or in pairs in savanna, grassland with scattered bushes and occasionally along main roads. Perches conspicuously on outer branches, posts or wires, flying to the ground to seize insects and other small prey. 23 cm. **732**

2 BRUBRU *Nilaus afer*. Common resident. Small pied bird with rich rufous flanks in both sexes. Immature browner above, feathers edged white, underparts barred brown. Male makes a drawn-out, far-carrying whistle 'trrioooo', the female sometimes replying with a softer, wheezy 'wheee'. A widely distributed woodland and savanna species. Active and restless, usually in pairs which work their way through the upper and mid-strata, calling frequently. 15 cm. **741**

3 PUFFBACK *Dryoscopus cubla*. Fairly common to common resident. Identified by pied appearance with distinctive, white-edged wing feathers and crimson eyes, female with white forehead and eyebrow, male with black cap. When excited male erects back feathers to form a puff (see illustration); may fly from tree to tree like this while calling 'chick-weeu, chick-weeu . . .', this uttered less frequently while feeding. In flight the wings make a distinct purring sound. Pairs, often in bird parties, occur in broadleafed and *Acacia* woodland and riverine forests of the north and east where they feed in the canopies of the larger trees. Often noisy and conspicuous. 18 cm. **740**

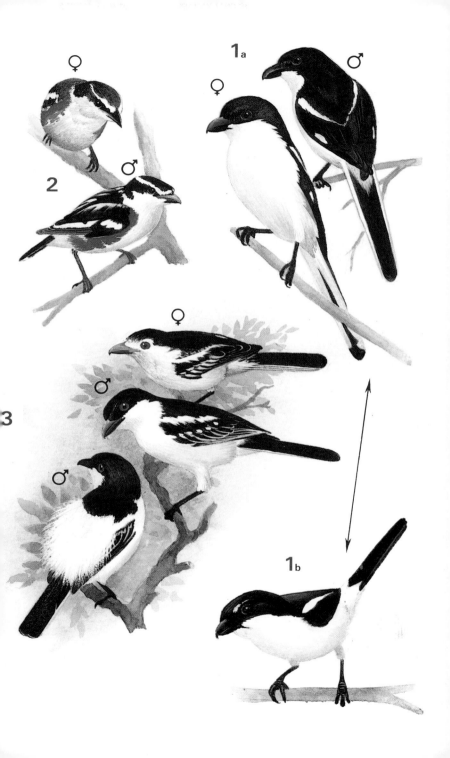

1 SOUSA'S SHRIKE *Lanius souzae*. Rare, exact status not established; recorded once from the extreme north-east. Told from the Redbacked Shrike (pp.272-273) by *dull* brown wings and tail, bold white wing-bar reaching to shoulder, and dusky underparts, only the throat being white. Tail feathers very narrow. Female has tawny flanks and immature is narrowly barred blackish on underparts. Has a low, scraping call note. Normally occurs sparsely in broadleafed woodland where it still-hunts like other *Lanius* shrikes. 17-18 cm. **734**

2 SOUTHERN BOUBOU *Laniarius ferrugineus*. Rare, possibly resident, but exact status not established; occurs sparsely in the southeast. Cinnamon colouring of underparts sometimes extends in pale wash to throat, but *always richer on flanks, belly and vent;* cf. Tropical Boubou (4) which has even wash of creamy-buff on underparts. Female duller, browner on upperparts. Immature mottled brownish on upperparts, barred brown on flanks. Calls in duet, first bird 'ko-ko' replied to by 'kweet', or 'boo-boo' replied to by 'whee-oo', or a liquid-sounding 'phooweeol' replied to by 'hueee' or 'churrr', with variations. Secretive, remaining concealed in the lower stratum of dense bush. 23 cm. **736**

3 SWAMP BOUBOU *Laniarius bicolor*. Common, localised resident. Differs from (2) and (4) in underparts being *pure white;* sexes alike. Immature with buff feather-edges to upperparts, ashy barring on underparts. The calls are a mellow 'whoooer' replied to by a harsh, ratchet-like 'kack-ack-ack-ack' or 'wheeee' replied to by 'kh-kh-krrrrrrr'. Pairs occur in mature riverine forests and papyrus of the northern wetlands. Less secretive than other boubous, often perching openly while calling. 22-23 cm. **738**

4 TROPICAL BOUBOU *Laniarius aethiopicus*. Common resident. Differs from Southern Boubou (2) in having an *even* pale cinnamon or ivory wash over entire underparts; sexes alike. Immature has feathers of upperparts edged buff. Has various duetting calls, a mournful 'whoooer' replied to by a harsh 'zhreeee', or a deep 'wha-wha-wha' replied to by a simultaneous 'zrang-zrang-zrang' plus other whistling and twanging sounds; calls generally sounding harsher, more mechanical than those of (2). Usually in pairs in riverine forests, thickets on termitaria and dense bush. Secretive, remaining in the lower stratum. 23-25 cm. **737**

5 CRIMSON BOUBOU (CRIMSONBREASTED SHRIKE) *Laniarius atrococcineus*. Common resident. Upperparts like other boubous but underparts entire crimson. Very young birds are ash-grey below, finely barred black. Calls in duet, both sexes calling almost simultaneously, a sharply delivered 'qui-quip-chiri' or 'pee-eeoo, pee-eeoo' or a sharp 'bilk-bilk, bilk-bilk' replied to by 'kzzeeeee' with variations. Widespread in pairs in *Acacia* savanna and thorn thickets in Kalahari scrub. Frequents the lower stratum and forages on the ground, hopping about with raised tail. 22-23 cm. **739**

Bush shrikes. Colourful shrikes with olive-green and grey upperparts and yellow or orange and yellow underparts. Most frequent dense bush and have distinct calls.

1 BOKMAKIERIE *Telophorus zeylonus.* Rare, exact status not established; has been recorded only near Lobatse in the south-east and Bokpits in the south-west. Black lores and gorget on yellow underparts distinctive; immature duller, lacks gorget as illustrated. Both sexes call in duet, a variety of ringing phrases, eg. 'bok-makiri', 'kok-o-vik', 'bok-bok-chit', 'wit, wit-wit' or 'pirrapee-pirrapoo', each sequence repeated at about three-second intervals. Usual habitats are bushy hillsides and valleys with grassy patches, farmlands and suburbia. Feeds on the ground. 23 cm. **746**

1 J

2 GREYHEADED BUSH SHRIKE *Malaconotus blanchoti.* Uncommon resident. Much larger than the previous species with distinct grey hood, *very heavy bill* and white patch before a yellow eye. The immature has the head mottled brown, bill horn-coloured. The characteristic call is a haunting, drawn-out 'hoooooooooop' or 'hoooooooo-ip'; also makes a 'clip-clip . . .' sound. Singly or in pairs in mixed woodland, riverine bush and thickets, feeding and calling mostly from the mid- and lower strata. Hard to see, even when calling. 25-27 cm **751**

3 ORANGEBREASTED BUSH SHRIKE *Telophorus sulfure-opectus.* Common resident in the north and Limpopo system, becoming scarcer in the south-east. Male distinguished by yellow forehead and eyebrow, black mask plus yellow underparts with an orange breast, this much reduced in the female. Immature lacks eyebrow and mask, lores and throat white in first plumage. Calls a musical, much-repeated 'poo-poo-poo-pooooo' or 'pipit-eeez, pipit-eeez . . .'. Usually in pairs in mixed riverine bush, thornveld and *Acacia* thickets, feeding and calling from the mid- and upper strata. Not secretive but difficult to see unless calling. 18-19 cm. **748**

Tchagra shrikes. Heavy-billed, similarly coloured shrikes which feed on or near the ground, creeping about in the lower stratum of their preferred habitat and moving from bush to bush in low, rather heavy flight. Often reveal their presence by distinctive calls.

1 BLACKCROWNED TCHAGRA *Tchagra senegala.* Uncommon to fairly common resident; sparse in the west and south. Told from the previous species by *black* crown; immature has crown mottled brown and black, the bill horn-coloured. Normal call a loud, ponderous and rather flat-sounding 'CHEER-tcharee, trichi CHEER-tcharoo, cheeroo, cheeroo'. Pairs also duet with a variety of grating, churring and whistling sounds. Singly or in pairs in thornveld and woodland, especially favouring thorn thickets, frequenting the lower stratum, but also occurs in quite open habitat. Widespread. 21-23 cm. **744**

2 THREESTREAKED TCHAGRA *Tchagra australis.* Fairly common resident. Smaller than the previous species, distinguished by *grey-brown* (not black) crown, this and white eyebrow separated by narrow black line; flight pattern similar to that of (1). Immature similar, duller. The alarm note is a guttural 'churr'. In the summer the male displays by flying steeply upwards to above tree height, then planing down with quivering wings while calling 'tui-tui-tui-tui-tui . . .' in a descending cadence. Widespread, primarily in thornveld but also occurs in the fringes of broadleafed woodland. Singly, spending much time on the ground beneath bushes where, if disturbed, it hops onto some low branch before hopping or flying into cover. 19 cm. **743**

Helmetshrikes are characterised by intense sociability, usually in groups of six to twelve. Nomadic unless breeding, they move from tree to tree continuously while maintaining a noisy chattering comprised of harsh whirring and grating sounds plus bill-snapping. Sexes alike.

3 REDBILLED HELMETSHRIKE *Prionops retzii.* Uncommon resident. Entirely black except for white vent and tail-tips; immature browner. Parties occur in broadleafed woodland and well-developed riverine forests, feeding in the tree canopies and on the trunks. 22 cm. **754**

4 WHITE HELMETSHRIKE *Prionops plumatus.* Fairly common resident; less common in the south-east. Identified by pied plumage and butterfly-like flight; immature with browner crown. Parties occur in broadleafed, *Acacia* and mixed bush savanna, frequenting the mid- and lower strata. Restless, flying from tree to tree in low, straggling procession. 20 cm. **753**

Starlings. Family STURNIDAE. A well-known family of frugivorous and insectivorous birds with strong, slightly arched bills and sturdy legs. Many species are gregarious, especially at roosts. Their calls are mainly various unmusical squeaks and squawks. Unless otherwise stated the young resemble adults.

1 WATTLED STARLING *Creatophora cinerea.* Fairly common to common resident. A pale species, the male particularly so when breeding, at which time the head may be ornamented with yell ' and black skin plus wattles as illustrated (b), or have only the wattl. ; (c), or may resemble the female (a). Non-breeding male like female but darker winged; then both sexes appear drab. The call is a rasping, squeaky sound. Occurs in flocks in dry grassland with scattered bush patches, arid thornveld and dry woodland on Kalahari sands, often near cattle posts. Highly gregarious at all times, widespread and nomadic when not breeding. 21 cm. **760**

760

2 REDWINGED STARLING *Onychognathus morio.* Common localised resident in the east and south-east; a few sight records for the Okavango Delta perhaps indicate some wandering. Similar to the next species but larger, with dark eyes and red-brown flight feathers, female with grey head, breast and mantle streaked black. Has a variety of pleasant, loud whistles, the most usual being a drawn-out 'spreeooo'. Normally flocks frequent rocky cliffs and valleys or buildings in suburbia. Red wings striking in flight. 27-28 cm. **769**

769

3 PALEWINGED STARLING *Onychognathus nabouroup.* Rare, possibly localised visitor but exact status not established; two records only of flocks in the arid south-west. Differs from the previous species in white flight feathers (striking in flight) and orange eyes; ranges do not overlap. Has similar melodious whistles to (2). 26 cm. **770**

770

4 PLUMCOLOURED STARLING *Cinnyricinclus leucogaster.* Fairly common summer resident. Male unmistakable. Female quite different, having brown upperparts, white underparts heavily spotted with brown and a yellow gape; immature like female, eyes brown. The call is a series of pleasant, slurred notes. An arboreal, frugivorous species, widespread in mixed woodland and savanna. In pairs when breeding, otherwise in flocks of mostly one sex. 18-19 cm. **761**

761

1 GREATER BLUE-EARED GLOSSY STARLING *Lamprotornis chalybaeus*. Common resident. A short-tailed glossy starling, larger than the next species and differing from (3) in having a *blackish ear patch, royal blue belly and flanks* and generally a more iridescent appearance, especially on the wing coverts. Also has two distinct rows of black spots on the wing coverts. The call is 'sque-ear, sque-eear-eear'. Occurs in pairs when breeding, otherwise forms flocks in broadleafed woodland and savanna in the north and east; comes readily to human settlements, feeding on the ground. 21-23 cm. **765**

2 LESSER BLUE-EARED GLOSSY STARLING *Lamprotornis chloropterus*. Rare, status not established; recorded twice in Kasane. Likely to occur sporadically in that region. Smaller but closely similar to the previous species, flanks more magenta. Immature distinctive as illustrated. The song is 'chirp-chirrup-treerroo-chirp-treee'; on take-off and in flight calls 'wirri-girri'. 20 cm. **766**

3 CAPE GLOSSY STARLING *Lamprotornis nitens*. Very common resident. Differs from the previous two species in *lack of a dark ear patch*, underparts uniformly coloured blue-green. In poor light can appear blackish, in good light is peacock-blue or green. Immature drabber with much dull, blackish feathering. The call is a pleasant 'trrr-treer-treer-cheer', often by several birds at once. Ubiquitous, preferring *Acacia* savanna, mixed woodland and scrub plus human settlements, forming flocks when not breeding. 23-25 cm. **764**

4 SHARPTAILED GLOSSY STARLING *Lamprotornis acuticaudus*. Rare, exact status not established; several sight records for the extreme north-west. Identified by wedge-shaped tail, otherwise similar to the previous species. Has blackish ear patches, but male with diagnostic *red eyes*, female with *orange-red eyes*. Immature darker, *underparts dull grey-brown, the feathers tipped buff*, eye brown to yellow; cf. immature of (2). Voice unrecorded. Occurs in broadleafed woodland; in flocks when not breeding. 26 cm. **767**

1 BURCHELL'S GLOSSY STARLING *Lamprotornis australis.*
Common resident. Largest, lankiest of the glossy starlings. Like the
following species has *dark eyes* but differs in being larger-bodied,
shorter-tailed and longer-legged. Folded wings extend halfway down
tail. Has a blackish mask extending from bill to ear coverts, the
plumage blue with a purple wash. Immature duller, brownish below.
The call is a squeaky 'churrik-urr, churrick-urrik-kerr . . .'. Widespread, pairs, small parties or flocks frequenting woodland and
savanna. 30-34 cm. **762**

2 LONGTAILED GLOSSY STARLING *Lamprotornis mevesii.* Fairly common resident. In common with the previous species has *dark
eyes* but differs from it in having a long, graduated tail, the legs
appearing shorter and the body smaller in comparison to its overall
length. The folded wings do not extend beyond the base of tail. Lacks
dark ear patches, the head, mantle and tail blue washed purple, wings
greenish. Immature duller. Flocks make a chattering 'trrreer-eeear'.
Found in small flocks in riverine and broadleafed woodland. 30-
34 cm. **763**

Oxpeckers. Family BUPHAGIDAE. Related to starlings but with very
sharp claws for clinging to the fur of large mammals. Their bills are
used to comb the animals' fur for ticks and blood-sucking flies, the
tails used as props as they clamber all over their hosts.

3 YELLOWBILLED OXPECKER *Buphagus africanus.* Fairly common resident. Differs from the next species in larger size, yellow bill
with red tip, orange eyes surrounded by narrow yellow eyerings plus
pale rump and upper tail coverts. Immature duller with dusky-brown
bill. Makes a hissing 'kuss, kuss' sound. Flocks are found in association with buffaloes, giraffes and cattle in the north. 22 cm. **771**

4 REDBILLED OXPECKER *Buphagus erythrorhynchus.* Common
resident. Differs from (3) in having an entirely red bill, red eyes and
larger yellow eyerings; lacks a pale rump. Immature has bill blackish
with yellow gape. Makes a hissing 'churr' and a 'tzik, tzik' sound. Is
found on antelopes, giraffes and cattle in all but the arid regions.
20-22 cm. **772**

Sunbirds. Family NECTARINIIDAE. Small, insect and nectar-eating birds with downcurved bills adapted to flower-probing. Males with iridescent plumage and yellow, orange or red pectoral tufts which are displayed in excitement. Some males undergo an annual 'eclipse' when they adopt drab plumage resembling that of the female. Young birds also resemble females. At food sources males spend much time chasing females and other males in swift, erratic flight.

1 WHITEBELLIED SUNBIRD *Nectarinia talatala*. Common resident. Male has blue-green head, mantle and upper breast (*appears blue in good light*) separated from *white* underparts by a purple band; pectoral tufts yellow. Has no eclipse plumage. Female has brown upperparts, white underparts; cf. next species. Has a distinctive song, 'chu-ee, chu-ee, chu-ee-trrrrr', repeated frequently. Usually in pairs in dry mixed woodland, *Acacia* savanna, riverine bush and suburban gardens. Male sings for long periods from a bush-top. 11,5 cm. **787**

2 MARICO SUNBIRD *Nectarinia mariquensis*. Common resident. Male differs from male of next species in larger size and longer, more curved bill; from male of (1) in *deep claret-red* breast-band (although occasionally this can appear quite scarlet) and *dark* underparts belly to tail; has no eclipse plumage. Female larger, longer-billed than female of (3), underparts below dusky throat richer yellow, more heavily streaked. Immature starts with yellow underparts and black bib (see margin illustration); as the yellow fades with ageing plumage can resemble female Black Sunbird (pp. 288-289). The call is a brisk 'chip-chip' or a husky 'schitz-schitz' becoming a long, stuttering series ending in a pleasant warble. Singly or in pairs, widespread in dry thornveld, riverine and hillside bush. 13-14 cm. **779**

3 PURPLEBANDED SUNBIRD *Nectarinia bifasciata*. Rare, exact status not established; a few records for the extreme north. Both sexes very similar to previous species but smaller, the bill shorter and less curved, female paler yellow on underparts. Male in eclipse like female but with dark wings and tail, the rump blue-green. Has a distinctive call 'tsikit-y-dik'. The song, often by two birds in unison, is a high-pitched, hesitant trill 'tsip tsip tsip tsippity-tsirrily-tsirrily, tseep'. An active, nomadic species which favours riverine thickets. 10-11,5 cm. **780**

4 MIOMBO DOUBLECOLLARED SUNBIRD *Nectarinia manoensis*. Rare, status not established; very few records from north of Francistown. Male distinguished from other male sunbirds by *scarlet* breast-band, yellow-buff belly and vent plus blue uppertail coverts; pectoral tufts yellow. No eclipse plumage. Female has drab yellow-grey underparts without streaking. Calls a sharp 'chip' or 'zzik-zzik' and has a jumbled song of high-pitched sizzling notes. Occurs in broadleafed woodland, usually in pairs. 13 cm. **784**

288

1 SCARLETCHESTED SUNBIRD *Nectarinia senegalensis*. Uncommon resident. Male unmistakable; no eclipse. Immature male with rudimentary chest-patch and pale underparts well spotted blackish, female with heavily marked underparts as illustrated. A large sunbird with long, well-curved bill. Makes a high-pitched chattering and a much repeated 'cheep, chip, chop' from a prominent perch. A noisy and conspicuous species occurring in a variety of wooded habitats in the north, including riverine woodland and savanna. 13-15 cm. **791**

2 BLACK SUNBIRD *Nectarinia amethystina*. Uncommon localised resident. Male lacks the scarlet breast of the previous species, appearing all-black with iridescent green forehead plus purple throat and shoulder patches; no eclipse plumage. Female has bold creamy moustacial streak, dark speckled throat, creamy-yellow underparts. The call, often given in flight, is 'tschiek' or 'zit'; also makes a stuttering 'chichichichichi' and has a pleasant, subdued warbling song uttered for long periods while concealed in foliage. Pairs and single birds are found in woodland, savanna and riverine bush plus suburbia. Lively and conspicuous at a food source. 15 cm. **792**

3 COPPERY SUNBIRD *Nectarinia cuprea*. Rare, exact status not established; a few records for the extreme north. Breeding male has upperparts, head and breast metallic golden copper with greenish reflections on head and throat, purple on rump and tips of wing covert feathers, tail and rest of underparts velvety-black; male in eclipse plumage resembles female but has tail and wings black, rump and wing covert feathers coppery. Female has upperparts olive-brown, underparts yellow, unstreaked. Has a harsh 'chit-chat' call and a high-pitched 'chiki-chiki-chiki' alarm note plus a soft warbling song. Frequents the fringes of riverine forest. 12 cm. **778**

1 DUSKY SUNBIRD *Nectarinia fusca.*
Rare localised resident; largely confined to the south-west with irregular sightings outside of its home range. Full breeding plumage of male as illustrated; male in eclipse plumage as margin illustration; may breed like this. Female hardly distinguishable from female of Whitebellied Sunbird (pp.288-289). Male has a loud warbling song reminiscent of Whitebellied Sunbird 'chuee-chuee-trrrrr' or 'tiroo tiroo tiroo sweet-sweet-sweet' with variations. Found in Kalahari scrub and woodland plus rocky outcrops in dry watercourses. 10-12 cm. **788**

2 COLLARED SUNBIRD *Anthreptes collaris.* Uncommon localised resident. A small, distinctive, short-billed sunbird, both sexes metallic green on upperparts with rich yellow underparts, the male with green throat plus blue and purple collar. The song is 'chip-chip-chip-chip, chirreee...chirreee-chirreee'. Pairs frequent riverine forests where trees and creepers are in flower, often joining mixed bird parties and hawking flying insects, but quiet and unobtrusive. 10 cm. **793**

White-eyes. Family ZOSTEROPIDAE. Very small, yellow-green birds which glean insects from leaves and probe flowers for nectar. Unless breeding they occur in flocks which fly from tree to tree where they search the foliage closely, often in the inverted position. The sexes are alike. Young birds are duller and initially lack the white eye-wattles.

3 YELLOW WHITE-EYE *Zosterops senegalensis.* Fairly common localised resident. Smaller and yellower than the previous species, upperparts paler. The song is a brisk, short, repeated phrase similar to that of (3) 'chu, tri-tri-tri-tri, treechu-tree-tree-treechu-treechu'. Flocks occur in the riverine forests and woodlands of the north and north-east, feeding mostly in the canopies. Behaviour much as (3). 10,5 cm. **797**

4 CAPE WHITE-EYE *Zosterops pallidus.* Common resident. Slightly larger than the next species and more greenish in colour, upperparts darker, underparts variable being greyish (a), greenish (b) or whitish with buff flanks. The contact call is a melancholy 'phee' by members of a party while feeding. The song is loud with an urgent quality 'perpwee, perpwee, choo, trree-choo-trree-choo, trree-choo-trree-choo-trree', this phrase repeated many times from a treetop; also has a subdued warbling song uttered from the depths of a bush. Gregarious when not breeding, flocks feeding on flowering trees and creepers in almost any wooded habitat in the east, plus suburbia. 11-13 cm. **796**

Weavers, sparrows and allies. Family PLOCEIDAE. A very large group of conical-billed, mainly seedeating birds. Many breed colonially and weave complicated nests which themselves help in species identification. See nest drawings on pages 302-303.

1 YELLOWTHROATED SPARROW *Petronia superciliaris.* Fairly common resident. Yellow breast-spot *not* a field character; lacking in immature. Best identified by *broad white eyebrows*; cf. Streakyheaded Canary (pp.318-319) which has similar broad white eyebrows but lacks the white wing-bars of this sparrow. Sexes alike. The usual call is a rapid 'chree-chree-chree-chree'. Usually seen in pairs, occasionally flocks at a food source, in well-developed woodland, savanna and riverine forest. Frequently common around settlements. On the ground it *walks*; does not hop like other sparrows. 15-16 cm. **805**

2 GREYHEADED SPARROW *Passer griseus.* Common resident. Identified by entirely grey head and single white wing-bar; bill black when breeding, otherwise horn-coloured. Sexes alike. Immature more streaked on mantle. Makes a repetitive 'cheep-chirp', the first note ascending, the second descending, plus an occasional trill. Widespread and normally gregarious, sometimes in large flocks; in pairs when breeding. Feeds on the ground where it *walks* (does not hop), occurring in *Acacia* savanna, dry broadleafed woodland, around cattle posts and human settlements. 15-16 cm. **804**

3 HOUSE SPARROW *Passer domesticus.* Common resident. Male distinguished by grey cap and black bib; cf. larger, brighter, Great Sparrow (pp.296-297). Female and immature duller, paler, with offwhite eyebrows. The call is 'chissip' or 'chee-ip'. Pairs and small parties occur in association with human habitation, breeding under the eaves of houses. An introduced species now found in most towns; seldom found in a natural environment. 14-15 cm. **801**

4 REDBILLED BUFFALO WEAVER *Bubalornis niger.* Fairly common resident. A distinctive blackish bird with a red bill plus white feathers on flanks and wings. Immature greyish with much mottling on sides of head and underparts, the bill horn-coloured to orange. The call is a mellow 'triddlyoo-triddlyoo-triddlyoo-triddlyoo'; makes chattering sounds at the nest. Pairs and small flocks are found in thornveld and dry mixed woodland, especially in association with baobabs and other large trees in which the large communal nests are built; see illustration on p.302. Patchily distributed and nomadic when not breeding. 24 cm. **798**

5 REDBILLED QUELEA *Quelea quelea.* Fairly common to locally and temporarily abundant resident. Small, brownish weaver with red bill and legs in both sexes when not breeding; breeding female only has yellow bill. Breeding male variable as illustrated, otherwise resembles non-breeding female, as does the immature. Individuals make a 'chee-chee' sound which becomes a loud chattering in a flock. Widespread, occurring in large gatherings, sometimes many thousands, which are nomadic when not breeding. Occurs mainly in dry thornveld or agricultural lands, flying flocks resembling columns of smoke. Breeding colonies may cover large areas of bush. 13 cm. **821**

1 REDHEADED QUELEA *Quelea erythrops*. Rare, exact status not established. Positively identified only in the extreme north-east. Breeding male distinguished by bright red head and stout horn-coloured bill, at other times resembles the female. Flocks make a twittering sound. Irregular and nomadic throughout its range, flocks frequenting moist grasslands, marshes and woodland where they feed on grass seeds. 11,5 cm. **822**

2 SCALYFEATHERED FINCH *Sporopipes squamifrons*. Common to locally abundant resident. Identified by very small size, pink bill and 'bearded' appearance. Sexes alike. Immature duller, lacks scaling on forehead, bill horn-coloured. Has a shrill, sparrow-like song; the normal call a chattering 'ching, ching, ching' by birds in a group. Widespread, small parties frequenting arid thornveld, *Acacia* savanna, human settlements and stockyards, feeding on the ground. 10 cm. **806**

3 SOCIABLE WEAVER *Philetairus socius*. Locally common resident. Pale beak offset by black face and throat diagnostic; a small, pallid, highly gregarious weaver. Sexes alike, immature with upperparts more spotted, no black face or throat. Groups make an excitable chipping sound at the nest. Flocks occur in the vicinity of their communal nests in the dry south-west and the extreme south-east. The massive nests are placed in a tree, frequently a camel-thorn, and accommodate many pairs of birds for both breeding and roosting. 14 cm. **800**

4 CAPE SPARROW *Passer melanurus*. Fairly common to locally common resident. Black and white head and breast pattern of male distinctive, female told from female House Sparrow (pp.294-295) by richer colouring, greyer head and *black bill*; immature similar. Normal call 'chirrup' or 'chissik'; the song a continuing variety of 'chirrup, chreep, chroop, chirreep . . .' notes. Often occurs near human habitation where tame and confiding, otherwise in farmlands and dry savanna; in flocks when not breeding. 15 cm. **803**

5 GREAT SPARROW *Passer motitensis*. Uncommon resident. Told from House Sparrow (pp. 294-295) by larger size, richer colouring. Immature, according to sex, like dull version of adult. The call is a typical sparrow-like 'chirrup, chirroo, t-t-t-t-t'. Widespread but sparse in dry thornveld, *seldom near human settlements*. Usually in pairs. 15-16 cm. **802**

6 WHITEBROWED SPARROW-WEAVER *Plocepasser mahali*. Common resident. Distinguished by bold white eyebrows and, in flight, by white rump and uppertail coverts; may have breast spotted or white. Sexes alike, immature similar but bill horn-coloured. Call a harsh 'chick-chick', the song a melodious, rambling assortment of liquid notes 'cheeoo preeoo chop chop, cheeoo trroo cheeoo preeoo chop chip . . .'. Pairs and loose flocks are found in woodland and savanna, usually near their nests, nest-building at all times of the year. 18 cm. **799**

Weaver nest illustrations appear on pp.302-303.

1 CHESTNUT WEAVER *Ploceus rubiginosus.* Very rare vagrant; one record of small flock near Maun. Non-breeding male resembles female, both sexes then told by *grey bill* and brownish plumage. Usually in flocks in arid thornveld and dry riverine bush. 14-25 cm. **812**

2 SPECTACLED WEAVER *Ploceus ocularis.* Uncommon localised resident. Distinguished by pale eyes and black streak through eyes to ear coverts, male with additional black bib. Immature like female, bill horn-coloured. The characteristic call is a descending 'tee-tee-tee-tee-tee-tee-tee'. A non-social weaver found in pairs in riverine vegetation of the northern wetlands and the eastern stretches of the Limpopo River. 15-16 cm. **810**

3 BROWNTHROATED WEAVER *Ploceus xanthopterus.* Uncommon resident. A small, short-tailed weaver, male with black bill and brown patch on throat and lores, female with pale bill and no brown on throat. Immature like female. The call is a typical weaver nasal twanging and trilling. Occurs in pairs and flocks in reedbeds when breeding or in riverine forests when not breeding. Always near water. 15 cm. **818**

4 GOLDEN WEAVER *Ploceus xanthops.* Fairly common resident. A large yellow weaver, the breeding male with a golden wash to underparts, heavy bill, pale eyes and plain upperparts diagnostic of both sexes. Immature like female but duller, darker on upperparts. Makes a harsh 'chip' and sustained swizzling. In pairs or small flocks in reeds and waterside trees of the northern wetlands, being rather inconspicuous when not breeding. 18 cm. **816**

5 THICKBILLED WEAVER *Amblyospiza albifrons.* Rare, localised resident of the northern wetlands. Heavy bill and dark appearance (for a weaver) diagnostic. Immature like female, bill yellower. Nesting birds make a continuous low chattering, otherwise silent. Pairs and small parties occur sparsely in reedbeds and riverine woodland. 18 cm. **807**

298

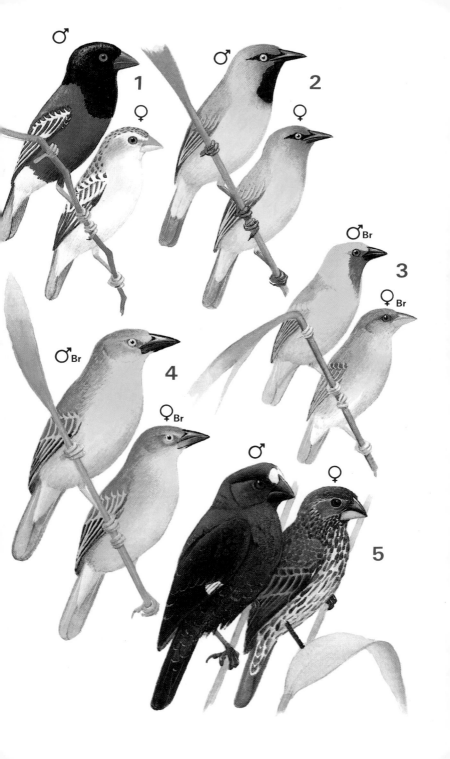

Weaver nest illustrations appear on pp.302-303.

1 MASKED WEAVER *Ploceus velatus.* Common to locally very common resident. Breeding male distinguished from the next species by *red eyes* and more yellow crown (black mask extends across *forehead* only). Non-breeding male resembles female, breeding female has yellower underparts and redder eyes. Immature duller, greyer on underparts. The call is a sharp 'zik' plus a prolonged swizzling when breeding. Gregarious and widespread, small flocks occurring in a wide variety of habitats including suburbia. Breeds colonially in reedbeds or trees, colonies largest when close to water. Nomadic when not breeding. 15 cm. **814**

2 LESSER MASKED WEAVER *Ploceus intermedius.* Fairly common localised resident. Breeding male differs from male of previous species in having *pale yellow eyes* and a black mask extending *over the top of the head*; female more yellow than female of (1) at all times. Immature like female but whitish on belly. Makes a typical weaver swizzling sound, especially noisy when nesting. In *Acacia* savanna and mixed woodland, nesting in trees in small colonies, often near water. 15 cm. **815**

3 SPOTTEDBACKED WEAVER *Ploceus cucullatus.* Uncommon localised resident. Breeding male of northern race (a) (normally found in Botswana) told by entirely black head and spotted back; in eastern race (presence of which along the Limpopo River requires confirmation) by *entirely yellow crown* and spotted back; see illustrations. Female has dark eyes, underparts entirely yellow when breeding; non-breeding female like non-breeding male, both with horn-coloured bills. Makes a husky swizzling when breeding. Occurs in various waterside habitats in the north, usually in small flocks, breeding colonially in reeds or trees near water. When breeding males display by hanging upside down beneath the nest, swinging from side to side with quivering wings and making swizzling sounds. Nomadic when not breeding. 17 cm. **811**

4 REDHEADED WEAVER *Anaplectes rubriceps.* Fairly common resident. Breeding male unmistakable, non-breeding male and immature like female. Normally silent but makes a squeaky chattering at the nest. Pairs occur in thornveld and broadleafed woodland, breeding in isolation or in small colonies, the nests, being built of twigs, remain conspicuous for long periods. Nomadic and inconspicuous when not breeding. 15 cm. **819**

300

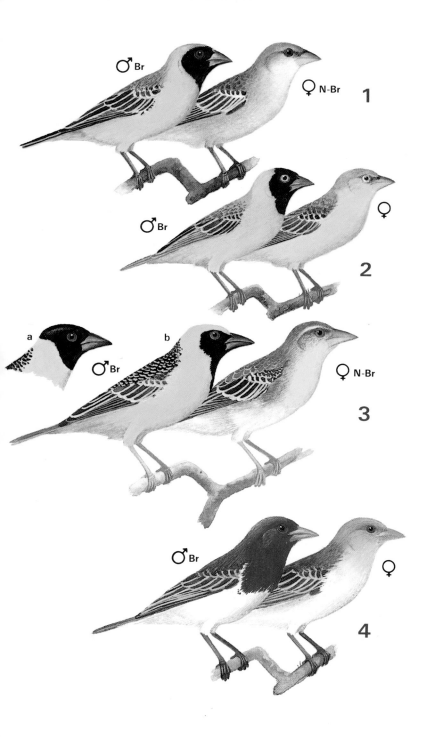

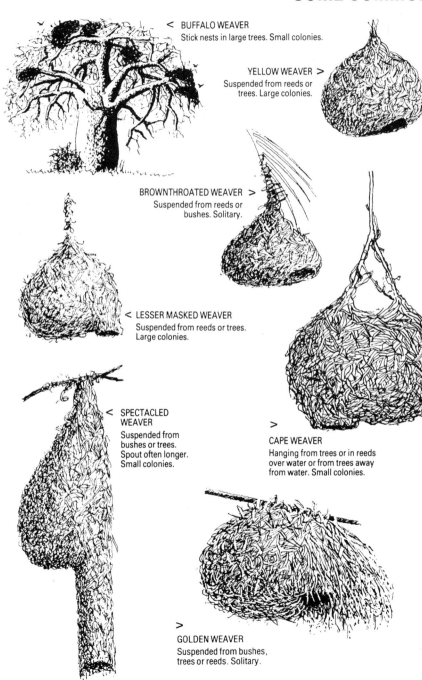

< BUFFALO WEAVER
Stick nests in large trees. Small colonies.

YELLOW WEAVER >
Suspended from reeds or trees. Large colonies.

BROWNTHROATED WEAVER >
Suspended from reeds or bushes. Solitary.

< LESSER MASKED WEAVER
Suspended from reeds or trees. Large colonies.

< SPECTACLED WEAVER
Suspended from bushes or trees. Spout often longer. Small colonies.

>
CAPE WEAVER
Hanging from trees or in reeds over water or from trees away from water. Small colonies.

>
GOLDEN WEAVER
Suspended from bushes, trees or reeds. Solitary.

WEAVER NESTS

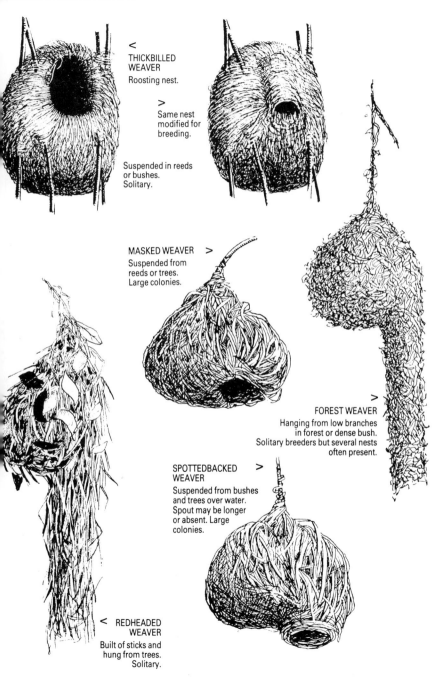

< THICKBILLED
WEAVER
Roosting nest.

> Same nest
modified for
breeding.

Suspended in reeds
or bushes.
Solitary.

MASKED WEAVER >
Suspended from
reeds or trees.
Large colonies.

> FOREST WEAVER
Hanging from low branches
in forest or dense bush.
Solitary breeders but several nests
often present.

SPOTTEDBACKED >
WEAVER
Suspended from bushes
and trees over water.
Spout may be longer
or absent. Large
colonies.

< REDHEADED
WEAVER
Built of sticks and
hung from trees.
Solitary.

Widowbirds and bishopbirds. Reed and grass-loving weavers, the males predominantly black when breeding, some with long tails; they habitually puff out their plumage in display. Non-breeding males resemble females, as do immatures, the various species then being difficult to identify. Ball-type nests are placed in long grass.

1 REDSHOULDERED WIDOW *Euplectes axillaris.* Uncommon localised resident. Breeding male identified by short tail and red shoulders. Male makes a husky 'tseek, wirra, wirra, wirra, wirra' when displaying. Occurs in reeds, papyrus and grasses fringing the waterways of the northern wetlands. Male conspicuous in summer when breeding, at other times form flocks and are difficult to tell from other non-breeding members of the family. 19 cm. **828**

2 REDCOLLARED WIDOW *Euplectes ardens.* Rare, exact status not established; recorded once near Gaborone. Breeding male has red frontal collar only; smaller than Longtailed Widow (pp. 306-307), tail more slender, bill black (not grey). In display male makes a weak 'kizz-zizz-zizz-zizz' with tail spread while in flight or from a perch. Frequents rank grass in *Acacia* bush. 15-40 cm. **831**

3 WHITEWINGED WIDOW *Euplectes albonotatus.* Fairly common to locally common resident, but sparse in the north. Breeding male recognised by yellow and white shoulders, bluish bill and broad tail. Male displays conspicuously in summer from a perch, tail fanned and uttering a twittering call. Frequents marshes, moist valleys, rank vegetation bordering cultivations and road verges in otherwise dry thornveld and mixed bushveld, usually in small flocks. 15-19 cm. **829**

4 RED BISHOP *Euplectes orix.* Fairly common to locally common resident. Breeding male unmistakable. When breeding male calls a wheezy, spluttering 'zik-zik-zik...zayzayzayzayzay'. Occurs in flocks in association with reeds, rank grasses and cultivations in damp localities. The male displays with puffed-out plumage in flight over its breeding territory or from a conspicuous perch. Forms nomadic flocks when not breeding. 14 cm. **824**

5 GOLDEN BISHOP *Euplectes afer.* Fairly common to locally common resident. Breeding male unmistakable. Has a high-pitched buzzing, swizzling call 'zzzzzzz zzit zzit...' when breeding. Occurs in damp localities, near dams, along streams, in moist grassland and grassy pans during the summer; otherwise wanders widely. 12 cm. **826**

1 LONGTAILED WIDOW *Euplectes progne.* Rare localised resident; occurs in the south-east, more commonly in wet years. Breeding male unmistakable, being pale-billed, larger, broader-winged and heavier-tailed than the Redcollared Widow (pp.304-305), red and cream shoulders conspicuous. Non-breeding male told by large size and red shoulders, being larger than the female and all others in this family. Normal call is a repeated 'chip . . . chip . . . chip . . .' but when breeding the male has a subdued swizzling song. A grassland species, favouring damp localities with rich growth. In summer the male displays conspicuously in low flight over its breeding territory, wings flapping slowly and deliberately, tail hanging downwards. When not breeding forms nomadic flocks. 15-60 cm. **832**

2 YELLOWRUMPED WIDOW *Euplectes capensis.* Rare, status not established; one record from 70 km north of Nata. Possibly occurs more regularly in that region since it is known to occur in adjacent Zimbabwe. Non-breeding male retains yellow shoulder-patch. Prefers marshy regions near streams and in hills. 15 cm. **827**

Waxbills, finches, twinspots and mannikins. Very small, mostly colourful, conical-billed weaver-related seed-eaters, immature birds being dull versions of the adults. Gregarious when not breeding. Nests usually of a loose ball-type with a side entrance, constructed of fine dried grasses and placed in a bush or on the ground; a few species use an old nest of a true weaver. All forage on the ground.

3 MELBA FINCH *Pytilia melba.* Common resident. Both sexes identified by bright red bill, male with distinctive red forehead and throat plus golden breast; differs from next species in larger size, *pale grey* head, *green* wings and black (not green) barred underparts. The usual call is a single, low 'wick' but also makes a plaintive whistle and has an attractive, variable song. Widespread except in the dry interior. Occurs in thickets in *Acacia* savanna and along watercourses, often with waxbills and firefinches. 12-13 cm. **834**

4 GOLDENBACKED PYTILIA *Pytilia afra.* Rare, exact status not established; recorded from widely separated points in the north. Differs from the previous species in smaller size, brown and red bill, green (not black) barred underparts and distinctive *orange patch on wings*. The call is a piping 'seee', the song a soft rattling sequence of notes. Pairs frequent broadleafed woodland and savanna, but are nowhere common. 11 cm. **833**

♂Br
1

♂Br

2 ♀

♂N-Br

♀

♀

3

♂

B JACK

1 BROWN FIREFINCH *Lagonosticta nitidula*. Uncommon localised resident. A small brown firefinch with pink face and throat plus *grey (not pink)* legs; cf. female of (2). Sexes similar. The call is a flat, unmusical 'tsiep, tsiep' or 'weet-weet-weet', the song a reedy 'swee-dee-see-swee-kee-dee ...'. Small flocks occur in thickets of riverine forests in the Chobe-Linyanti-Okavango region. Often feeds on footpaths, flying into nearby bushes when disturbed. 10 cm. **843**

2 REDBILLED FIREFINCH *Lagonosticta senegala*. Fairly common resident. Both sexes have *red uppertail coverts* (cf. previous species), male with extensive red on head and underparts, eyes with creamy-yellow orbital rings, *bill pink*, culmen brownish, *legs pink*. Female almost entirely brownish but larger than previous species, *bill, lores and legs pink*; immature may lack pink bill. The call is a nasal 'fweet, fweet'; has a short fluty song. Occurs in pairs and small parties in *Acacia* savanna and in suburbia. Frequents thickets and rank grasses. 10 cm. **842**

3 BLUEBILLED FIREFINCH *Lagonosticta rubricata*. Not recorded in Botswana but occurs sparsely in the Marico region of western Transvaal, may therefore be expected occasionally along the Limpopo system. The bill appears black. Upperparts from bill to lower back plain rich brown, much browner than (4) with *no pink wash* (but see note of caution under that species), male with underparts rich red, belly black, female paler on belly. Has a characteristic trilling, bell-like call and a stuttering alarm note not unlike that of (4). Frequents riverine thickets and rank grass patches. 11 cm. **840**

4 JAMESON'S FIREFINCH *Lagonosticta rhodopareia*. Fairly common resident. Bill blackish in both sexes, nape and mantle washed pink (but note: some individuals lack this pink wash and are then similar to (3)), rest of upperparts less dark than (3), underparts of male rose-pink (not red); female more orange-pink on underparts. Immature male more uniformly brown above, underparts rose-pink with brownish wash on lateral breast, flanks and underbelly; cf. (3). Has tinkling 'trrr-trrr' alarm notes plus various musical calls 'tewee-tewee...' or 'fweeee' or 'zik, zik'. In thickets and rank grasses in thornveld, riparian and secondary growth around cultivated lands. 11 cm. **841**

J ♂

4

1 LOCUST FINCH *Ortygospiza locustella*. Rare, exact status not established; two birds only collected in the Okavango region. Very small, ground-feeding bird; male unmistakable, female with darker upperparts than the next species plus *orange-brown wings*. The call is a querulous 'pink-pink'. Frequents wet grasslands in flocks, feeding in patches of bare ground. Flushes reluctantly then makes off in fast, dipping flight for some distance before resettling. 9 cm. **853**

2 QUAIL FINCH *Ortygospiza atricollis*. Fairly common resident. Sexes similar as illustrated, male with black cheeks and upper breast; told from the female of the previous species by brown (not orange-brown) wings, white facial markings and rufous underparts. The call is a querulous, metallic 'tirrilink' given in flight and often the only clue to the species' presence. Pairs and small flocks frequent grasslands, especially over-grazed regions, pan fringes and similar damp localities. Occasionally takes off in brief flight, suddenly descending again. In courtship the male towers high then plummets down while making a clicking sound. 9,5 cm. **852**

3 CUTTHROAT FINCH *Amadina fasciata*. Fairly common resident. Male unmistakable. Female told by all-over scaly appearance and pale bill, smaller, darker than female of next species. Has a thin 'eee-eee' call and a rich warbling song. Occurs in nomadic flocks unless nesting, frequenting thornveld, savanna and suburbia in the eastern and north-eastern regions. Forages on the ground. Some evidence of movement into the Delta region during winter. 12 cm. **855**

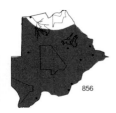

4 REDHEADED FINCH *Amadina erythrocephala*. Fairly common to locally common resident. Larger than the previous species, male with entirely red head, female paler, plainer, bill dark horn. The call is a distinctive double note 'chuck, chuck' becoming a noisy twittering in a flock. Unless breeding occurs in flocks in dry thornveld and grasslands where it forages on the ground; a frequent visitor to waterholes. Widespread and nomadic. 12-13 cm. **856**

5 BRONZE MANNIKIN *Spermestes cucullatus*. Rare, status not established; recorded sporadically in the south-east, once at Kasane. Adults distinctive, immature dull brown with black bill as illustrated. The call is a wheezy 'chik, chik, chikka' or a rapid 'tsree tsree tsree' becoming a shrill twittering in a flock. Small, highly gregarious birds frequenting a variety of well-bushed habitats; thickets in thornveld and savanna, plantation fringes and suburbia. Feeds on the ground or by clambering about grass stems to reach the seedheads, when flushed flies off to a nearby bush, eventually returning in ones and twos. 9 cm. **857**

1 ORANGEBREASTED WAXBILL *Sporaeginthus subflavus.* Rare, locally uncommon resident; regular in the south-east, elsewhere very sporadic. Very small but distinctive species with yellow underparts, orange rump and undertail coverts, red and black bill; immature like female but bill black. Has a rapid tinkling flight call and a soft 'chit-chit' contact call while feeding. Occurs in small flocks, usually near water or marshy regions in reeds or rank grasses and sedges. Very active and mobile, making off in straggling sequence before suddenly dropping down again. 8,5-9 cm. **854**

2 BLACKCHEEKED WAXBILL *Estrilda erythronotos.* Fairly common resident. Female and immature duller than male, less red. The call is 'foo-weee' rising on the second syllable. Widespread and in small nomadic flocks when not breeding, frequenting dry *Acacia* savanna and thornbush along dry watercourses. Seldom plentiful. 12-13 cm. **847**

3 BLUE WAXBILL *Uraeginthus angolensis.* Common resident. Both sexes unmistakable, immature paler than female. The characteristic call is a high-pitched 'weet-weet'. Pairs and small parties, frequently with other small seedeaters, are found in thornveld, thornbush thickets along watercourses, old cultivations and suburban gardens in the east and north. 12-14 cm. **844**

4 COMMON WAXBILL *Estrilda astrild.* Fairly common resident. Red bill and facial mask plus red central belly distinctive; immature similar but with blackish bill. The call, usually from many in a flock, is an assortment of shrill notes 'chewi-chee, chewi-chee' descending on the second note, plus 'chee-churr, chee-churr, chip, chip, tri-tri-CHEE, tri-tri-CHEE...'. Flocks occur on grassy riverbanks, reedbeds and rank vegetation bordering cultivated lands, seldom far from water. Very active birds, flying off in straggling procession from place to place. Feeds on the ground or on seedheads. 13 cm. **846**

5 VIOLETEARED WAXBILL *Uraeginthus granatinus.* Common resident. An unmistakable long-tailed waxbill, the tail appearing broad in flight; immature duller than female. The much repeated call is 'tiu-woowee'. Pairs, often in company with other waxbills, are found near dense thickets in dry thornveld and *Acacia* savanna, being widespread, particularly in arid regions. 13-15 cm. **845**

312

Whydahs and widowfinches. Family VIDUIDAE. Small, ground-feeding, seedeating finches which are brood parasites, laying their eggs in the nests of mostly waxbills. Male whydahs in breeding plumage have very long tails and are pugnacious towards other small birds; when not breeding they resemble the confusingly similar females. At times males may be seen in transient plumage with traces of the breeding colours visible. Immatures are very plainly coloured, the species almost indistinguishable. See overleaf for description of widowfinches.

860

1 PINTAILED WHYDAH *Vidua macroura*. Fairly common resident. Male in breeding plumage distinctive; the red bill is retained in non-breeding plumage when it can be distinguished from (3) by black legs. Courting male hovers over females, describing a circle in the vertical plain, while calling a continuous wispy 'peetzy-peetzy-peetzy . . .'. In normal flight the male calls 'tseet-tseet-tseet'. Occurs in the habitat of its host, the Common Waxbill (pp. 312-313) but also in adjacent light woodland. Male usually accompanied by up to six females; larger groups when not breeding. 12-34 cm. **860**

862

2 PARADISE WHYDAH *Vidua paradisea*. Fairly common resident. Distinctive plumage of breeding male (a) similar only to rare Broad-tailed Paradise Whydah (pp.316-317) but differs in *tapering tail-feathers*; transitional plumage as (b). Female and non-breeding male have whiter head-stripes than previous species. Has a short sparrow-like song and utters an occasional 'chit'. Occurs in *Acacia* savanna and broadleafed woodland. Courting male holds the two short upper tail feathers erect (cf. Broadtailed Paradise Whydah); also hovers over females in slow, bobbing flight causing the tail to undulate. Parasitises the Melba Finch. 12-38 cm. **862**

861

3 SHAFTTAILED WHYDAH *Vidua regia*. Fairly common resident. Breeding male distinguished by red bill, orange-buff underparts and *bulbous ends* to tail-shafts. Female and non-breeding male have similar but less distinctive head markings than other whydahs, but this is the only whydah with *red legs at all times*. The call is a series of variable sharp notes 'chit-chit-tsip-trrippy-tsip-chit...'. Singly or in small flocks, females predominating, in dry *Acacia* savanna and grassland with scattered thornbush. Widespread and nomadic when not breeding. Parasitises the Violeteared Waxbill. 12-34 cm. **861**

1 BROADTAILED PARADISE WHYDAH *Vidua obtusa.* Rare, status not established; a few records only for the north-east. Breeding male differs from the Paradise Whydah (pp.314-315) only in the *wide tail feathers*, not tapering as in that species. Female and immature of both species indistinguishable. Behaviour much the same as for Paradise Whydah, its occurrence in the north-east linked to that of its host, the equally rare Goldenbacked Pytilia. 12-38 cm. **863**

Widowfinches. Small, all-black brood parasites of the firefinches (pp.308-309), being strictly host-specific. Plumage of breeding males as illustrated. Non-breeding males resemble females, illustration (2); immatures more russet-brown. Males are usually identified by bill and leg colouring plus song, which mimics that of the host, but in Botswana bill and leg colours do not always follow the normal patterns. For instance a race of the Steelblue Widowfinch (4) has a white bill and red legs, the Purple Widowfinch (3) can have pink legs while the situation is further complicated by the possibility of the occurrence of a new species of widowfinch, parasitising the Brown Firefinch (pp. 308-309), with the same bill and leg combination as (4). *Great caution is therefore called for when attempting specific identification of this little-studied group.* Widowfinches are solitary or in small groups during summer when the males sing from a prominent perch, at other times are gregarious.

2 BLACK WIDOWFINCH *Vidua funerea.* Status not established; no confirmed records for Botswana. Male in breeding plumage usually identified by *white bill and red legs and feet*, however note that a race of (4) also has a white bill and red legs; the certain identification of this species in Botswana is probably impossible. The call is a rapid 'chitchitchitchit'; also has a chirping song-phrase interspersed with the tinkling notes of its host, the Bluebilled Firefinch. Suitable habitat includes thornveld, mixed bushveld, savanna and road verges. However its host the Bluebilled Firefinch is also not yet known in Botswana. 11 cm. **864**

3 PURPLE WIDOWFINCH *Vidua purpurascens.* Rare resident; only regularly observed in the south-east. Male in breeding plumage identified by *white bill and pale pink to whitish legs and feet.* The song is a mixture of harsh notes and the trilling of Jameson's Firefinch, its host. Occurs in mixed bushveld, savanna, thorn thickets and riparian woodland. 11 cm. **865**

4 STEELBLUE WIDOWFINCH *Vidua chalybeata.* Uncommon resident. Male in breeding plumage normally identified by *red bill, legs and feet* but the local race *okavangoensis* has a white bill (see further discussion under family description above). The song incorporates the 'fweet fweet' notes of its host, the Redbilled Firefinch. Its distribution follows a similar pattern to that of its host where it is found in dry thickets in mixed bushveld, savanna, riparian woodland and old cultivations. 11 cm. **867**

316

1 CUCKOO FINCH *Anomalospiza imberbis.* (Family PLOCEIDAE). Rare, status not established; a few records from the extreme northeast. Adults resemble a yellow weaver (to which they are related) but the black bill is shorter and stouter. Immature has two-coloured bill as shown. Male calls 'tsileu tsileu tsileu', also makes a weaver-like swizzling. Frequents grassland and bush savanna. A parasitic weaver, its hosts being cisticolas and prinias. 12-13 cm. **820**

Canaries and buntings. Family FRINGILLIDAE. Sparrow-sized songbirds, canaries with strong conical bills, usually notched tail-tips and undulating flight, buntings strongly terrestrial and with weaker, narrower bills. Many species markedly nomadic.

2 YELLOWEYED CANARY *Serinus mozambicus.* Fairly common resident. Told from male of next species by smaller size, bolder facial markings plus grey crown and nape; sexes alike. Immature as illustrated; paler below, even whitish, lacks grey on head and nape. Calls 'tswirri' and has a lively, shrill song delivered in short bursts. Occurs in small parties and flocks in all types of woodland, thornveld, savanna, riverine bush and suburbia in the north, east and southeast. Feeds on the ground and on grass seedheads, flying into trees when disturbed. 12 cm. **869**

3 YELLOW CANARY *Serinus flaviventris.* Fairly common resident. Male differs from previous species in larger size, richer yellow underparts, lack of any grey on nape or crown, and less contrasty facial markings. Female distinctive, darker above *with yellow rump*, whitish below with lightly streaked breast. Immature like female, greener above. The male sings a sustained jumble of shrill trilling and warbling notes from a bush-top. Normally occurs in pairs over most of Botswana, but more common in open savanna, *Acacia* woodland and villages. Forages on the ground and comes regularly to drink at water points. 13-14 cm. **878**

1 BLACKHEADED CANARY *Serinus alario*. Status not established; several sight records in southern Botswana require confirmation. Main illustration (a) shows the southern race while (b) shows the northern race of the male which is most likely to occur in Botswana, but black markings of head and breast very variable and similarity to male Cape Sparrow (pp. 296-297) should be noted. Female inconspicuous, sparrowlike with chestnut back as illustrated; immature even duller, more streaky above. Calls 'sweea' or 'peechee' and has an unmelodious, jumbled song. Small flocks normally frequent arid hills, foraging on the ground and in bushes. 12-15 cm. **876**

2 BLACKEARED CANARY *Serinus mennelli*. Rare, status not established; a few records of single birds in the extreme north-east, this being the western extremity of its Zimbabwe range. Distinguished by combination of streaky crown, *black mask* and streaked breast; cf. next species. Mask browner in female and immature. The call is a sibilant 'see-see-see', the song a rapid 'teeu twee teu, twiddy twee twee . . .'. Occurs in broadleafed woodland. 13-14 cm. **882**

3 STREAKYHEADED CANARY *Serinus gularis*. Uncommon resident of the north-east and south-east. Told from the previous species by larger size, *bold* white eyebrows (these and streaked crown diagnostic) and duller, unstreaked underparts; the mask not distinct as in (2). (See also Yellowthroated Sparrow (pp.294-295) which also has bold white eyebrows.) Sexes alike; immature similar to adults but *does have brown streaking on underparts*. Has a pleasant, melodious song delivered in short bursts and a 'tirririt' call note. Singly, in pairs or in small parties in woodland, savanna and riverine bush. Inconspicuous and seldom numerous. 16 cm. **881**

4 BLACKTHROATED CANARY *Serinus atrogularis*. Common resident. A small brown canary *with a yellow rump* (the rump yellower, more contrasty than that of either female Yellow Canary or female Yelloweyed Canary (pp. 318-319)); black throat *may be absent* or vestigial. Sexes alike, immature like adult but more streaky on underparts. Calls 'twee' in rising pitch and has a strong, sustained song of mellow phrases. Small flocks feed on grasses and weed-seeds in woodland, savanna, fallow farmlands, waste ground and on road verges, visiting water points daily. Widespread. 11-12 cm. **870**

1 LARKLIKE BUNTING *Emberiza impetuana.* Uncommon to locally fairly common resident. A small, nondescript, cinnamon-washed bunting, mostly lacking in diagnostic features. Sexes alike, immature closely similar. The call, uttered at take-off, is a nasal 'chut', the song a rapidly delivered 'trrrooo-cheeoo-cheep-trree' repeated frequently with variations. Usually found in flocks of ten to fifty strong, occasionally larger, in arid grassland and dry woodland, visiting waterholes when these are available. Highly nomadic, flocks sometimes 'erupting' temporarily into new regions. 13-14 cm. **887**

2 ROCK BUNTING *Emberiza tahapisi.* Fairly common resident. Distinguished by cinnamon colouring plus black, white-streaked head; female and immature with brown-streaked crown. The short, distinctive song is repeated at frequent intervals 'tee-trrr, chirri-chee' or 'swiddle-swiddle-saaa'. In pairs, occasionally small flocks, on rocky or stony slopes with or without bushes plus dry *Acacia* savanna. Normally recorded in the eastern half of the country but occasionally recorded in the north-west and central Kalahari. Unobtrusive but for distinctive call-note. 13-14 cm. **886**

3 GOLDENBREASTED BUNTING *Emberiza flaviventris.* Common resident. Distinctive and unmistakable; head-stripes in female yellowish, in immature brownish. The normal call is 'pret-ty-boyeee', sometimes answered by the mate 'sitee'; the song is a frequently repeated 'chipchipchipchipchip-teee, teeu-teeu-teeu-teeu'. Widespread, pairs and small groups occurring in broadleafed woodland, thornveld, savanna and around cattle posts. 16 cm. **884**

4 CAPE BUNTING *Emberiza capensis.* Rare, status not established; recorded only in the east and south-east. Slightly larger than (2) and told from it by pale buff (not cinnamon) underparts plus white throat and brown-streaked crown, cinnamon on wings only. Sexes alike, immature similar, duller, more streaky on breast. The call is 'cheriowee', the song, uttered from a rock or bush-top, is a shrill 'cheep, cheep, tip, cheeucheeu, tip-cheeu-tip-cheeu'. The dates of the very few observations suggest that birds are on passage early and late summer. 16 cm. **885**

322

GLOSSARY OF TERMS USED

Acacia deciduous trees of the genus *Acacia*. In Africa these are thorny, with bipinnately compound leaves (each leaf is again divided into small leaflets) and small, powderpuff-like or elongated flowers.

Accipiter sparrowhawks and goshawks. Long-tailed, short-winged raptors with long, unfeathered legs and long toes. They specialise in catching small birds (or small mammals in the larger species) in swift pursuit from a standing start.

Afrotropical region Africa south of the Palaearctic region, the Tropic of Cancer roughly forming its northern limit. Formerly called Ethiopian region.

Aggregation a gathering (of birds) brought about by some common interest such as a temporary food availability, after which individuals disperse separately.

Albinistic white or partially white plumage resulting from a lack of normal colour pigmentation.

Brood parasite birds which deposit their eggs in the nest of another species; in Botswana these are cuckoos, honeyguides, whydahs and the Cuckoo-Finch.

Broadleafed woodland woodland comprised of trees with broad leaves as opposed to thornveld where trees of the genus *Acacia* are dominant.

Bush refers to any terrain with trees of moderate height as opposed to the taller, more luxuriant growth of woodland or riparian forest. See also Bushveld.

Bushveld a terrain with mixed trees of moderate height (5 m–10 m) in which the trees frequently touch each other below canopy height; sometimes in dense thickets and usually with a grassy groundcover.

Calcrete a white, stony, calcium-carbonate surface deposit found commonly in regions of low rainfall.

Conspecific being of the same species.

Crepuscular active at dusk. When applied to birds it usually infers that they are active in the half-light hours of *dawn* and dusk.

Culmen the upper ridge of a bird's upper mandible.

Dam a man-made water impoundment, usually with a retaining wall at the opposite end to the inflow.

Delta a river mouth with several diverging branches forming a triangle. In Botswana refers to the inland Okavango Delta.

Desert a region of extremely low rainfall, usually less than 25 mm annually. The only true desert region in Botswana lies in the extreme south-west.

Dispersal a more or less random centrifugal movement away from a locality.

Display in animals denotes actions that have become specialised in the course of evolution; threat display, courtship display, social displays, etc.

Egg-dumping the habit among secondary females in such social species as the Ostrich, guineafowls and others, of laying their eggs in the nest of another female of the same species, usually the dominant female of a flock. Also refers to random egg-laying in places other than nests by immature or unmated hens of any species.

Endemic a species found only in one region.

Falcon	small, swift-flying raptors with pointed wings that specialise in catching flying birds by means of a rapid descent from above, known as a 'stoop'. Falcons build no nest, using instead a cliff ledge or the unused nest of another raptor.
FF	females.
Flats	level ground.
Fledgling	a young bird that has recently acquired its first feathers.
Flock	a group of birds that moves as a more or less cohesive unit.
Floodplain	grasslands that become inundated by river spillage.
Graduated tail	a tail in which the central feathers are longest and all others progressively shorter, the outermost being shortest.
Gregarious	living in flocks or communities.
Immature	refers to any bird beyond the nestling stage but not yet adult.
Intra-Africa migrant	birds that migrate regularly, with a consistent pattern of movement, within the African continent.
Irruptive	an irregular movement into a new region, often brought about by climatic conditions and usually of a temporary nature.
Juvenile	a young bird below sub-adult stage.
Kalahari thornveld	thornveld with stunted, scattered or more or less continuous *Acacia* or *Dichrostachys* tree species on Kalahari sand and calcareous soil with tufty grasses.
Leaf-gleaner	a bird that seeks insects from the leaves of the tree canopy.
Local movement	a mass movement of birds, not necessarily regular, within a comparatively small area.
Malar	the area on the side of the throat immediately below the base of the lower mandible.
Melanistic	darkness of plumage colour resulting from abnormal black pigmentation.
Migration	a regular movement of birds (or other animals) between two alternative regions inhabited by them at different times of the year, one region in which they breed and the other region used by them when not breeding.
Miombo	broadleafed woodland in which trees of the genus *Brachystegia* dominate; common in Zimbabwe with small regions in north-east Botswana.
Mixed bushveld	a region of mixed tree types, including both broadleafed and thorny species, growing more or less continually or in clumps, to an average height of about 7 m–10 m.
MM	males.
Montane	mountainous country.
Mopane	.a broadleafed, deciduous tree, *Colophospermum mopane*, found in much of the north and north-east of Botswana. May grow to a height of about 10 m, the leaves rounded, heart-shaped and reddish when young.
Morph	an alternative but permanent plumage colour.
Moustacial streak	a streak or line running back from the base of the bill in some plumages.

Nomad	a species with no fixed territory when not breeding.
Palaearctic Region	the northern hemisphere, incorporating North Africa, Europe, Scandinavia and Asia.
Pan (or flood-pan)	a natural depression which fills with water as the result of rainfall or river spillage.
Parkland	regions of woodland with well-spaced trees, little secondary growth and a grassy groundcover.
Passerine	birds that habitually sing or call and that have 'normal' feet, with three toes facing forward and one facing backward; excludes birds with webbed, lobed, or zygodactylous feet.
Pectoral	the breast region; in birds especially the lateral breast regions.
Range expansion	the process in which a bird increases its breeding range; a spread into regions not previously occupied.
Raptor	a bird of prey; one that hunts and kills other animals for food.
Recurved bill	a bill that bends upwards, e.g. Avocet.
Riparian	of or on riverbanks.
Riverine forest	the trees fringing a river, usually evergreen and more luxuriant than trees of the surrounding country and often with an understorey of dense thickets and secondary growth. In the more arid regions growth is less well developed, then often referred to as Riverine Bush.
Sexual dimorphism	differences in appearance between male and female of a species.
Soft parts	the parts of a bird's body not covered by feathers; bill, eyes, legs and feet plus any unfeathered skin.
Speculum	a patch of iridescent colour on the wings of some birds, notably ducks.
Still-hunt	watching for prey (usually on the ground) while perched.
Sub-song	a bird song of lower than normal pitch, sometimes of longer than normal duration.
Scrub	brushwood or stunted bushes.
Tail-streamer	elongated tail feathers, often the central or outer feathers.
Teak	the tree *Baikiaea plurijuga* which grows extensively in Zimbabwe and in small regions of north-east Botswana.
Thicket	a number of shrubs or trees growing very close together.
Thornveld	a bush habitat or woodland comprised of *Acacia, Albizia* or *Dichrostachys* trees, all of which are thorny.
Understorey	the lowest stratum in (usually) forest or woodland; secondary growth consisting of young trees, small bushes and annual plants.
Veld	a term used loosely in reference to various types of terrain, thus grassveld, bushveld, etc.
Watercourse	a dry riverbed; a permanent channel resulting from water run-off during periodic rains.
Waterhole	any natural or man-made waterpoint used by animals for drinking.
Woodland	regions with trees of moderate height and well-developed canopies which are so spaced as not to interlock; may cover flat ground or

hillsides, with or without well-developed secondary growth or ground-cover.

Zygodactyl feet which, in certain non-passerine birds, have two toes directed forward and two backward: cuckoos, barbets, woodpeckers, honey-guides and others.

REFERENCES USED

A Check List of the Birds of the Bechuanaland Protectorate and the Caprivi Strip. Reay H.N.Smithers (1964). Trustees of the National Museums, S.Rhodesia.

Newman's Birds of Southern Africa (Updated). Kenneth Newman (1988). Southern Book Publishers, Johannesburg.

Roberts' Birds of Southern Africa. Gordon L. Maclean (1985). John Voelcker Bird Book Fund, Cape Town.

The Birds of Zambia. C.W.Benson, R.K.Brooke, R.J.Dowsett, M.P.S.Irwin (1971). Collins, London.

The Birds of Zimbabwe. M.P.S.Irwin (1981). Quest Publishing, Zimbabwe.

Babbler. Nos. 1-15. Magazine of the Botswana Bird Club, Gaborone.

EXAMPLES OF BIRD HABITATS
IN BOTSWANA

Semi-arid bush and shrub savanna fringing a pan in the Mahuasehube Game Reserve, south-west Botswana. Conspicuous birds would be Redcapped Lark, Greybacked Finchlark, Capped Wheatear, Doublebanded Courser, Black Korhaan and Greater Kestrel. The distant woodland would shelter insectivorous species such as the Redeyed Bulbul, Titbabbler, Pied Barbet, Crimson Boubou and various summer-visiting warblers. *Photo: Duncan Buchart.*

A southern Kalahari pan in tree and bush savanna. Typical habitat of the Ostrich, Kori Bustard, Black Korhaan, Caspian Plover (late summer), various larks, the Titbabbler, Pied Barbet, Cape Turtle Dove, Hoopoe, Black Crow, Kalahari Robin, Blackchested Prinia, Marico Flycatcher and Scalyfeathered Finch with summer influxes of Lesser Grey and Recbacked Shrikes plus various warblers. *Photo: Wendy Borello.*

329

Central Kalahari tree and bush savanna. Frequented by the birds mentioned for the more southerly regions (previous page) plus such species as the Rufouscheeked Nightjar, Spotted Dikkop, Sabota, Fawncoloured and Rufousnaped Larks, Swallowtailed Bee-eater, Lilacbreasted Roller, Grey and Yellowbilled Hornbills, Lesser Masked Weaver, Gabar and Pale Chanting Goshawks, Blackbreasted Snake Eagle and Blackshouldered Kite. *Photo: K. Newman.*

Calcrete deposits are a feature of much of the southern and central Kalahari. Here they are seen in semi-arid tree and bush savanna near Tshane Pan, Kgalagadi district. *Photo: Wendy Borello.*

The Barolong flats in south-east Botswana, together with the more southerly Pitsane flats, harbour such species as the Shortclawed Lark, Orangethroated Longclaw, Marsh Owl, Secretarybird, Orange River Francolin, Namaqua Sandgrouse, Rufouseared Warbler and Sociable Weaver while the rare Blue Crane is an occasional visitor. The various local pans are often rich in waterbirds. *Photo: Don Aldiss.*

Acacia/Combretum mixed woodland on the Limpopo River, a region rich in barbets, woodpeckers, hornbills, woodhoopoes, kingfishers, mousebirds, swallows, bulbuls, tits, thrushes, flycatchers, shrikes and sunbirds. *Photo: Brian Bushell.*

Mopane/Croton/Combretum tree savanna on rocky hills in the eastern region. The birds are many and varied, often occurring in parties made up of several species. Notable are the Shorttoed Rock Thrush towards the south and the Sooty Babbler among the granite boulders of the more northerly hills. *Photo: Don Aldiss.*

Delta grasslands of the Makgadikgadi Pans Game Reserve, home to the Pinkbilled and Rufousnaped Larks, Black Korhaan, Greater Kestrel, Capped Wheatear and Pied Crow. During the summer Lesser and Redfooted Kestrels, European Bee-eaters and Caspian Plovers may be seen in large numbers. *Photo: Wendy Borello.*

Palm savanna with northern Kalahari tree and bush savanna near Nxai Pan. The palms are frequented by Palm Swifts and Rednecked Falcons while other conspicuous birds are Arrowmarked Babbler, Grey, Yellowbilled and Bradfield's Hornbills, Grey Lourie, Lilac-breasted Roller, Forktailed Drongo, Pied Crow, Anteating Chat, Threestreaked and Black-crowned Tchagras plus Plumcoloured and Cape Glosy Starlings. *Photo: K. Newman.*

Sua, the easternmost of the Makgadikgadi Pans, is a rich haven for waterbirds. Flamingoes are usually present in large numbers while pelicans, Caspian Terns, Grey-headed Gulls, Avocets, Spoonbills, and many species of herons and ducks can usually be seen. The shorelines are frequented by several species of waders, small plovers and larks, including the Clapper Lark and Chestnutbacked Finchlark. *Photo: Duncan Buchart.*

Dry, stunted mopane scrub and mopane woodland are a feature of much of the region between Nxai Pan and Savuti during drought periods and, at such times, are virtually devoid of birds with the exception of a few hardy species. *Photo: Wendy Borello.*

Aerial view of the Okavango Delta showing extensive aquatic grasslands and fringing riparian forests. Many species of herons abound, including the Slaty Egret and Little Bittern, as do Marabou, Saddlebilled and Openbilled Storks, Spurwinged Geese, Longtoed Plovers, Darters and Reed Cormorants. *Photo: K. Newman.*

The water fig *Ficus verrucolosa* grows extensively in the Okavango waterways and is used by a variety of waterbirds for both roosting and nesting. Darters, Reed Cormorants, Openbilled and Marabou Storks, Purple, Squacco, Rufousbellied and Greenbacked Herons, Little Bitterns, Great White, Yellowbilled, Little, Black and Slaty Egrets sometimes combine to create huge breeding colonies. *Photo: K. Newman.*

Lily-covered lagoons such as this are a feature of the Okavango Delta and are frequented by Pygmy Geese, Whitebacked, Whitefaced and Fulvous Ducks plus African and Lesser Jacanas. The fringing riparian forests harbour the Swamp Boubou, Heuglin's Robin, Brown Firefinch, Whiterumped Babbler and Pel's Fishing Owl among others. *Photo: K. Newman.*

A pan in well-developed mopane woodland in the Kwhai River region. Conspicuous birds in this woodland are Redbilled, Yellowbilled, Grey and Bradfield's Hornbills, Little and Swallowtailed Bee-eaters, Longtailed and Burchell's Glossy Starlings and Redheaded Weavers. Following rain the pans are frequented by ducks, waders and several heron species. *Photo: Wendy Borello.*

Broadleafed woodland of the north-eastern Kasane Forest Reserve, the dominant trees being *Brachystegia* species. This woodland harbours a rich avifauna, the birds often occurring in loose parties of mostly insectivorous species. A typical party might include the Longbilled Crombek, Southern Black Tit, Fantailed Flycatcher, Chinspot Batis, Golden-breasted Bunting, Greyheaded Sparrow and Cardinal Woodpecker. *Photo: Steve Spawls.*

INDEX TO SCIENTIFIC NAMES

337

INDEX TO ENGLISH NAMES

340

SETSWANA BIRD NAMES

This list of Setswana bird names has been derived and reconciled from Campbell's *Guide to Botswana* (1983), Robert's *Birds of Southern Africa* (1984), and two recent, original lists collected in the field. It is patently obvious from the attempts to reconcile these sources that the list as presented is not definitive or even correct. However, rather than shy away from producing Setswana bird names, we hope that this effort will stimulate the Tswana-speaking users of this fieldguide to contribute by providing criticisms, corrections, additions and explanations so that a more definitive list can be produced. It would be ideal to place the Setswana names in the species descriptions alongside the English and scientific names for each bird. Any contributions would be gratefully received by the Botswana Bird Club, P O Box 71, Gaborone.

Number	English Name	Setswana Name	Number	English Name	Setswana Name
001	Ostrich	Ntshe, Mpshe	182	Greater Kestrel	Nketshane
	pelicans	Leya, Lekurra, Kukara, Sehudi		francolins (Coqui, Crested, Orange River)	Lesogo, Letsogo, Letsiakarana, Letsikarane
	cormorants, Darter	Timeletsane	189	Crested Francolin	Leatsiakaradi
	herons	Kokolohutwe		francolins (Redbilled, Natal, Swainson's)	Kgwale, Sogonoke
063	Grey Heron	Segwepe			
064	Goliath Heron	Mogolori	194	Redbilled Francolin	Magobenyane
	egrets	Nalangwe	199	Swainson's Françolin	Rrakooukhibiou
071	Cattle Egret	Nalangwe wa oikgomo, Letlhapelapula, Mmamoleane, Manawane, Modisane		quails, buttonquails	Tshosabanne, Lephurulwane, Lephurrwane
	bitterns	Kgapu	203	Helmeted Guineafowl	Kgaka
081	Hamerkop	Mamasiloanoke, Mamasilanoka	207	Wattled Crane	Mogologi
			208	Blue Crane	Kokolehutwe, Mogolori
	storks	Lekolwane, Lekolowane, Mokotatsie	209	Crowned Crane	Leowang
			213	Black Crake	Mmamathebe
084	Black Stork	Lekolwane lelentsha	224	Lesser Gallinule	Tweetwee
088	Saddlebilled Stork	Molombwe		moorhens, Redknobbed	
089	Marabou Stork	Gube		Coot	Kgogonoka
091	Sacred Ibis	Koklehutwe	230	Kori Bustard	Kgori, Thulakome
095	African Spoonbill	Mmalbwane	231	Stanley's Bustard	Kgorithamaga
	flamingoes	Nonyaneyatladi	233	Whitebellied Korhaan	Mokagatwe
	ducks, Pygmy Goose	Sehudi	237	Redcrested Korhaan	Mokgweba
	geese, Knobbilled	Legou, Phalabogogo	238	Blackbellied Korhaan	Mokgweba
	Duck, SA Shelduck		239	Black Korhaan	Motatau, Motlatlagwe, Tlatlagwe
101	Whitefaced Duck	Lewewe			
102	Egyptian Goose	Leharatata	240	African Jacana	Mogatsakwena
115	Knobbilled Duck	Ranko, Sefalabogogo	225	Crowned Plover	Thatswana wa motlhaba, Letlhatswane, Letheetsane, Lethejane, Lerweewee
116	Spurwinged Goose	Sehudi sesephatswa, Letsikwe			
118	Secretarybird	Tlhame, Tlhangwe, Mmamolangwane, Klongwe, Thamu	258	Blacksmith Plover	Thatswana wa noka, Lethulatshipi
	vultures	Lenong	261	Longtoed Plover	Thatswana wa oi kubu
122	Cape Vulture	Diswane		dikkops	Monogwangwa, mongwangwa
123	Whitebacked Vulture	Kopajammutla			
124	Lappetfaced Vulture	Kgosiyama, Bibing	297	Spotted Dikkop	Tswangtswang, Kgoadire (but see also African Fish Eagle)
	kites, harriers	Mmankgodi, Segodi, Phakwe			
	buzzards, Chanting Goshawks	Segotsane, Segodi, Phakwe		coursers	Dakatswane
127	Blackshouldered Kite	Segoetsane, Phakalane	301	Doublebanded Courser	Legarasipi, Segolagola, Segwelegwele
	eagles, Hawk Eagles, Snake Eagles	Ntsu	344	Namaqua Sandgrouse	Legwar'agwara Lekwetekwie, Lekotokobii
131	Black Eagle	Ntswi			
146	Bateleur	Peteke, Petleke	346	Yellowthroated Sandgrouse	Legwaragwara phutimphabogoe
148	African Fish Eagle	Audi, Kgoadire (but see also Spotted Dikkop)	347	Doublebanded Sandgrouse	Mogwaragwara
	Lizard Buzzard, sparrowhawks, small goshawks, kestrels	Seggotsane, Phakalane		pigeons, doves	Leeba, Lephoi
			349	Rock Pigeon	Leebarope, Letseba
162	Pale Chanting Goshawk	Mankukonono	352	Redeyed Dove	Letseba oope
	falcons	Segwetsane	354	Cape Turtle Dove	Mhiri

343

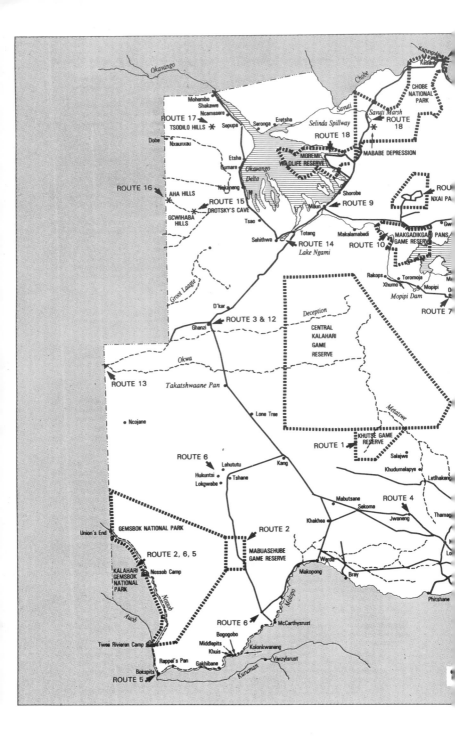